19

The Alderman's Tale

Don Mosey

The Alderman's Tale

WEIDENFELD AND NICOLSON · LONDON

Published in Great Britain by
George Weidenfeld & Nicolson Limited
91 Clapham High Street
London SW4 7TA

ISBN 0 297 81114 2

Typeset at The Spartan Press Ltd,
Lymington, Hants.

Printed in Great Britain by
Butler & Tanner Ltd, Frome & London

Contents

Prologue

It seems to be fashionable in some quarters to sneer at any story of a Northerner who emerges from humble origins to fashion some sort of better life for himself. It may, therefore, come as a surprise to the sneerers to learn that we enjoy a cliché of our own – to look down our noses at a fair number in the effete South who seem to us to achieve success through influence and string-pulling rather than honest toil.

It takes a good deal to persuade a cricket-lover in Yorkshire, Lancashire, Derbyshire and Nottinghamshire – most of all, perhaps, in Glamorgan! – that his (or her) hero has an equal chance of being selected for an England Test place with a man who plays for Middlesex, Surrey or Kent. One might even add, 'or one born in South Africa or the West Indies!' Similarly, as this book may indicate, I find it difficult to believe that a grammar schoolboy from the provinces could ever compete on equal terms with a public school product from the Home Counties for a position in BBC cricket commentary circles.

But there is more to life than arguing such points. Certainly there has been more to mine than an in-the-end unavailing attempt to beat 'the system'. There has been fun and laughter all along the way; friendships made and experiences shared; new adventures round every turn in the road; new lessons to be learned and a certain amount of wisdom acquired.

And that, surely, is *really* what life is all about?

DM

1 *Myself When Young*

The first twelve years of my life were spent in a tiny farm cottage – so tiny in fact that it can only be described as one-and-a-half up, one-and-a-half down – in the Worth Valley, a couple of miles from the centre of the textile and engineering town of Keighley in Yorkshire. Today the area of Bracken Bank is an ocean of council housing estates; in the 1920s it consisted of one farm, two attached cottages, of which ours was one, and on a slightly higher elevation, fifty or sixty yards behind us, a single incongruous row of sturdy, stone-built houses standing sentinel over the farm. In the first, westernmost of these lived my maternal grandparents with my mother's brother, Arthur Ruddock, and his wife, Mabel. Over the next fifteen years they were joined by six children so I was never going to be short of playmates, particularly as one of the other houses of Elmwood Terrace – which still stands, now presiding over the council houses – was occupied by a family called Stott that included innumerable children. I was fascinated to learn that the eldest of these, a married girl, had a son who was older than her youngest brother. It took me years to come to terms with the fact that Harold Stott was uncle to a boy older than himself!

My only memory of my Grandfather Ruddock is of seeing his body brought downstairs when I was three years old and hearing the word 'cancer' spoken for the first time. He was buried in Nab Wood cemetery at Saltaire where my mother's family originated and every Friday, until I was five and thus required to go to school, I travelled on a bus with my mother and grandmother to put fresh flowers on his grave. As the trip usually involved continuing into the middle of Bradford where the ladies carried out some minor shopping it took on the trappings of an adventurous outing for me rather than a solemn occasion.

My grandmother was a remarkable lady. She was lame for the whole

3

time I knew her but I never learned how or why. She had had some schooling and had spent half of each day learning her three 'Rs', the remainder working in a wool-textile mill. Yet she knew, and taught me before I was seven, the entire succession of English kings and queens from the Norman Conquest to the reigning George V. She had an encyclopaedic knowledge of Queen Victoria's family and could recite the entire string of forenames of all of them. From her I learned that the Prince of Wales, much in the news in the 1920s and even more so in the following decade, was named Edward Albert Christian George Andrew Patrick David, and I wondered what on earth his family called him! She drew an old-age pension of ten shillings (50p) a week and when I accompanied her from time to time to collect it from the Post Office on Ingrow Bridge I marvelled at the wealth incorporated in that one brown note. Thursday was 'baking day' at No. 1, Elmwood Terrace, just as Monday was 'washing day', and as the family of Uncle Arthur and Auntie Mabel grew so did the number of loaves, scones and rock buns which showered from the oven from Thursday morning until late afternoon.

The fire in the hearth served the dual purpose of warming the room and baking the bread and cakes in the oven which was fixed into the wall alongside the fire and heated by coals in a cavity underneath it. As there was no space in the oven for anything else at the same time, Thursday lunch (or dinner as it was to us) came from a huge pan of broth which bubbled away on the fire during the morning – carrots, turnips, onions, potatoes and lots of pearl barley, together with thick crusts of home-made bread. It was full of nourishment, and I hated it. Until I was five I was present on those occasions when my mother helped her mother and her sister-in-law in cleaning the house daily, which seemed vast compared with our own cottage. In fact it consisted of a kitchen-living room, which was all-purpose, and a 'front room', which was kept in a state of pristine Victorian cleanliness and never seemed to be used except, perhaps, on Sunday if 'company' arrived. Upstairs were two bedrooms but there remained the attic and the cellar, a great, gloomy dungeon of a place with a stone flagstone floor where rows of pots containing home-made jam were stored.

My own family cottage at No. 1, Bracken Bank Farm, had the same sort of flagstone floors, partly covered by an extremely modest carpet and home-fashioned rugs, contrived by 'tatting' odd fragments of discarded material on to a hessian base. The kitchen was minute, with one tiny window looking out on to the farmyard, and it was scarcely a kitchen since most of the cooking had to be done on the fire in the living-room. Yet it did contain a small gas-ring cooker, a stoneware sink which was where the family ablutions were also performed, a hand-operated mangle with wooden rollers and a dolly-tub in which clothes and bedding were soaked before going through the mangle.

Sanitary facilities were outside. I remember they were up-graded in the late 1920s so that a falling-down building of stones was replaced by a brick-built edifice but there was still no flushing system; men came once a week to empty the hideous, noisome tubs and for an hour or two I suppose the atmosphere was vilely polluted but, never having known anything else – and with the farmyard ever-present, right on top of us – I cannot remember noticing anything untoward.

The front window looked out over a small garden filled with antirrhinums, phlox, Sweet William and Michaelmas daisies so there was always colour throughout the summer, and we looked right across the valley to the hamlet of Hainsworth, perched on its hill, and to the moors beyond, gashed by the quarries from which the mills and houses of Keighley had been built. There were bilberry bushes covering great stretches of those moors, and blackberries to be found everywhere, so, with raspberries grown in one corner of our garden and gooseberries grown by Uncle Arthur on an allotment some distance away, there was always seasonal jam-making in progress and delicious fruit pies emerging from the oven. Coal for the fire was stored in another tiny outhouse ('t'coil 'oil') where, behind the door, hung a zinc bath in which I (and subsequently my two brothers) were scrubbed clean every Friday night with additional sessions if our games had sent us home more than usually begrimed. It never occurred to me to wonder when my parents were able to take their baths; it was only years later I fathomed the reason for being sent on errands or extra visits to grandmother at what seemed to be eccentric moments.

We were in no way connected with the farm, except in the geographical sense. The farmer was a tenant of the Clough family who owned the huge spinning mill in the valley bottom, as were we and our neighbours, the Mitchells. This was because my father – and my mother, until I arrived on the scene – were employed at Clough's and thus it was a sort of grace-and-favour residence which we rented. My father was the most thoroughly decent human being I have ever known. He had 'served his time' as an engineering apprentice and had just time to complete those indentures before he went into the Army in 1917. Either with typical perverseness, or perhaps because of his address (Bracken Bank Farm), he was posted to a cavalry regiment!

He lost a brother in the Dardanelles while one of my mother's brothers was killed in France, and another was so severely affected by poison gas that he never fully recovered and suffered breathing problems for the rest

5

of his remarkably long life. The war had a profound effect upon my immediate family but then just about everyone my parents knew had similarly been touched by the horrors of 1914-18. I remember reading bound copies of the *Illustrated London News* and I looking aghast at pictures of the muddy, shell-pocked battlefields of the Somme with stunted, decapitated trees and the rotting remains of horses strewn everywhere. Every one of these might have been carrying my father and I wept to see them.

He was demobilized from the Army to find the country in deepest recession and the engineering trade affected more desperately than most. There was just no work for him at all that involved his specialist skills. But he was now married; it was his *duty* to find work and provide a home for his wife. No man who 'thowt owt abhat 'issen' went on the dole; there *must* be something for him to do to earn some money. And Dad counted himself lucky to find part-time employment, for three days a week, in one of the dirtiest parts of Clough's mill – the combing. It brought him thirty shillings (£1.50p) a week. But it also left him with four days a week in which to find other means of supplementing that income. He collected debts owing to doctors from their 'panel' patients, acted as groundsman to Ingrow United Football Club and Knowle Park Congregational Cricket Club, and went hay-making on local farms in July. My God, how he worked. But as I grew older I never heard one word of complaint from him. He regarded work as a privilege, not as a right. If he had to go out and spend days or weeks searching for something to earn a few bob, then that was what had to be done. He never drank; his one luxury was one ounce of pipe tobacco a week and if we found ourselves short of anything his tobacco was the first sacrifice to be made. He mended the family's shoes and mother repaired our clothes, and I can never remember being hungry in my whole adolescent life. I am quite sure my parents were hungry – often – but my brothers and I never knew what it meant to go without a proper meal.

As children, my cousins, my brothers and our friends the Stotts never found any difficulty in entertaining ourselves. Just beyond Elmwood Terrace was a disused quarry, known to us as 'T'Delf', with rock faces, rockfalls, hillsides covered in brambles, birds' nests in abundance, trees to be climbed, and fissures which we imaginatively magnified into caves by squeezing through the narrowest of openings. In short, with the exercise of the most modest imagination we had an adventure playground of vast extent and no trace of man-made artificiality. Beyond t'Delf was a field perfect for sledging in winter and beyond that a walk over the fields brought us to Holme House Wood (which was never called anything but Old Mouse Wood with absolute belief in the accuracy of the name) with its clear stream and a carpet of bluebells every May and the smell of wild garlic heavy throughout the long days of summer. Beyond that – and these walks were as nothing to our frail legs; it was the only way to get around – were the Sylvan delights of Newsholme Dene, again with a stream and, joy of joys, half a dozen swings. There was Oakworth Park with its terracotta grottoes forming a great labyrinth to seven-, eight-, and nine-year-old minds. There was fishing in the River Worth, credited in Keighley's coat of arms as being the founder of the town's industrial fortunes (because it powered the woollen mills) but dismissively referred to by us as 't'beck'. There was delight in being the one to spot the first daisy, then the first buttercup in the meadows. There were the moors to roam and explore, horse-chestnut 'conkers' to be gathered and the seasonal berries to be taken home . . . proudly, in the knowledge that one was contributing something to the household budget. There was a huge variety of wildlife – it was not unusual to see a fox well within the borough boundaries of Keighley – and the whole area was one vast playground.

Down in the valley bottom the Worth Valley branch of the London, Midland and Scottish Railway was not the tourist attraction it is today (and God bless the Preservation Society for keeping it for posterity) but a major means of communication between the villages and hamlets *en route* . . . Ingrow, Damems, Oakworth, Haworth and Oxenhope. Damems had a fascination all of its own. A cluster of farms and cottages with a population of less than a hundred, it was reputed to have the smallest station on the whole LMS network until the stationmaster, a man named Grimshaw, had a house built for him to save a walk of three or four miles from his home on 'Ingerra Loin Top'. This had the effect of doubling or trebling the size of the station and so Damems lost its record! But I remember Mr Grimshaw as a tall, lean, spare man with a dog, a whippet, which accompanied him to work and which was said to spend its days happily ratting in t'beck while its master went about his chores of signalling trains, issuing and collecting tickets and opening and closing the level-crossing gates. The walk from Bracken Bank to Damems was a pleasant one, a path trodden for years, perhaps centuries, along field-bottoms and over stiles; it is sad now to see it all engulfed in concrete and tarmac, bricks and mortar.

The lingua franca of our juvenile community was West Riding Yorkshire at its sloppiest and most slovenly, some way removed from what we called 'Oxford English' as spoken by BBC announcers. Not that we had a radio until I was nine years old because we simply could not afford to buy a 'wireless set' outright and my parents were absolutely firm in their refusal to become involved in hire-purchase. They had seen too many families unable to keep up payments on essential items like furniture and bedding and who had suffered the ignominy of seeing the goods publicly re-possessed. The stigma of not being able to pay for articles which had been 'bought' far transcended the inconvenience of losing them. My brothers and I were brought up on the strict principle of what you can't afford you do without and so firmly was this impressed upon me that when the time came for me to 'buy' a house for the first time I agonized for days (and, more particularly, nights) before I could bring myself to sign the mortgage agreement. Debt of any kind was anathema, and hire-purchase in my family meant, quite simply, debt.

But I had been in homes which did have a radio and the beautifully modulated enunciation of the speakers made no impact on me in a personal sense. That was what the BBC was about – talking posh. There was no way in which it could ever affect my life. It was simply not part of my world. No one I knew, or ever expected to meet, spoke in that way. If anyone had ever suggested that one day I might broadcast (if not in Oxford English, then in relatively civilized cadences) I would have said he was potty. People like me, and those I knew, just did not dream dreams like that. They were far beyond the realms of possibility.

The basic principles of verbal communication in my environment were simple: never go to the trouble of enunciating a word correctly, using all its syllables and letters, if there is a short cut. The aspirate was unknown to me during the early years of my life. 'Always' was 'ollus', 'I will' was 'Al', 'will not' was 'weern't' and 'my' was 'mi'. A common greeting between two acquaintances would be, 'Nathen then, ah etter?' Translation: 'Now then. How are you?' Response: 'Reight (pronounced as in "eight"). Ahettar?' ('Right. How are you?') I use the letter 'h' in that context merely to indicate the elongation of the letter 'a'. Interspersed with these lazy bastardizations were genuine, or almost genuine, bits of dialect. Thus, if I caught my trousers while trespassing over a barbed-wire fence, it was necessary to confess that I had 'rivven mi britches'. A pair of braces was 'a set o' galluses', a cardigan was a 'ganzy', a bowler hat (often to be seen at funerals) was a 'billy-cock,' a boater (seen mostly in films) was a 'straw benjie'. One didn't simply 'go' anywhere, one 'went off'. '*Setting* off' was different; it meant either one was going on holiday or at least out for the whole day to somewhere special. My vowels were broad, my accentuation ponderous.

This was the way we communicated with each other, in the family, amongst friends. To think of doing otherwise never occurred to me, and if it *had* occurred it would have smacked of treachery. I had a vague sort of idea at the back of my mind that I admired people who spoke 'proper' but I could not have put it into words. They were different, a race apart. One could never become one of them; they were, as my grandmother put it, 'born to it'. It was the natural order of things. Grandma had a keen perception of the natural order – there were those born to take charge and those pre-destined to serve. One did not nurse ideas above one's station. Yet she steadfastly voted Conservative, as did my parents, as I have always done!

If I had no burning desire to improve my speech, I most certainly required a wider knowledge of things. I positively thirsted for knowledge. It was a long time before I understood that wisdom is more desirable than knowledge *per se*, but at the age of five I could hardly be expected to make such judgements. That was the age at which I started attending Ingrow St. John's Church of England School, next door to the parish church of that name. I doubt if the school had more than fifty pupils. Certainly, in a very short space of time I knew the names of all of them and, sixty years later, I can remember most of them. Eric Dalton was older, and my hero. Kathleen Wilkinson was the prettiest girl and I loved her; poor Minnie Parker was my (country) dancing partner and I hated her.

There were three teachers: Mr Francis Jervis, the head; Miss Thorne and Miss Miles, the latter taking the youngest children for their first few years so that the major part of formal tuition fell on the shoulders of Miss Annie Elizabeth Thorne who intrigued me by pronouncing St. Patrick with an exaggeratedly long 'Ah' . . . St. P*ah*trick. On the walls of the three classrooms were reminders of our great Empire: pictures of elephants towing loads of teak in Burma, African women bearing hands of bananas on their heads, and West Indians cutting sugar cane. Our maps showed great areas of the world coloured red and we were taught that the sun never set on the king's possessions. It took me a long time to work this out.

The playground seems tiny when I pass it now but it was entirely adequate for the number of scholars with the obligatory set of cricket stumps chalked on one wall during summer. The gate opened on to the road to Halifax and a flight of steps led to the chancel end of St. John's parish church.

Lessons concentrated severely on the basics of education plus a fair amount of time devoted to religious matters. We all knew the Ten Commandments by heart and we could all recite the Catechism though I doubt if any of us knew what it meant. While I was never to master the finer points of mathematics when it involved matters like the time taken for a bath to fill, or empty, I was given a grounding in simple arithmetic (which has never deserted me) through the agency of the 'times-table'. At some stage of every day we would be required to go through the litany of 'two twos are four, three twos are six,' right up to 'twelve times', all chanted with metronomic rhythm in plaintive sing-song tones. All this was charted along one wall of the classroom to refresh our memories though one was not allowed, of course, to refer to it when one was dragged from the chorus to do a solo.

But for me the highlight of the week was always Friday afternoon when, as we wound down towards the weekend, Miss Thorne introduced us gently and painlessly to literature, reading by instalments from a selected children's classic. The first one I remember was *The Water Babies* which had the additional attraction of having been written by Charles Kingsley while staying at Malham and Arncliffe, both Dales villages not too far away from Keighley (although in terms of the sort of distance we normally travelled as children they might as well have been in Tibet). Nevertheless, the mere fact gave us a sort of sense of personal involvement. The allegorical aspects of the book were a bit too much for most of us, I suspect, but following a straightforward, literal line, it gave us pleasure. But it was as nothing compared with the delights of Kenneth Grahame's *The Wind in the Willows*. I felt at the time that I would very happily have listened to the story being told over and over again, every Friday afternoon for the rest of my life. To this day I look upon stoats and weasels with distaste but at badgers and moles with tremendous affection, even if it has not always been shared by farming and gardening friends.

One chapter per week was our ration of the story and so four of them had passed pleasantly enough with the establishment of the central characters and their various, different personalities. Then came the Friday when we reached the chapter called 'Dulce Domum' and at the end of it I walked home in a sort of daze. At seven I was quite incapable of understanding what had happened or even of explaining to my parents who were almost unnerved to find me spending an entire evening deep in thought, without any physical activity of any kind. Vaguely I was conscious that we had reached a new dimension in Friday story-time. Generally my fellows and I demanded action of some sort in the narrative, or at any rate dialogue. How, then, could I come to terms with the impact upon me of a sentence like, 'The sheep ran huddling together against the hurdles, blowing out thin nostrils and stamping with delicate forefeet, their heads thrown back and a light steam rising from the crowded sheep-pen into the frosty air . . . '?

Or 'Most of the low latticed windows were innocent of blinds and to the lookers-in from outside, the inmates, gathered round the tea-table, absorbed in handiwork or talking with laughter and gesture, had each

that happy grace which is the last thing the skilled actor shall capture –
the natural grace which goes with perfect unconsciousness of observa-
tion.'?

Severely limited in vocabulary as I was, literal-minded in appreciation
of the words I did know, this was mysterious to me, like the writing of
someone in another language. If you *stamped*, you did so in a definite
manner, leaving no one with illusions about the purpose of the action.
How, then, could one – even a sheep! – stamp with *delicate* forefeet?
'Innocent of blinds' – what could that mean? I struggled with this first
conscious encounter with a figure of speech and beseeched explanations
from my parents who in turn struggled to provide them. My introduction
to the bel canto of words was an almost traumatic experience. Vaguely I
was conscious of having been moved by the words I had heard and I
didn't know why. The battle to achieve understanding was as emotional
an experience as the effect of the words themselves. And with hindsight
I see just what a highly emotional child I was. History, for instance, was
taught by word of mouth, in story form – and not from text books.

After hearing Miss Thorne's strictly Tudor version of the brief reign
of Richard III I went home in floods of tears, partly because of the
intense pathos with which she invested the alleged murder of the little
princes and partly because I identified it all so closely with the lives of
myself and my first brother, five years younger! It took me several adult
years to dismiss this crude and probably inaccurate picture of Richard of
Gloucester from my mind and a later acquaintance with Shakespeare
didn't help, either.

This was history of blood and guts rather than the repeal of the Corn
Laws and the Act of Union. Crecy and Agincourt were patriotic
triumphs rather than brilliant examples of tactical genius. Richard the
Lionheart was a noble hero rather than a rebellious son and a neglectful
monarch. In short, our earliest English history was learned in strict
black-and-white terms; no shadings or overtones. It made it relatively
simple to translate it into terms of my own scenarios, enacted on the
empty moortops or in the more immediately available 'Delf'.

And so those earliest years passed oh-so-pleasantly. If we were poor it
did not register particularly because everyone we knew was in similar
circumstances. A Saturday penny was all the pocket money we expected
or required, always with the knowledge that one half of it had to be
reserved for the Sunday School collection the following day. I had
enough to eat, clothes to keep me warm, a whole vast playground round
about me, friends to share these pleasures if I required company and the
imagination to create my own world if I wanted to play alone. It was an

extremely private world, populated by giants from the pages of history, or the sports pages of newspapers and magazines, and often from my own fantasies which were many and colourful.

At home, I preferred to kick a football about beside the cottage on my own rather than in an organized game with a group of friends because I was able to indulge in more private dreams. In my mind I created a team, then a whole league, and played out an entire season of 'fixtures' – there were few shock results or heart-breaking reverses in *my* league. Artificially created entertainment was, therefore, rarely required. Occasionally the older girls of the Stott family took their younger sisters to the Oxford Hall cinema, a bit of a fleapit two or three miles away, and very kindly hauled along one small boy who usually emerged, terrified, from some silent horror film which rendered him sleepless for the following week. Imagination can work both ways. We sat on wooden bench seats only a few feet from the pianist who ingeniously provided a suitable accompaniment to the action. But while this sort of excursion had its technical attractions, I much preferred to be roaming the moors or the woods in a world of my own creation.

Meanwhile at St. John's School we had moved on to *Treasure Island* and at home I read *The Count of Monte Cristo*. I recall Edmond Dantes taking for ever to tunnel his way out of the Chateau D'If and sharing his experience of frustration and despair. Unwittingly, I had quietly absorbed another lesson in creative writing. In my final year (aged ten) at the little school, the headmaster, Mr Jervis, took over literary instruction. He had a beautiful, melodious voice and my Friday afternoons were now spent spellbound as he described to us the plot of first *Macbeth* and then *Hamlet*, told simply as stories. My first introduction to William Shakespeare was thus not as a playwright but simply as a writer who could think up rattling good yarns.

I was heartbroken to have to leave St. John's at the age of eleven. I had been happy there; I had felt secure in my small circle of friends with whom I shared moortop adventures and playground competitions. But the Education Act required me to move, at eleven, to the big, sprawling and impersonal world of Ingrow Council School. Mercifully, within months I had won a scholarship to take me to Keighley Boys' Grammar School and a whole new world opened up for me. In those few brief months, however, two significant things happened.

First, a teacher named Miss Dorothy Bentley detected some faint ability to write essays and encouraged me energetically to develop that first crude skill. A spelling mistake brought down her wrath, it seemed, more severely on myself than on other members of the class and I was made to write out the word correctly twenty times. I resented it bitterly at the time, but I have never ceased to thank her, in my mind, in the years that followed. The second window on the world through which I looked at Ingrow Council gave me my first glimpse of the great composers. Miss Dorothy Riley, who taught mathematics, was (unknown to me) a musician of some accomplishment and along one wall of the classroom where she regularly taught was a series of charts listing the most notable classicists: Beethoven, Ludwig van (1770-1827), German; Berlioz, Hector (1803-69), French . . . through to Wagner, Richard (1813-83), German, and Weber, Carl Maria von (1786-1826), German. And so, with maths having little appeal for me, I spent long, drowsy afternoons absorbing the detail of Miss Riley's musical tradition. If I emerged from Ingrow Council School with little knowledge of arithmetic beyond the principles of addition, subtraction, multiplication and division, I at least knew the names and dates of most of the world's greatest composers.

I had, in fact, 'discovered' music a couple of years earlier when, in the mid-thirties, we acquired our first wireless set at home. It had taken an immense effort of saving by my parents, and it helped to change my life. Winter evenings found me sprawled upon a rug in front of the fire pursuing my favourite hobby at that time – copying out maps of various countries from an old atlas – while listening to every programme put out by the BBC. This led me to switch from collecting the 1934 issue of cigarette cards of famous cricketers (by standing outside tobacconists and asking grown-ups who emerged with a new packet of Players for the card which was enclosed in each of them) to collecting the series issued by a rival firm of manufacturers, 'Stars of the BBC'. In this way, while by no means being disloyal to Messrs Herbert Sutcliffe, Hedley Verity, Bill Bowes, Douglas Jardine, George Geary, Tommy Mitchell and Co, I made the acquaintance of people like Henry Hall, Olive Groves, the two Leslies, Roy Fox, Jack Payne and other radio personalities.

If that list includes a fair proportion of dance-band leaders it is no way significant; theirs was not music which interested me. But one evening I listened to a broadcast of Oscar Straus's 'A Waltz Dream' and I was captivated by the pure melody of the score. By sheer chance, a travelling company came to the Keighley Hippodrome (a place of entertainment I had never visited) the following week and I begged to be allowed to go to see their performance of that very same 'Waltz Dream'. This caused much heart-searching. The cost of even the most modest seat in 't'theatre' was more than that for a wooden bench at the Oxford Hall Cinema. The family budget, if stretched and juggled, might run to one seat but certainly not two. I would have to be allowed out beyond the normal eight o'clock curfew (nine on long summer evenings, which I regarded as perfectly normal and natural and accepted without rebellion) and that had never happened before. But my folks finally agreed, supplied me for the first time in my life with three whole pennies, and I walked into town, climbed a thousand (it seemed) stairs to the upper balcony known as 'up in t'gods' and listened entranced. I deliberately avoid saying 'watched entranced' because while the presence of those on stage gave substance to the performance as compared with my recent experience on radio, it was the marvellously tuneful score on which my attention was really focussed. It was the most pleasant and painless of all possible introductions to Music with a capital 'M'. By the time I was fifteen I was a devoted listener to opera and on the rare occasions when it was possible to watch a performance – *very* occasionally, in Bradford – I was queuing on the doorstep long before the theatre opened. Since that time I have listened in wonderment to Tauber, Gigli, Bergonzi, Domingo and Pavarotti, to Joan Cross, Joan Hammond, to Joan Sutherland and Kiri Te Kanawa, to Janet Baker, Elizabeth Harwood, Maria Callas, Victoria de los Angeles, Kathleen Ferrier, to Norman Allin, Norman Lumsden, Forbes Robertson and scores more. All the experiences have been important but none more significant to me than that first experience of operetta – probably by a hack company – at Keighley Hippodrome.

It was fairly easy to develop this new interest in Keighley in the 1930s because the strong nonconformist element in local churches, and even stronger tradition of choral music in them, meant annual performances of 'Messiah', every winter.

With the cost of their visits underwritten by wealthier supporters of the various churches, most of the finest singers in Britain regularly visited Keighley to sing in 'Messiah' and the Sunday performances of Handel's masterpiece were preceded by a Saturday night 'secular' concert in the Sunday School. Operatic arias, duets, trios and quartets were heard in all their glory and I haunted every performance.

It was about this time that I switched my religious allegiance from Methodism to Church of England. Since I was just about able to walk I had attended a Primitive Methodist Chapel at Bogthorn, about half-a-mile from my home. Now, as my boyish treble was heard around the house essaying snatches from works far beyond my ken, my mother enrolled me in the choir of the parish church of St. John. Now I added Stainer's 'Crucifixion' and 'Olivet to Calvary' to my musical repertoire and was actually paid for doing so. Every three-monthly period brought 'pay', which never exceeded ninepence in my case though some boys received more and I savagely put down this differentiation to dislike of me by the organist and choirmaster, 'Fatty' Fortune, rather than to any musical shortcomings on my part. I loved robing myself in surplice and cassock and Eton collar for matins and evensong, glorified in it when we were required to sing a descant to the hymns and revelled most of all in the ceremonial of processional and recessional hymns when some special church occasions required us to walk solemnly down the aisle to our places in the choirstalls rather than simply take our places there at the start of the service. The sermons were tedious, it is true, but surreptitious games of 'Hangman' and 'Battleships' whiled away the time quite pleasantly. There were annual delights like the choir outings, on one of which we travelled by coach to Liverpool where I was awed by the majesty of the ocean-going liners of the Cunard and White Star fleets and by a drive through the recently opened engineering marvel of the Mersey Tunnel. At Christmas we trudged around the homes of the wealthier parishioners and sang carols for them in houses larger and grander than anything I ever expected to see in my life. And we were financially rewarded for that, too. It is hardly surprising that I wondered why I had 'wasted' so many years in Methodism!

It *wasn't* wasted time, of course. If twice-daily attendances at Sunday School did not basically make me a better Christian and even if it did result in my 'signing the pledge' at a time when I had no idea what alcohol was – let alone be in a position to promise to abstain through the whole of my future life – it at least taught me certain disciplines, and most of all it gave me a certain respect for the people who gave up their time every weekend to try to make a bunch of unruly kids into rather more civilized human beings. And in purely material terms there were the annual prizes to look forward to, for regular attendance. They enabled me to found a library with the adventure stories of Henty and Ballantyne and finally to reach the ultimate delight of the 'William' novels of Richmal Crompton. It is difficult to decide what modern youngsters would make of them and certainly my own two boys by-passed them but to me, around the eleven and twelve years mark, they were books which I simply could not put down.

For more regular reading, on a weekly basis in fact, I was allowed two publications a week from the D. C. Thomson stable in Dundee – *The Wizard* on Tuesday and *The Hotspur* on Friday. These were in turn swopped with my schoolfellows for the other Thomson story-magazines, *The Adventure* (Monday), *The Rover* (Thursday) and *The Skipper* (Saturday). *The Hotspur* was by some margin my favourite, dealing only with school stories, and the personalities of Tubby Ryan, 'Deadwide' Dick Doyle, Cyrus Judd and Kit Delaney, battling with the irascible Mr Smugg at the Red Circle School, were as real and as important to me as Billy Bunter and Hurree Jam Singh were to those who favoured the Frank Richards characters at Greyfriars. They induced a fervent admiration for the public school principles of fair play and fundamental decency, concepts which I felt in those earlier years were so far from anything I would experience personally that they took on an air of mysticism. It therefore came as a profound shock to me, even in mature middle age, to find that a public school education can by no means guarantee those qualities. But all that was in the future. . . .

2 *Golden Days*

John Drake, the bachelor landlord of an inn near the parish church of Keighley, died on 23 May 1713, leaving property to yield a salary for the Master of a Free School, the town's first, who was to be qualified to teach Latin and Greek and must remain unmarried. Three years later the foundation stones were laid. His bequest, however, was not of such dimensions that would allow the building of a noble Queen Anne or early Georgian pile and the building in which I began my more advanced schooling was strictly and hideously Victorian, the original foundation of Mr Drake's schoolroom having long since (1870) been moved into the Mechanics Institute in the town centre.

Yet I cherished a soft spot for old Drake and his contemporary Jonas Tonson for it was as a Drake and Tonson scholarship boy that I went to Keighley Boys' Grammar School in 1936. It was blessed with a superb headmaster, Neville Hind, and a dedicated staff, most of whom spent a major part (if not all) of their working lives there. Gilbert Swift, then recently qualified at Carnegie College as a physical education teacher, Captain of Fylde and of the Cumbrian County rugby teams, was a heroic figure as my first sports master, and more than fifty years later he is still my very good friend. Arthur Pickles, who lived to be well over ninety, more than anyone else taught me to have a proper respect and affection for the English language and my debt to him was incalculable. Percy Morgan, a burly Welshman with beetling brows, who spent a lifetime furthering the cause of school rugby, gave me my first lesson in humility by writing a report which said, 'Good. But not as good as he thinks he is.' Arnold Birch taught maths so I was never going to achieve a rapport with him; I have had a mental block on matters scientific all my life but he was the greatest cricket enthusiast on the staff and devoted hours of his off-duty time to searching for a boy good enough to be recommended to the Yorkshire nets. Miss 'Frizzy' Berrington was my first form-mistress and in my opening week under her care she uttered an admonition which turned out to be strangely prophetic: 'Mosey – if it was possible for you to earn a living simply by talking there might possibly be some future for you.' It was a moment I recalled with huge personal delight when once invited back to address the school on Speech Day.

We did not dwell on matters of tradition, contenting ourselves with praying in a vague and scarcely heartfelt way for the souls of Messrs Drake and Tonson at the annual Founders' Day service, yet to some of us with a more romantic turn of mind there was a certain pleasure in reflecting that the school, and its predecessors, had been opening up minds for more than 200 years. My introduction to rugby football marked the start of a love affair which has lasted, with growing affection, for more than half-a-century. To me it is still the greatest sporting brotherhood in the world and I delight in the friendship of members of it in New Zealand, Australia, South Africa and the USA as well as in Britain. I have always contributed more in enthusiasm than skill but my love of the game has remained undiminished since I played for the first time.

School Camp, to which a hundred or so of us repaired every July, opened up more undreamed-of joys. This had been established for thirty years or so when I first went to the beautiful site three miles outside Kirkcudbright, on the southern coast of Galloway. The rocky coastline provided another adventure playground to which I warmed immediately; the great sweep of Senwick Woods could be transformed (with only a bare flight of fancy) into African jungle; the wreckage of an old, wooden sailing ship conjured up visions of piracy, especially when coupled with the name of John Paul Jones who had actually raided that part of the British coastline during the American War of Independence; there were smugglers' caves, acres of sands, traditional tales of former Camps handed down from one generation to the next. This was a wonderland to me and I exhausted myself trying to explore every inch of it – on foot or on my brand-new bicycle.

An hour's bike-ride away was Threave Castle, home of the Black Douglases, a grim, square keep on its island in the River Dee, and though I was to learn later that the custodian's version of the castle's history owed as much to his imagination as to recorded fact, it was enough for me at the age of eleven to accept without question the gory tales of old Archibald the Grim and his bloodthirsty line. I combed the shelves of the local library for every book I could find on the history of mediaeval Scotland and by accident stumbled upon H. V. Morton's *In Search of Scotland* and *In Scotland Again*. At once I became his most devoted slave.

Those were golden summers which fickle memory tells me gave us weeks of unbroken sunshine with no trace of rain. To this day I can recall no place on earth which has given me such unalloyed happiness. Every year, at some stage, I return to Kirkcudbright to recall it, often in the company of Gilbert Swift, occasionally with other now-venerable school contemporaries. Sadly the camp does not exist in the form in which we knew it but the field where we pitched our tents is just the same, as are the rocks, the beach and the woods, and there is still a magic in the air.

In my second year at school (1937) my father was at last able to return to the trade for which he had originally been trained. The emergence of Germany as a military power once again had awakened Britain to the need to strengthen its own Navy, Army and Air Force and engineers were needed. I can remember his joy when he was able to come home one evening and announce that he had got a job which would pay £4 a week. This meant riches untold in terms of the family budget and since his new job was in the village of Eastburn, five miles away on the other side of Keighley, we could rent a bigger and more modern house half a mile from the John Lund works. It seemed an enormous wrench and upheaval, leaving the only home I had ever known, even though we would enjoy the incredible luxury of a bathroom and flush toilet of our very own for the first time! On the Sunday lunchtime before our move I cycled to Eastburn to inspect the village of 600 people which was to be my new home, noting the great sweep of moorland that seemed to tower over the village, with a great gaping hole of a disused quarry. There would be ample compensation for my loss of 't'Delf'. And Peter Walton, a boy in my form at KBGS lived in Eastburn so it would not be too difficult to ease myself gently into a new circle of friends.

Eastburn in 1937 had one general store, a Co-op, a baker's, the regulation fish-and-chip shop and one pub, the White Bear. My choirboy days now came to an end because there was only a Methodist chapel in the village without even a resident minister so the sermons were mostly handled by lay preachers. After the war a 'council' housing estate virtually doubled the size of the place and after that came the great sprawl of the modern Airedale Hospital which is as big as, if not bigger than, the village itself. Eastburn was never the same again. But in those lazy days of the 1930s I loved it. At Ingrow, my company had been largely that of the prolific Stotts – most of them girls – or my cousins, the Ruddocks, who were all slightly younger than me. When you are six or seven years old you have not overmuch time for four- or five-year-olds. Now, in Eastburn, it was good to have as my regular companions five boys of roughly the same age.

Together, over the next few halcyon years, we explored every inch of the surrounding moors, the course of the River Aire, attended school and Sunday School, and discovered girls. Up to that point I had presumably been unaware of a biological difference between the sexes but this was long before the so-called permissive society and relationships were strictly chaste. Nevertheless, I conceived a certain passion at the age of twelve for a young lady named Joan Smith who lived in Ingrow and had taken up employment at the Ritz Cinema, virtually next door to KBGS, as an usherette. On her way to work in the early afternoons she was known to pass slowly outside the school's tarmacadam recreational area – a vision of beauty with a mane of flowing blonde hair. My previous acquaintance with her gave me a certain prestige amongst my schoolfellows since a coy 'Hello, Donald' addressed through the railings which surrounded the school 'yard' represented a considerable sexual advance. The young lady was the first I remember to break away from life in the town by sending a photograph of herself to the Butcher Film Corporation, being offered a contract, changing her name to Sandra Dorne and becoming Keighley's first celebrity in my lifetime. I basked in a certain amount of reflected glory for years after that and even corresponded with her during my subsequent wartime service. Alas, by the time I returned she had been snatched away from any possible resumption of our vague and distant contact.

But at least it gave a tiny feeling of fame-by-association even if I had to wait until Ms Dorne (née Smith) had established herself, and for providing me with the first example of get-up-and-go I had ever experienced I have always felt indebted to the lady. It was all too easy in the 1930s to accept the inevitability of a lifetime which would be spent in the environment of one's birth . . . to accept that one would, as a natural process, drift into employment in either a textile mill or an engineering workshop. If one happened to be a little brighter than the next chap it might mean a position 'in the office' (ie a clerical position) and that would mean a social status at least one degree higher than that of those who merely trudged to and from work wearing overalls. Yet the examples were now before me if I wished to observe them. . . .

Two of the senior boys of KBGS were J. C. (Jack) Hatch and Asa Briggs. The first of these progressed to Sidney Sussex College, Cambridge, and went on to become a most distinguished scholar on modern historical themes, author of a dozen learned works on Africa – and even a member of MCC! In due course he became Lord Hatch of Lusby. The second also graduated as a brilliant historian, again concentrating on nineteenth-century trends and ultimately *the* authoritative figure on the development of the British Broadcasting Corporation – Lord Briggs of Lewes. Their generations of schoolfellows (four years apart) sent out a stream of luminaries into education, the arts, into science and industry – but probably two-thirds of their classmates remained firmly rooted in Keighley or its immediate neighbourhood. There was no easy way out, but the opportunities were clearly there. My problem was always going to be that mental block on matters scientific. I simply could not fathom the mysteries of mathematics beyond simple and straight-forward arithmetic; physics and chemistry might just as well have been taught to us in Sanskrit for my understanding of them. And to pass the School Certificate examination, the doorway to further education, it was essential to pass in mathematics. There was no way I was ever going to do that, notwithstanding modest skills in the arts, and therefore my schooldays were always clouded by that one distant shadow, drawing ever closer as I climbed through Second, Third, Fourth and Fifth forms.

Nevertheless, and despite my spending an inordinate amount of time working off detentions imposed for lack of attention to subjects which did not interest me, I recall those four-and-a-half years at KBGS with tremendous affection. There was always at least one, and usually three or four, masters willing to give up Saturday mornings to organize extra cricket matches; I was playing league cricket on Saturday afternoons from the age of eleven (after serving my apprenticeship as scorer and bag-carrier); there was rugby for house teams and the school second XV; and there was great pleasure in learning more of English, French and German, of history and geography. All this was coupled with close friendship with two classmates, Howard Chester and John Scott Atkinson. Together we formed the most regular trio in detention but academically we had our moments. Chester, I suspect, would still be my friend today but sadly he was lost during the war, flying with the RAF. Almost equally sadly, I lost touch with Atkinson when our lives took different courses on leaving school but I treasure one memory of his complete disruption of an English class.

He had recently conceived a passion for angling and brought into Form 4c a small tin of bait – maggots! – which he intended to put to good use on the River Aire. We were doing *The Tempest* for School Certificate and that afternoon were performing Act IV with Atkinson cast as Trinculo while another boy took the role of Stephano in the scene where the two try on 'the glistering apparel' left for them by Ariel. Poor Atkinson had enough problems in enunciating the line, 'I do smell all horse-piss,' to the accompaniment of clearly audible sniggers all round but in attempting to don an imaginary 'jerkin' he dropped the box of maggots from his pocket on to the floor. The mere sight of the obscene mass of squirming white grubs was enough to send his companion leaping for cover while a gale of laughter, audible throughout the entire school, swept through the class. As the usual trio trooped resignedly into detention the following Friday afternoon it was voted the most spectacularly well-merited punishment of the week. Whatever became of Atkinson, J. S.? He was a major figure in a part of my life which is precious to me. He was but one of many Atkinsons amongst my schoolfellows, just as Butterfields, Laycocks, Binnses and Whittakers abounded amongst the 560 boys of KBGS. They have gone round the world and made their mark in a thousand different ways. The Old Boys' Association linked us in later years.

Indeed, when I worked in Manchester, we formed an official sub-branch to welcome more recent school-leavers who were joining Manchester or Salford Universities and to offer them our hospitality. Others did something similar elsewhere to manifest the pride and affection we felt for the old school. Unlovely as its surroundings were, its name meant a great deal to so many hundreds of us, and to the staff who had seen us through those formative years. Even when a stroke of a Ministerial pen savaged two-and-a-half centuries of service to the community and sent the grammar school plunging into the gloomy abyss of comprehensive education, some of those masters soldiered on, hating almost every minute of their new working lives but still retaining a loyalty to what had gone before. It finally broke the heart of Gilbert Swift, whose entire PE-teaching life had been spent there. He had captured the imagination, earned the respect and admiration of innumerable school-boys. After his wartime service he returned to lead the old boys' Rugby team, Keighlians, to win the Yorkshire Shield (for junior sides, of which they were one) and the Yorkshire Cup (for senior clubs) in the same 1947-8 season. It had never been done before; it has never been done again.

But when the day came when he had to appeal, in morning Assembly, for *volunteers* to fulfil the fixture which was the pride and joy of his Rugby season, against Bradford Grammar School, an appeal which fell on deaf ears amongst his comprehensive flock, he could take no more. He retired early and mercifully has been able to spend time reflecting on the thirty glorious years he had known rather than the last few miserable ones. All this, of course, lay in the future and there was no thought in the 1930s of the senseless and tragic destruction of the country's grammar schools. Those of us who had been fortunate enough to gain places at KBGS were grateful for the opportunities which opened up to us. I cannot think there were many who did not benefit in some way.

Meanwhile, back in the village of Eastburn, six of us were growing together through our teenage years – Peter Walton, Steve Thompson, Cedric Kenyon, Harry Walmsley, Eric Barsby, and myself. Only Cedric is no longer with us. Peter, who has spent his whole life there, keeps us in touch with each other as he did throughout the war years when the others were away. But in 1937-9 we had no thought of our own involvement in war. My own first reaction to the announcement on 3 September 1939, was a feeling of panic that my father might once again be called to serve in the Army.

We had spent the previous three years getting into the usual scrapes – a minor orgy of streetlamp-breaking resulted in an appearance in Juvenile Court and the severest possible punishment at home – but by and large it was a reasonably well-behaved period of our lives. During the summer holidays we played cricket virtually non-stop from first light to sunset – there seemed to be no rain that I can remember! – or roamed the moors behind the village or the river bank in the valley-bottom. Once again, it seemed easiest to create our own world and our own fun from the natural environment. On Sundays, wearing the obligatory suit and collar and tie, more sedate pastimes were required and we walked for miles and miles over those moors, conversation never flagging and laughter rarely far away from our lips. If we were ever bored I do not recall the occasion and I have never watched the wonderful *Last of the Summer Wine* on TV without thinking the writer, Roy Clarke, must have had some sort of similar experience in *his* youth. We were a mixture of William, Ginger and Douglas with Foggy, Compo and Clegg. We discovered caves or built 'hides' on the moors or the woods, and when winter froze the pond in the quarry-bottom we improvized games of ice-hockey without skates. Seasonally, we indulged in more formal pastimes which arrived with mysterious regularity on the scene – like marbles and whip-and-top – and in October we threw sticks into the horse-chestnut trees to knock down our conkers.

In 1938 – the year I was taken by an uncle on a never-to-be-forgotten visit to London to see Len Hutton score his 364 against Bradman's Australians – I was so fascinated by the cricket tourists that I broke with tradition to spend a number of summer evenings exclusively in the company of one of the younger village boys. Duncan Townson was two or three years the junior of The Six and two or three years is a yawning gap when you are a teenager. Nevertheless, Duncan was brighter and more imaginative than the rest of us and, moreover, he showed promise of being a better cricketer than any of us. And even more to the point, he had *his own bat*! Thus, when he approached me with the suggestion of playing our own two-boy Test Match in the playground of the village school (about the same size as the one I had known at Ingrow St. John's), it was a novelty I could not resist. The 'schoolyard' was the necessary venue because the walls provided the fieldsmen we needed with only a couple of practitioners.

The rules were very simple. When 'England' batted, one of us had to adopt the style of each batsman in turn while the other took on the roles of the 'Australian' bowlers. Television being unknown to either of us, all we had seen of the tourists at that start of that season was on the cinema newsreels but we had picked up the main characteristics. And as we were by no means ambidextrous the bowling of Fleetwood-Smith presented certain difficulties – even more so than that of Verity, or the left-handed batting of Paynter and Leyland. I have to confess that the 'series' began to lose something of its appeal for me when Hammond/Townson batted for three complete evenings, Duncan arguing that this was the Second Test at Lord's and the England skipper was on his way to a score of 240. It was for the most part, however, great fun while it lasted and it lasted until Hardstaff/Townson sent an off-driven six through a school window and parental negotiations ensued on the matter of joint payment for the damage.

It is interesting to reflect that immediately after the war the young Townson partnered Eddie Paynter on many occasions when the little left-hander was breaking every Bradford League record as a Keighley batsman and went on in due course via KBGS and Cambridge, to spend most of his life teaching at Sevenoaks School where two of the pupils to pass through his hands were Chris Tavare and Paul Downton. It is quite probable that Duncan regarded this as a straightforward glimpse of his future while we played that childhood Test series; what was most definitely not envisaged was that one day I would tour with both Tavare and Downton and talk to them of those long-remembered occasions in Eastburn.

Looking back, it seemed so easy to entertain ourselves in those teenage years and I often wonder how our attitudes might have been changed if we had known television. Setting aside for a moment (though by no means disregarding) the influence it has on matters like violent crime I find myself regretting as much as anything its destruction of conversational values and the way TV has seemingly damaged youngsters' capacity for creating their own pleasures – of quite simply doing things for themselves. When I was well into my sixties I became quite (possibly unreasonably) angry to read in a newspaper a report from the pleasant village of Bentham at the extreme western tip of Yorkshire about an anonymous letter to the village's community newspaper from young people aged fifteen to seventeen. 'In Bentham there is rarely anything happening for our age so we sit (sic) and wander the boring streets of Bentham,' it read. 'If people are so bothered about us, why don't they help us by putting discos on, opening up the youth club for the day during the holidays, a special youth club for our age?'

The letter accused 'old Benthamers' of not understanding teenage needs and then threatened: 'If nothing is done, I fear Bentham will become a place where damage is done most nights. Also people will be staying up all night as we will not care for them as we have our fun and also there will be a definite increase in house parties. So BE WARNED, help us and we will help you.'

Apart from one's immediate reaction – that 'the younger generation of Bentham,' as the letter was signed, might well take a few lessons in expressing themselves a little better – I am afraid I was saddened and sickened by that report; it was not entirely surprising to learn the police had told the town council that lack of parental control was a contributing factor to the problem. My contemporaries and I did our share of 'hanging about street corners' as a preliminary to deciding how to spend our evening; if the outcome of that decision was activity which brought a complaint to our parents we found ourselves in twice as much trouble. If we were caught scrumping apples and had our backsides kicked our parents did not prosecute the kicker for assault but gave us an extra clip round the ear and a lecture on our behavioural shortcomings. Looking at the six of us who spent those years together I cannot believe that the policy did any irreparable damage to our characters or personalities. But then, of course, we did not have the benefit of social workers and educational psychologists.

3 *Into Journalism*

The Second World War had been in progress for exactly thirteen months when I passed my sixteenth birthday. Thoughts of a university education had disappeared with an abject failure, as expected, in the science part of my School Certificate examination. In odd moments of honesty I acknowledged to myself that with just a little bit of effort I could have managed at least the maths part of the exam but as such reflections led directly to an acceptance that I had let my parents down after their many sacrifices for me I tended to dismiss them. My brother Derek, five years younger, was now taking up *his* scholarship to KBGS and the third of us, Stuart, was only three years old. At least I no longer had to worry about my father being called up as he was now helping to make planes for the Blackburn Aircraft Corporation in Leeds; otherwise, the war seemed destined not to touch us in the village. We learned to identify the aircraft which now droned overhead in greater numbers than we had ever seen before – the very sight or sound of one in the thirties had been enough for us to look up at it – but it was invariably 'one of ours'. Our first wartime holiday, to Morecambe, was under canvas at my insistence because there was to be no more camping at Kirkcudbright for six years and I remember a dash into an air-raid shelter with young Stuart complaining loudly at the interruption of his sleep. No bombs were dropped until the 'planes crossed Morecambe Bay to Barrow and that was the first even remote hint of hostilities I was to experience for three years or so.

Meanwhile, the time had come for me to start work and in those last few months of 1940 I had been scouring the columns of the (Bradford) Telegraph and Argus for some sort of job which seemed even remotely inviting. All I could really show for my four-and-a-half years in grammar school was a reasonable acquaintance with the English language, a prize-winning fluency in German, a modest grasp of French, and a certain familiarity with some aspects of history and geography. I was not exactly highly qualified and only vaguely aware that what school *had* done for me was stimulate the working of my mind. If anyone asked what I hoped to do to earn a living I answered, 'I would like to write,' but there was not an extensive market for my essays. I sent one of them to a magazine which had begun publication in 1939 called *The Yorkshire Dalesman*, and was rewarded with a pleasant and encouraging letter from the editor-proprietor, Harry J. Scott.

This did not cut much ice when I went for an interview with the Keighley branch office representative of *The Yorkshire Post*, and his vacancy for a junior reporter went, quite rightly, to a boy I had known at school, George Emmott. In fact he went on to edit, in due course, the *Manchester Evening News*. But I had built up my hopes of a career in journalism so high that I was in despair when I was turned down. Then, unknown to me, my mother stepped in. A bright, intelligent lady, though her formal education had been modest, she was determined that her boys were going to have a chance, somehow, of making a better life for themselves than she and my father had been able to enjoy. She arranged an interview for me at the *Craven Herald and Pioneer*, the weekly paper printed in Skipton – equidistant from our village but in the opposite direction. I got the job, and a lifetime's love-affair with the communications medium began in December 1940.

I went home for lunch after my first morning, my face reflecting the sheer delight I felt, without giving any great thought to the fact that it meant still more sacrifices for my folks. I was not to receive any pay for my efforts. On the contrary, the directors of the CH & P required my gratitude that they had generously waived 'the paying of a premium for training me.' It meant that my parents, far from having another earner in the family, now had to find the money for a bus-pass between Eastburn and Skipton, plus the cost of shorthand lessons! With utter selfishness, I put such thoughts behind me as I excitedly described the office, the files of newspaper copies going back deep into the nineteenth century, my first colleagues, and the wonder and excitement of it all as I used a typewriter for the first time and laboriously hammered out my first words to be printed in the paper. They were: 'Appended are the results,' and they constituted the lead-in to a printed form bearing the results of a dog show!

The editorial staff consisted of the Editor, Walter Kendall Gott; the chief reporter, John Mitchell; *the* reporter, Charlie Branston; and now a trainee-junior, me. Within a fortnight Mr Gott had joined the Army and a week after that Charlie joined the RAF. John became Editor and I became The Staff. The two years that followed may well read to modern youngsters like some form of Dickensian drudgery; to me they were wonderful, wonderful years which I still recall with unbridled pleasure. I regarded myself as immensely privileged to be on my way to becoming a newspaper reporter. Though I most certainly worked harder than I had ever done in school and than I was ever to do in the future, I never, quite honestly, gave that a thought. The shorthand lessons – from a young lady in a neighbouring village who worked as a shorthand-typist – tailed off after only a few months because of the sheer volume of duties in Skipton. I never got beyond the halving and doubling chapter in Pitman's Guide and my speed increased purely and simply through practice so that in later years when I was specializing in court work I could do 180 words per minute without ever having completed a course of lessons.

Not only had I to take down notes of immensely long weekly lectures – one form of entertainment for the public in those dark, austere wartime years – by Dr Arthur Raistrick, a noted geologist and archaeologist, but John Mitchell, taking his position as the local newspaper editor very seriously, began to use me as a secretary, dictating dozens of letters a week. The *Telegraph and Argus* branch office reporter in Skipton, Percy Illingworth, contributed to the *Herald* a great number of column-inches (by arrangement) on matters like Council meetings and farmers' meetings, and the Editor weighed in with a column of 'gossip notes' called 'A Craven Man's Diary', but just about everything else in the editorial pages was either written, or sub-edited, by the trainee. Almost every day there were paragraphs to be telephoned to the *Yorkshire Evening Post* ('transferred charge call, please, to Leeds 32701') and the *Yorkshire Evening News* ('Leeds 27341') – fifty years later it is absolutely no effort to recall the numbers, so frequently did I ask for them in the name of 'Mitchell, Skipton.' This was 'lineage' with the payment going to the Editor, though it was only after the war that I learned this. I saw not a penny of the money and to be honest I never thought that money might be involved. I was blissfully happy to think that a story I had telephoned might appear in one or both of the Leeds papers.

Every day began with a call to the police station to check whether there had been any road accidents, and every Monday morning I did the rounds of the homes of all local clergymen to inquire what had happened over the weekend in their churches. Proofs of every word to appear in the paper next Friday had to be read – advertisements as well as editorial matter – with no copy-holder. It was a matter of reading three lines of the page-proof, then checking it against the original 'copy'. And I loved it all . . . every syllable, every comma and semi-colon. I was naive – oh *so* naive – but my enthusiasm rarely wavered.

It was my sheer ingenuousness which (almost) gave me the first 'scoop' of my young and innocent life. On the back of an advertisement for a lost sheep from way up in the Dales I was startled to find a message: 'Have two sides of ham, five dozen eggs and a couple of chickens which I will bring in next Saturday.' This, in wartime, austerity-bound Craven! I had uncovered a branch of the Black Market. Just as I was about to rush off to the police station with the evidence I noticed that the note was addressed to an extremely well-known local personality who actually worked for the Craven Herald Ltd. I took it to him first, thus saving him from a hefty fine and myself from the sack!

I can remember being given only one piece of training (in return for the waiving of that premium) by the Editor. It was, quite simply, to get all the facts and to get them right. It was from the printers that most of my tuition came, notably the works foreman, Reg Billows, a marvellous man who corrected my spelling, improved my grammar, revolutionized my punctuation and was always available to dispense sound advice on any subject when I required it. I owe him more than I could ever repay. In 1942 we were joined by another man for whom I conceived a tremendous affection – Harry J. Scott, he who had sent me that encouraging note three years earlier. He had sunk all his savings into *The Yorkshire Dalesman*, publishing it from his home in the beautiful village of Clapham, some twenty-five miles away. Wartime restrictions on the use of paper had meant the 'pegging' of the circulation of his little magazine which made it an uneconomical enterprise. By taking up part-time work on the *Herald* he managed to keep the *Dalesman* afloat throughout the war years so that from 1945 onwards he was later able to expand its scope, dropping the 'Yorkshire' from the masthead, and building up a flourishing publishing business with a readership which extends to expatriates all over the world who love the countryside. I thought I knew a little about nature and wildlife, country customs and people, until I met H. J. Scott. Apart from being my tutor in so many aspects of journalism he was one of the kindest and most generous-hearted men I have ever known.

The part of the job I liked least was having to call at the homes of war casualties to collect biographical details and, where possible, a photograph, but as in everything else in my new world there were lessons to be learned like tact and discretion and compassion. Just before he joined the Army I had met Noel Wild, a contemporary of Charlie Branston, who was a reporter with an East Lancashire group of newspapers (ultimately becoming Editor of the Nelson Leader), and I had begun a correspondence with Noel which lasted right through the war. He was a Desert Rat of the Eighth Army with marvellous stories to relate (within the limitations imposed by censorship) with a good journalist's touch, while I kept him in touch with the scene at home – his mother and sister lived in Skipton – with what I hoped was a developing sense of literary humour. We have been firm friends now for fifty years and our every meeting is punctuated with laughter at frequent intervals. These are the good things of life.

Skipton was a good place to be spending those first two or three years of the war. We were subject to austerity and rationing like everyone else. Though air-raids or airborne invasions never threatened us we had to observe black-out regulations, to immobilize cars at night, to carry gas masks and to contend with painted-out road signs. Troops were stationed in the town, amongst them the handsome film star Richard Greene who caused much fluttering of hearts amongst our girls. Down the valley at Keighley Girls' Grammar School the numbers were swelled by the arrival of evacuees from a London school including a young lady named Patsy Sloots who was destined to become the film starlet Susan Shaw. There was interest and excitement for us without any of the dangers. Life went on as before with the Dales farmers and their wives thronging Skipton's wonderful old cobbled High Street on Saturday mornings on their weekly visit to town. I loved – still love – that street with its Norman Church at its top, side by side with the great Castle of the Romillys and Cliffords.

Skipton calls itself 'The Gateway to the Dales' and it is a splendidly accurate title for beyond the castle for thirty, forty, and fifty miles to the west and the north the countryside opens out into the glorious valleys of the Aire, the Wharfe, the Nidd, the Ure, the Swale and the Ribble. It is enchanted country, rich in legend and in pre-history. It is a land of high moorland and gentle pastures, of great limestone fells and caves and potholes which honeycomb their slopes; of woods where rich carpets of bluebells follow in the wake of primroses and violets; of lakes and rivers and waterfalls; of tiny, hidden villages where the cattle (and the unmarried daughters) were secured from the Scottish rievers. From north to south this wonderland stretches for something like fifty miles with only a slightly lesser girth from east to west. And this was my 'beat' as a trainee-reporter. Not that I was able to venture far into it during those early years. Intelligence from the far-flung outposts was contributed by a host of village correspondents who reported on a quite astonishing variety of fund-raising efforts on behalf of different branches of the war effort. The news came on a variety of types of paper. Miss Woodhead of Dent sewed together her several pages a week with cotton thread; Miss Seed of Bentham seemed singularly fortunate in being able to get chocolate because her notes on whist drives, church services – and the inevitable war casualties – were written on the inside of wrappings which had once covered bars of Cadbury's Blended Chocolate (no dairy milk in those hard days).

In Skipton, the metropolis of the huge rural area of Craven, there were Salute the Soldier Weeks, Wings for Victory Weeks, savings campaigns and, on one never-to-be-forgotten occasion, an exhortation to our farmers to make even greater efforts of production voiced by the Joint Parliamentary Secretaries to the Ministry of Agriculture and Fisheries (in the Coalition Government), respectively Mr Tom Williams MP and the Duke of Norfolk. Percy Illingworth, who covered the event for the *Herald*, came into the office the following morning to report that His Grace, the Earl Marshal of England, had signally failed to get on the same wavelength as his audience, which was not entirely surprising since *he* was largely concerned with pedigree dairy herds managed for him by underlings while *they* were all about hardy herds of moorland sheep. When the time came for questions (reported Percy) one of these gnarled veterans of the fells stepped out into the aisle of the town hall and delivered the following comment: 'I've nowt to ask but I'd just like to say summat. If 'is Royal 'Ighness the Duke of Norfolk can be t'joint Parliamentary Secretary to t'Ministry of Agriculture and Fisheries I see no damn reason why I can't be t'bloody Prime Minister of England.'

Notwithstanding the terrible events which were taking place all round the world, in *my* little world it was possible to find something to laugh at almost every day. And yet the war, in other ways, was never very far from us. When I reached the age of seventeen-and-a quarter it was possible for me to volunteer for the Services. My parents, not unnaturally, were against it but the final word came from the directors of the Craven Herald Ltd who solemnly held a board meeting to discuss this weighty matter and decided that I could not be spared to throw my nine-and-a-half stones into the war effort. However, a new junior was taken on to our ration-strength – Bill Mitchell, later to join Harry Scott at *The Dalesman* magazine and to become, in due course, its Editor as well as a considerable author and lecturer. When my next request was submitted to the directors they graciously agreed and off I went to the recruiting office in Bradford one Saturday afternoon. I had had probably the best grounding anyone could possibly have in grass-roots journalism; I loved the life passionately and my sights were now firmly fixed on Fleet Street. But that would have to wait for a while.

My war had so far been an unreal affair. I now took a train to London, to the Aircrew Receiving Centre at Lord's Cricket Ground, medical category A1, and four-and-a-half years later emerged from the depot of the Army Education Corps at Buchanan Castle (on the bonny banks of

Loch Lomond), category C4. In between I had seen France, Egypt, India, Persia, Iraq, Transjordan and Palestine, developed a taste for travel, acquired a bent foot and one or two other bits and pieces which were not quite perfect and learned just a little about life. I had joined up as a teetotal non-smoking virgin and an insufferable prig. I returned still a non-smoker and not quite so much of a prig. My girlfriend had deserted me, causing the sort of anguish known to those who have experienced the sharp pangs of first love, but there was now a whole new post-war world to explore. I was actually demobilized in York at 10 a.m. in June 1947, and by 2 p.m. I was in the office at 38, High Street, Skipton, desperately anxious to resume my career. This rebounded on me in due course because as I was entitled to thirteen weeks' leave (with pay) and as I now resumed work immediately, I eventually found myself in trouble with the Income Tax Inspector, having incurred a debt it took me six years to discharge!

My first thoughts now were to pick up the threads, to establish as quickly as possible that I had not forgotten anything I had learned and, once assured of this, to press on with 'the career'. Skipton and The Dales were very much livelier than I had known them, the clouds of the war having lifted. I volunteered to cover every story which was just a bit more than run-of-the-mill on a rural weekly paper. The discovery of a couple of skeletons in a cave high up in the limestone country proved a great help. Were they the bones of spies who had parachuted into the wide-open spaces of the Craven uplands? Were they the remains of German aircrew? Or were they the victims of an undetected crime? The inquest failed to establish any explanation and the mystery helped in churning out story after story not only for the Leeds papers but for the 'nationals' as well. At last I felt I might be getting somewhere. In the meantime there were diversions in a lighter vein.

A film was being made in Craven called *A Boy, a Girl and a Bike* with John Gregson, Honor Blackman and a sixteen-year-old nymphette called Diana Dors. The production was based principally in the lovely village of Burnsall, in Wharfedale, and I did several stories about it. One day, hitching a lift into Skipton in a taxi bearing the lively Miss Dors, I was startled when she said, 'I heard a joke last night but there was one word in it I'm not quite sure about. What's a penis?' I gulped and felt my face go crimson. The discomfiture was not helped by catching the eye of the taxi-driver in his rear-view mirror. 'Well . . . ?' demanded the sixteen-year-old. I gulped again. 'Look,' she pursued the matter impatiently, 'is it a prick?' The driver's shoulders heaved; the car swerved slightly. 'Yes,' I gasped. 'Well why didn't you bloody well say so,' came the petulant sign-off line. Miss Dors addressed no further word to me, and I had none to offer to her.

I was still a prig.

I was also twenty-two, earnest, ambitious. Charlie Branston had returned from the RAF, Bill Mitchell from the Royal Navy and in our collective absence the *Herald* had taken on two extra juniors. One was Ron Evans, destined to become Director of Programmes with HTV in Bristol in due course; the other was my brother, Derek, who has been a weekly paper editor for twenty-nine years and was awarded the MBE in 1990 for his services to journalism. Even with more newsprint available and extra pages each week the *Craven Herald & Pioneer* was overstaffed. It was not so much a matter of their being insufficient work to keep us all busy. The directors of the paper had become used to the idea of having diligent enthusiasts toiling heartily through six years of war for nothing. They were now obliged to pay a wage of some kind to all of us (£4 a week in my case) and the weekly payroll now disturbed the economics of their operations. With my usual ingenuousness, this had escaped me and I had acute feelings of disloyalty as I wrote letters each week applying for jobs on bigger newspapers. My guilt was finally washed away when John Mitchell took me on one side: 'I have always thought you were an ambitious lad who wouldn't stay with us,' he said. 'Ron and Derek have to do their National Service and I'm sure they'll be away after that but in the meantime we've got to keep them here. Charlie doesn't want to move from Skipton so *he'll* stay. But we just can't afford the staff we've got. If you want any help in getting another job I'll give you a good reference.'

'Thanks. Yes. I would like that,' I replied. And the following week came the offer of a place on the reporting staff of the *Yorkshire Evening Press*, in York. I snatched their hand off. And, with the now princely emolument of £8 a week I married Josephine Ann Tillotson, a noted athlete, gymnast and hockey player of nineteen years, whose tolerance, fortitude, generosity and love have been greater than I deserved.

There can be few more pleasant places to start married life than York, especially to someone with a keen interest in mediaeval history. The editorial staff of the *Evening Press* were, without exception, a delightful bunch of people and my first year's experience of a paper which was published daily was pleasant in the extreme. I was warmly welcomed by the Rugby Union Club, played a lot of cricket locally as well as back in the West Riding and my first taste of Assize Court reporting fired my enthusiasm as no specialist branch of journalism had done up to that point. Hitherto I had simply regarded myself as a reasonably competent all-rounder, happy to turn his hand to anything that came up on the diary.

Now I found myself waiting for the Assizes to come round with sharp anticipation. Possibly there could have been no better starting point to stimulate this interest than York.

To reach the court meant walking past Clifford's Tower, astride its imposing *motte*, and the cell where Dick Turpin was reputed to have spent his last night on earth – tourist attractions which appealed to me no less than the hordes of visitors who milled about them. But it was *inside* the court that I felt the liveliest excitement no matter what the nature of the case being tried. The sheer majesty of The Law was something which impressed me profoundly – the trappings and the pageantry, the pronouncements in Norman-French and the legal jargon in Latin. But most of all I loved the *English* of The Law. The wit was of a calibre I had scarcely encountered outside the pages of a book; I admired the elaborate care devoted to an outline of the case designed to make matters clear to the least erudite juror; the exquisite courtesy of barristers to the judge, the judge to barristers and the barristers to each other. This was English as spoken on another planet compared with the rough, gruff argot which was my native tongue.

I had, in fact, taken the first crude, fumbling steps towards making myself intelligible in the spoken word after hearing the meticulous enunciation of Percy Illingworth, the *Telegraph and Argus* man in Skipton, when I first met him eight years earlier. Percy spoke with a delicate precision which was entirely different from that of anyone else I knew. He consciously searched for the most appropriate word to use in any given context. His philosophy seemed to be: if something is worth saying it is worth saying well, as accurately as possible. And I had made a mental note to try to follow his example. To do so in Percy's presence might have smacked of impertinence – at best, my motives might have been misunderstood – so I waited until other opportunities presented themselves. They came in abundance in my Service days, notably in India where a reasonable mode of speech was a passport to a better social life when off duty, especially when accompanied by an ability to play Bridge (at which I worked hard).

So by 1948, while retaining my Northcountry vowels, which I was pretty sure I would be unable to discard even if I had wanted to, I had tidied up and disciplined my speech to a certain extent. Sitting in court for days on end helped to extend the vocabulary and to cultivate new resonances. Just why I was doing this was something I would have found difficult to explain. Possibly, somewhere in my subconscious, there was the thought that as a journalist it was my job to write intelligible copy, and it was equally desirable for my conversation to be readily understood and as interesting as it was possible to make it. It was all about communication.

All this apart, I actually *enjoyed* those days in court for a whole range of other reasons. I was somehow a part, peripherally at any rate, of the process of The Law since it was my report that told the general public what happened to the criminals in their midst; friendships developed with police officers and, in due course, a number of lawyers; occasionally I saw what were seen by those same police and lawyers to be miscarriages of justice when juries returned 'wrong' verdicts; I saw 'guilty' decisions in murder trials and was unable to repress a faint shudder as the judge donned the symbolic black 'cap' and passed the death sentence; I watched as men (and a few women) went away for long stretches of imprisonment and wondered what it would be like for them; I heard brilliant and persuasive arguments by counsel and marvelled at their legal and verbal skills; and above all, as the more bizarre cases unfolded I learned the great Truth: that it is indeed stranger than fiction.

My particular friend on the editorial staff of the *Evening Press* was Len Sutton, the racing correspondent, who topped the table of newspaper tipsters in my year in York. He had excellent contacts in the many stables around York, Wetherby and Malton and from time to time produced a spectacular coup which he shared with me and with the paper's Rugby League correspondent, Bert Foster. The outstanding success was when he 'napped' a two-year-old filly (could there be a greater lottery?) called Beautiful Morning which romped home a winner at 33 to 1, earning Len the undying hatred of all *local* bookmakers. The unknown form of the horse, the massive unpredictability of that type of race and the presence of more fancied candidates all combined to induce those long odds from the on-the-course bookies. But the local housewives who liked a sixpence-each-way flutter found Len Sutton's confident tip too good to miss and invested heavily. It was the street-corner bookmakers who suffered.

Each Saturday the three of us – Len, Bert and myself – jointly invested in what I learned was called a 'Yankee' by picking four horses and backing them in six doubles, four trebles and an accumulator. We rarely made an outright loss, broke even more often than not and occasionally hit the jackpot as on the Saturday before I was married. Our chosen four (all Len Sutton's selections, needless to say) included a noble beast called Electric Whiskers which won at 100-6 and as it was coupled with three other, shorter-priced winners, Len was able to slip to me an envelope at the wedding reception containing my handsome share of the proceeds. Up to that point I was not entirely certain how I was going to pay for the honeymoon!

That was a good year in every possible way. There were off-beat moments like the one when I interviewed Sir John Barbirolli and learned that one of his ambitions was to walk round the city walls of York at midnight and I was able to fix up for him to do so. There was the time, more in keeping with my Hollywood-inspired view of newspaper work ('Hold the front page!' 'Stand by for a replate'), when *The Yorkshire Post* started scooping us on our own doorstep by reporting courts martial at Fulford Barracks about which we knew nothing on the *Evening Press*. Each morning for a fortnight I posted myself near the YP branch office and followed whichever of the Leeds paper's two representatives emerged first. Patience was finally rewarded when I trailed Peter Woods (later a BBC newsreader) to Fulford . . . to report, sure enough, a court martial. The YP were bunging a sergeant-major a quid to tell them when such occasions were due – my first introduction to cheque-book journalism. Our problem was solved by a quiet word with the sergeant-major: What would his commanding officer say if he knew one of his warrant officers was taking money to keep the Press informed? Thereafter the CSM still got his pound for ringing the YP – but he 'phoned us as well . . . for nothing.

Laughter was never very far from our professional lives. Whenever two or three journalists are gathered together an exchange of experiences from the daily round and common task can be guaranteed to throw up a whole series of anecdotes. And every day there was a gathering over morning coffee in a cinema restaurant in Coney Street or at lunchtime in the wonderful old Star pub in Stonegate. At that time the *Evening Press* was part of the Kemsley group of newspapers and Lady Kemsley had ventured north to visit the Royal Show when it was held on Knavesmire – the great recreational space to the west of the city. While on a visit to the local office, she had regarded a picture of a prize-winning bull as too indelicate to be printed in one of the group's newspapers, and had ordered the 'painting out' of the equipment that gave the animal its exalted status. This had led, inevitably, to a threat of legal action from the proud owner when the picture of his beast appeared in the *Evening Press*, mysteriously and miraculously emasculated!

The sports-writing staff of the *Evening Press* was not a large one and several people doubled up on duties between news and sport. The Assistant Editor, Wilf Meek, for instance, reported York City's football and was also a director of the club, too, which must have led occasionally to a conflict of interest. As a newsman with certain sporting interests I was asked from time to time to cross the editorial floor, so to speak, and I enjoyed these sorties into Rugby Union and cricket. It was during a

Rosebuds match (Yorkshire II v Lancashire II) at Scarborough that I first experienced the artistry of Johnny Wardle and, coincidentally, enjoyed strawberries and cream for the first time since my pre-war childhood. These were still days of austerity and food rationing was to continue for five or six years yet. And it was at York Cricket Club that I exchanged my first words with a young man playing for Yorks II v Northumberland who was to become one of my closest friends – and a broadcasting colleague as well – Freddie Trueman.

Occasionally I volunteered for an afternoon of sub-editing duties and sometimes, on a day off, I would spend an hour or two in the printing works (with the foreman's permission, of course – never upset the print unions!) watching how the pages were made up. This was going to be my job for the rest of my working life and I wanted to know everything I could find out about it. Beyond my liking for being in the High Court I harboured no thoughts of specialization. What did appeal to me was the hope that one day I would be able to turn my hand to any job on the editorial side of newspapers. It was a good life, one which held out the possibility of enjoying myself on most days of the week and being paid for doing so. How many people that I knew could say that? It seemed to me that if I had searched the whole field of employment I could have found no job more suited to my limited talent, none more calculated to provide job satisfaction, none in which I could more realistically nurture ambitions of rising to the top without academic qualifications. There was a whole world of newspapers and magazines 'out there' for me to explore if I could achieve the right degree of competence. The possibilities seemed endless. It was time for me to make the next move.

4 *In the Midlands*

It was a tremendous wrench to leave York, with all its natural beauty and its historic fascination, to part from the good friends I had made on the *Evening Press*, the days I had enjoyed on the cricket field and the beautiful racecourse, but ambition clamoured and I had 'lost' four-and-a-half years. I then made the catastrophic error of accepting a job as a reporter on the *Evening Telegraph* in Derby. It lasted precisely six weeks, including the month's notice I had to work after spending a fortnight discovering what a mess I had made of my second move! From the management's point of view at that time it was, I suppose, simply good business to work on the most parochial of lines and to have relatively experienced reporters covering things like parish council meetings. We hadn't even done that on the *Craven Herald*, leaving parish pump matters in the hands of village correspondents. But the *Evening Telegraph* seemed not to want anything written in a different way from the one in which it had been done since the paper was first printed. When one local parish council criticized its recreation ground supervisor I walked for miles after the meeting to find the home of the maligned official so I could give his point of view and 'balance' the story when I wrote it the following day. This brought a rebuke from the assistant editor who told me he wanted no 'fancy national paper stuff' in the *Evening Telegraph*.

And in purely mercenary terms, it took me that first fortnight, adding all my 'expenses' together, to reach a total of five shillings, or 25 pence in modern terms! We were not allowed to charge for meals, no matter how late our duties lasted (and parish councils can talk long into the night) and the news editor knew to the last ha'penny what the bus fare was to every far-flung outpost of the *Telegraph's* circulation area. There *were* talented journalists on the staff, of course – men like Frank Nicklin who went on to become a brilliant sports editor of *The People* and *The Sun*, and Angus

McPherson whom I never saw again after moving on from Derby but whose name frequently appeared in the *Daily Mail* as air correspondent, then defence correspondent – but many of my colleagues seemed resigned to what they took to be a normal newspaper life. Two things made life just a little more bearable during that hideous first fortnight.

On my first morning, doing the rounds of the police 'calls' (to check on road accidents; there was no way the Derby Borough Police were disposed to give information about more heinous 'crimes' to the local Press) I discovered in the Traffic Office one Sergeant Arthur Bassett, a former Welsh international winger who had joined the Halifax Rugby League Club just before the War and moved to the York Club in the mid-1940s. I had known him as a League star but had completely forgotten that he travelled from Derby to play each week; he, on the other hand, knew of my connection with York Rugby Union Club.

'What are *you* doing here?' he asked.

'I've joined the *Telegraph*,' I replied. 'Started today.'

'Right, man,' he grinned. 'Make your day off Wednesday and there's a game for you.'

I hadn't even started to think about Rugby but the unbridled delight of the news editor, when I returned to the office and asked for Wednesday to be my day off, was wonderful to behold. There was, if not open warfare between the paper and the police, a marked coolness which, it appeared, stemmed from the dislike of the Press by the Chief Constable, Colonel Horatio Rawlings, formerly of the Neath RFC. The Colonel was a pioneer of police Rugby and the presence in his force's team of a *Telegraph* reporter could only help towards a thawing of the cold war. Permission was joyfully given and four remarkable seasons began. It was not, in point of fact, an immediate way to the Colonel's heart. He rather resented the fact that a full XV could not be raised from his own ranks and the recruitment of guest players was permitted with grudging, rather than enthusiastic, consent. I was not the only outsider by any means. Derek Morgan, a young man with experience at the mighty Northampton Club, was qualifying by residence as a Derbyshire CCC all-rounder and he was a talented fly-half; Bob Tomlinson, who worked for the Post Office, played at scrum-half; Harry Parkes, a popular publican, was a speedy winger with much top-class Rugby behind him; and in the front row we had a bearded giant called Jackson whose first name I never knew although we became good friends because he was universally known as 'Jacko'. He was manager of the Butterley Estates on the Notts-Derbys border and a damn good forward.

Jacko was a regular player with the Derby Club and he brought to the performances of the Derby Borough Police XV not only valuable know-how but copious amounts of rum which, drunk before the game by his fellow members of the front-row union, caused a number of complaints from opposing teams that their heavy mob were emerging intoxicated from the first scrum as a result of inhaling the breath of their opposites. Jacko once got a non-travelling reserve card for an England trial and we looked on him with pride as well as enormous affection, particularly when he started to bring along to away games a hugely engaging Great Dane bitch called Juno. I can remember her name from forty years ago but not her master's!

Of the serving policemen in our ranks were Jim Bousher, a stalwart prop, Walt Scotford, hooker and a *Glorster* man much given to bursting into song after the match with that well-known West Country air, 'Whar be that blackbird too, I know where 'e be'; Jack Sergeant was a star who was regularly chosen for the British Police XV and was occasionally joined by Tony Jones, a gifted centre. And when we played sides from Army or RAF units Arthur Bassett was smuggled into the team under an assumed name. Colonel Rawlings would not allow the serious illegality of a Rugby League man playing in the Union ranks against other police sides but he turned a blind eye to the now veteran winger-cum-full-back turning out against clubs where he might not be known. There was an Ordnance Corps unit stationed not too far from Derby with whom we had a regular fixture due entirely to the presence in the Army ranks of a very young, red-haired second-lieutenant. We sensed from the first that something like ninety per cent of his side had been pressured into playing either by threats against their future happiness on that post or promises of an afternoon away from unappealling duties. In short, they weren't very good and they may well have been the only side we beat away from home during the four seasons I spent with Derby Borough Police. (When I quickly shook the dust of the *Evening Telegraph* from my shoes I moved twelve miles to Nottingham and continued the rugby connection.)

Fairly late in this career I was moved, in an emergency, from full-back to scrum-half for a match at the aforementioned Army unit. Arthur Bassett was making one of his rare appearances, some years after retirement and was not, one might say, at the peak of physical condition. Not being too familiar with the intricacies of half-back play I was relieved to see the ball emerge on 'our' side of the scrum with no sign of marauding flankers.

Without a thought for the fly-half who was waiting to find touch, I passed to the nearest available team-mate – Bassett, standing on my right. And by one of those miracles which do sometimes occur in a match (or used to, in less efficient days) he had a clear passage to the opposition line. Unfortunately, it happened to be some 100 yards away at the other end of the field. But old habits die hard and the old boy set off nobly, at least to make a show of it, and sadly for him the unorthodox tactics of the scrum-half had taken our opponents completely by surprise. Bassett had a good ten yards' start. Thus, on and on he ran, finally collapsing in an exhausted heap at the distant end of the field where he remained while the conversion was taken, the re-start effected and the next ten minutes of play ensued. When he was finally able to return to combat duty he sought me out without thought for other, more pressing matters taking place about him.

'If you ever do that again, bach,' he hissed, 'I'll bloody kill you.'

In common with most other Rugby teams we liked to acquire a trophy or two to be taken back to Derby from away games in the same spirit of harmless fun which decrees the prizes must be returned, intact and unmutilated, within the next week. We had, therefore, a particular fondness for visits to the Worcestershire County Constabulary whose headquarters and playing fields were at Hindlip Hall. The late Lord Hindlip had obviously been a successful big game hunter in his day for the hall was festooned with the trophies of many a safari. It was something like Aladdin's Cave to visiting sides bent on pillage, if not rape, and the after-match festivities were marked by much coming and going by the visitors and even more guarded patrolling by the home team. Nevertheless, we usually managed to embark for the return trip with a fair amount of plunder and on one notable occasion we left with a lion's head attached by ropes to the bonnet and a giraffe, sawn off at the neck, peering in perplexity through the sunshine roof, while most of the players were armed with knobkerries, spears and even the odd blow-pipe or two. As this took place in mid-December our delight in the acquisition of the giraffe diminished in direct ratio to the drop in temperature in the bus with its sunroof open on the return journey. The passage of the giraffe caused remark in most of the towns and villages through which we travelled, the temperature now at sub-zero levels but the pleas of those demanding the dumping of the camelopard met with stern rebuke from the team manager.

Detective Officer Ossie Lloyd was by far the most long-suffering member of the Derby Force. Apart from the headaches of getting together a team each week to fulfil the fixtures he had so lovingly arranged, he was charged with a thousand other duties connected with a wild and rebellious mob of social drinkers, the most difficult of which was ensuring that trophies were honorably returned to their rightful owners.

After a trip to Hindlip Hall his problems were magnified a thousandfold. British Rail at Derby Midland Station were not entirely sympathetic to his problems of sending the uppermost third of one giraffe in a freight van on a cross-country journey, not to mention the decapitated portion of a lion, the odd gnu or wildebeest and a fearsome selection of weapons of largely aboriginal origin. Forty years on I remember my seasons with that Derby side and my friendships with its members with immense affection and many a smile.

The second reason that made life a little more enjoyable was the 'digs' I found while my wife searched for a suitable flat. We settled, *pro tem.*, in the home of a man who bred terriers and boarded the pets of other dog-owners while they went on holiday. This gave me (as the world's No. 1 dog-lover who, after marriage, was not allowed a pooch of his own) the opportunity to exercise a whole pack of hounds of all shapes and sizes in a neighbouring park every evening I was available. It delighted me, irritated my wife and amazed our landlord whose attitude to the canine world was strictly commercial. He was grateful, nevertheless, to be relieved of irksome chores by such a willing volunteer and as a quid pro quo he initiated me into the mysteries of breeding. I was naively (I suppose) startled to find that not all certificates of pedigree are entirely reliable. Our host, for instance – I shall not name him since he may well still be flourishing in the business – had a champion with the most distinguished antecedents if not character. In fact it was a nasty, evil-tempered, permanently yapping creature which objected to being exercised on a lead. (In view of its value my instructions were *never* to let it off the lead.) Terrier bitches were shipped from all over the country to be mated with this anti-social cur, a sexual encounter which seemed to afford little pleasure to either party but which increased X's bank balance substantially.

But . . . X was keenly aware of all owners whose dogs would sooner or later be competing against his own strains in provincial and even national shows. The mere hint of competition sent X quickly across the road to the home of an elderly widow, Mrs Jordan, whose floppy, sloppy pet was originally from a good strain but had long since disappeared from the pages of the canine Debrett. Stud Dog Jordan had, however, lost none of his procreative qualities or his sexual appetites despite his years as a much-loved lap dog and any summons from X was greeted with much tail-wagging and licking of sensual lips. I have often wondered how many of Stud Dog Jordan's progeny have attained a spurious fame.

It was during my second week in Derby that I nipped across the border to the fair city of Nottingham and acquired a job on the *Journal*, a daily paper, and its companion evening publication, the *Evening News*. This was a

Westminster Press newspaper of Dickensian character and yet I stayed for four-and-a-half years! Just why this happened is a little difficult to explain so let me start by saying my wife and I loved the city (and still do). There were a lot of good journalists there, many of whom were destined to go on to better things; I was able to continue my social Rugby by returning to Derby once a week, and with the sometimes unreliable help of a 1932 BSA 500cc motorbike (a noble if venerable beast with a hand gear-change) I was able to return to Yorkshire to play cricket in summer; and the social life amongst the newspapermen and women was so good that it became increasingly difficult to tear oneself away.

In the early days there I joined the weekly knot of colleagues who congregated at the station each Thursday when there was a cheap-day excursion fare to London, to knock on the doors of Fleet Street news editors. Just before Christmas, 1950, I was finally offered a post in London – but returned home to receive the news that our first-born was due the following summer. This changed the whole direction of my life. Lusting after the glamour and potential glory of national newspaper reporting was one thing when my young wife and I could fend for ourselves. Leaving her and our son (the child was always going to be a son – no doubts on that score) in what I have always believed to be the cold, uncaring and impersonal atmosphere of the capital while I roamed the world was quite another thing.

My upbringing in a tightly-knit family where every waking thought of my parents had been for the welfare and future of their three boys convinced me that my career had to be in the provinces. It was in many ways illogical. Friends and colleagues took off regularly in search of better things, some of them to London, a few of them even with young families. But I was very much a product of my environment. Only when our two boys were old enough to look after themselves *and* their lady mother did I allow the wanderlust to take over and send me to the other side of the world for months on end. I certainly missed out on career opportunities and I have often questioned the wisdom of that decision.

In November 1949 I reported for duty at the office of the *Journal and Evening News* in Parliament Street, Nottingham. It was not an auspicious beginning. Along with my newly acquired motorcycle had come an RAF flying-suit, extremely handy on winter mornings with such an exposed form of transport. On the previous Saturday, playing for Derby Tigers against Notts Casuals, I had damaged the ligaments of my right knee, and now after climbing two flights of stairs to the reporters' room I presented a Bader-like figure, still in flying-suit and hobbling badly, as I introduced myself to the news editor Bob Bowley, and his deputy Jim Hall. About an

43

hour later, discreetly waiting until I was sitting alone, Mr Hall (terms of address were on a strictly formal basis) approached me uncertainly and then, taking the plunge, inquired solicitously, 'Do you suffer from a war-wound, Mr Mosey?' We had not met when I fixed up my appointment (I saw only the editor, a Mr Swinburne) so I suppose it was a reasonable misunderstanding but the inquiry took me by surprise. When I got the drift of the question I replied airily, 'Oh, no. I just damaged my knee last week playing Rugby.' Overcome with embarrassment, Mr Hall beat a hurried retreat and I don't think he ever quite forgave me in the next four-and-a-half years.

He was a decent sort, as was Bob Bowley, a gentlemanly journalist of the old school. Like most provincial papers, our columns were filled not only by staff reporters but by legions of district correspondents, telephoning reports that consisted largely of well-tried clichés strung together in a way that was designed to gain the correspondent as much space as possible, for he was paid on a basis of so-much-per-line. But there were no expert typists, equipped with headphones, to take down these reports as there had been in York and were, to the best of my knowledge, on all other papers worth their salt; copy-taking had to be done by the reporters. As the editor blithely explained when I hurried after him on my first day, 'Why should I pay copy-takers £10 a week when I can get the job done by reporters on £13 who are useful in other ways?' The logic could not be faulted. But the unspoken implication was plain: if we didn't like it we could always move on and someone less sensitive in terms of professional pride would be happy to take over.

And so there existed a state of war between reporters, fully-fledged members of the National Union of Journalists, and the district correspondents who were journalistic laymen. In the office matters were made even worse by the fact that we had *two* typewriters between (when we were all on parade) seventeen reporters. 'Copy' had to be taken in shorthand – to save the firm money on the cost of transferred-charge calls – and transcribed into longhand before being pushed through a hatch to the sub-editors. I couldn't think of another paper I had heard of where the subs would *accept* handwritten copy, let alone 'top-and-tail' it and put up the headlines. This unhappy situation reached its nadir on Saturday afternoons when all pretence of bringing out a *news*paper went by the board and the decks were cleared for action in production of the sports edition. In the circulation war with the *Evening Post* it was vital to get this on to the streets at the earliest possible opportunity. Even minutes counted in terms of street sales to those who (a) wanted to check their football coupons, and (b) to read Bill Botting's account of the Notts

County match, or Arthur Turner's on Nottingham Forest so they could mutter in disgust, 'This bugger has been at a different match ter me.' There was none of the sophistication of television in the Midlands at that time and radio results did not come up until after six o'clock on the regional programme. Those sports editions, all over the country, were absolute miracles of newspaper production. Every department worked in a state of frenzy.

The best shorthand-writers on the staff were given the job of taking a note from Bill Botting or Arthur Turner. The rest of us were left to deal with the shorter, but less accomplished, reports from our lay correspondents. Despite my volunteering for as much court work as possible as soon as I arrived in Parliament Street, no one seemed to have worked out that this required a pretty swift and reliable shorthand note. I did not trumpet the fact. And despite my interest in sporting matters no one seemed to have noticed that I might have some knowledge of things other than playing Rugby or cricket. Thus, by keeping a low profile on winter Saturdays, I found myself regularly employed on such matters of all-transcending importance as Langwith Junction Imps v Bilsthorpe Colliery Rangers, and half a dozen other matches of similar ilk. This was easy because the reports were largely duplicates of the previous week's string of clichés . . . 'Following a touchline dash, Smith sent a rasping cross-shot into the side-rigging,' . . . 'End-to-end-play ensued,' . . . 'The custodian was fully extended.' The phrases never varied from one week to the next. Never. So one simply sat with pencil poised, waiting for the name of a scorer, and then slotted it in amidst the welter of tired and well-worn descriptive passages which could simply be made up as one desired.

Thus were generations of *news* reporters from Nottingham brought up despising sports writers as cliché-ridden hacks of the worst type. Certainly it never crossed my mind for one fleeting fraction of a second that I might one day join them. I was a *news* man and proud of it, modest though my role might be at that moment. Some of my colleagues went even further. Not only did they know nothing about sport but they didn't want to know, either; in fact it became a sort of fetish in our newsroom to display the highest and most sublime ignorance of all sporting matters. Thus, strange messages dropped from time to time on the sport sub-editors' desk, like, 'Notts team to play Trent at Gillingham will be skippered by Artie Simpson,' which should, of course, have read, 'Notts team to play Kent at Gillingham will be skippered by R. T. Simpson.' Across the road at the *Post* they actually printed, and sent out on to the streets, 'Notts 283 for six, Bob White stopped play.' That classic has moved into the legends of the game to such an extent that it is regarded by many as apocryphal. It isn't. I actually saw it appear in the Stop Press column of the Nottingham *Evening Post*.

Observing the cricket-writing of the late forties had a certain appeal, particularly the writing of the two papers for which I worked. Dear old Arthur Turner had two styles. For the *Evening News* he ad libbed his copy to one of us in the office via the telephone; for the *Journal* he gave his report sober consideration before composing a piece in what we knew as his Cardus style. Forty years later I can recall with absolute clarity two extracts from those reports in our papers:

Notts v Lancs (*Evening News*): 'Tattersall beat both batsmen, and the stumps, at the same time which was fortunate for the former but unlucky for the latter when an lbw appeal was made against Hardstaff.'

Notts v Middlesex (*Journal*): 'A ball to Giles stood up, and spoke in a voice of evil, before slithering off the edge of the bat into the hands of Edrich, a Macchiavelli lurking in the slips.'

The deputy editor of the *Journal* in fact compiled a scrapbook of gems of this nature and kept it for years after moving on from the paper to another within the Westminster Press Group.

The Trent Bridge wicket in those days was the most notorious featherbed in the country, a graveyard for bowlers of every kind, and Notts were not an outstandingly good side by any means. Nevertheless, I fell in love with the ground at first sight. Parr's tree still stood in those days, round about square leg to a right-hand batsman when the bowling was from the Radcliffe Road end. And had not William Clarke, landlord of the Bell Inn in Angel Row (where the Nottingham branch of the National Union of Journalists held its monthly meetings 100 years later), married Mrs Chapman, widowed proprietress of the Trent Bridge Inn, and 'enclosed' her field at the back of the pub? Trent Bridge cricket ground was the very stuff of cricketing history and I loved its atmosphere, whatever the quality of the cricket. Every spare moment I found in summer was spent in taking a bus down to West Bridgford, talking my way in by flourishing an NUJ card, and spending whatever time was available watching county cricket.

By 1950 I had managed to talk the editor of the *Journal*, Ken Burnett, into acknowledging the importance of Test cricket by printing a Page One piece of sketch-writing on the day's play. Then, by impressing upon the *Evening News* that it was important to record the names of the first people in the queue at the turnstiles each morning, along with trivia of a similar nature, I had contrived a way of spending the whole duration of a Test match inside Trent Bridge while remaining gainfully employed. Thus, in

July 1950 I saw Cyril Washbrook's 102 and the local hero Reg Simpson's 94 prove all in vain as the West Indies won by ten wickets. As long as I live I shall remember the partnership of 283 by Everton Weekes and Frank Worrell, with Weekes stepping back outside his leg stump to cut the bowling of two leg-spinners, Roley Jenkins and Eric Hollies for four after four.

In 1951 came Dudley Nourse's South Africans and again there was a defeat for England. I got some 'quotes' from the touring skipper about his innings of 208 made with a fractured thumb and though I have long since forgotten what they were I do remember marvelling at the way he dismissed the injury as nothing worth talking about. Compton and Simpson scored centuries and Bedser, as in the previous year, bowled wonderfully on a pitch that gave him no help. There was no Test at Trent Bridge in 1952 but Freddie Trueman's destruction of India at Heading-ley and Old Trafford kept me happy, especially as I had seen the young Turk take his first hat-trick against Notts the previous summer. In 1953 came the Australians – the ultimate in Test-watching pleasure – and with great delight I accompanied the party (as a news reporter) on their visits to local industry . . . the Raleigh works and Players' cigarette-manufactur-ing factory . . . observing the young Richie Benaud, Alan Davidson who played his first Test at Nottingham, the great Lindwall and Miller, and Lindsay Hassett as Captain. There was, of course, no Bradman in the ranks but he was there just the same, as an expert comments man for the *Daily Mail*. Rain-affected pitches made it a Trent Bridge rarity – a bowler's delight – and once again Alec Bedser gave us a quite marvellous exhibition with fourteen victims for 99 runs. And the *Daily Mirror*, I recall with shocked horror, described it all in a back-page headline as 'One Big Yawn'.

Still there was no thought of any kind in my mind of taking up sports writing as a full-time occupation. Sport represented a hobby, a way of occupying one's leisure time and, in my conception of newspaper journalism, sport was a branch occupied by those not good enough to be newsmen. I was happy enough to chat to Bill Botting and Arthur Turner about their roles on the paper, about Tommy Lawton, the great England player of the previous era who was currently Notts County's centre-forward while Nottingham Forest were enjoying a run of success in the Third Division (South). The Notts Rugby Club (as it then was) had not the strength it was to achieve in the 1980s but 'my' winter game was their game and so conversations with Dennis Riley, the *Journal*'s Rugby correspondent, were pleasant enough. And now golf began to creep into my life for the first time.

There was no thought of actually *playing* the game; for one thing it required too much time and for another it seemed rather an expensive pastime to take up. But the paper had by now realized that the eccentric Yorkshireman who loved being cooped up in a courtroom for most of the day had an addiction to sporting diversions which could be useful. I had not the faintest idea what golf was about, much less its method of scoring, when I attended my first meeting of the Nottingham and District Winter Alliance at the Beeston Fields Club but the opposition reporter, Harry Richards, nursed me helpfully through the day; the officials were unanimously cordial and hospitable; and I came away feeling there were many less pleasant ways of passing a day. By now I was the newspapers' golf, tennis and athletics correspondent; deputy to the cricket, football and Rugby writers; and when a colleague named Dennis Cunningham went off to London I took over his coverage of ice hockey (Nottingham Panthers at that time being one of the six National League clubs), thus adding a new dimension to my sporting interests. It goes without saying that I covered my first ice hockey match without a single clue what the game was about, but by adopting the first principle of sports journalism (as I understood it, with patronizing arrogance) and stringing together a series of well-worn clichés I was able to spoof my way through until I had had the chance to learn what the national sport of Canada really involved.

Panthers' manager at that time was one Archie Stinchcombe, the Captain was Les Strongman and the record-scoring centre ice was Chick Zamick. All were superbly helpful and by spending a lot of off-duty time with them I was, in due course, able to pick up enough of the rudiments of the dazzlingly swift and exciting game to write a moderately intelligible report. In fact I thoroughly enjoyed my three seasons' flirtation with ice hockey. It had an entirely different ambience, and public, from any game with which I was familiar and I began to look forward to my Friday nights at the Nottingham Ice Stadium even though it meant an extremely late return home – result and scorers had to be telephoned to two national papers and one agency after filing my report for the following morning's *Journal*.

Now these extra-curricular activities (as I regarded my peripheral sporting activities) began to become a bit intrusive. Courts were my main preoccupation and with that went coverage of any major crime, and we had three 'good' (in the production of newspaper copy) murders during 1951. But that Saturday evening sports edition, with its match reports filling front and back pages, needed acres of 'notes' and comments to fill the *inside* pages and I found myself sitting in the Shire Hall, or the Guildhall, praying for a dull bit of evidence or a long-winded summing-up which I could précis from my shorthand note, while composing half a column of thoughts on golf, tennis, ice hockey and athletics. This did not exactly help to focus one's attention on *any* topic with anything like the necessary concentration but somehow we muddled through; I have never quite understood how.

The birth of No. 1 son, in the meantime, had been an event of considerable importance to my colleagues as well as to my wife and myself. Jo had been resident in the West Riding for three months when Ian eventually arrived on the scene on 29 August 1951. There was never any doubt in my mind that he was to be a Yorkshire cricketer, while Jo followed the philosophy ('humour the silly ass') that has enabled her to keep a semblance of sanity for so many years. The birth, in Keighley, was greeted by a shower of telegrams bearing such messages as, 'Have booked seats for Trent Bridge, 1971,' or, 'Size One bat available from Gunn & Moore.'

Meanwhile, back in Nottingham, the time had come to vacate the flat we had occupied for the past eighteen months. Five minutes' walk from the huge open tract known as The Forest, our flat was the obvious location for the inevitable party when the traditional Goose Fair came round in October. Parties were very much the order of the day in Nottingham journalistic circles during the early 1950s. Working conditions in both offices were difficult and if we hadn't all enjoyed a healthy social life we would have gone mad. Most of the reporters on both sides of the street were young flat-dwellers who regarded their work in the city as transient; we all hoped to move on to better things in due course. In the meantime we were going to enjoy ourselves. So on two or three nights a week, and most assuredly on Saturdays, there was a party at someone's flat. One way and another, we got through a fair amount of beer.

For 'rival' reporting staffs, we indulged in a good deal of inter-office fraternizing in our off-duty moments. On stories which afforded an opportunity to beat the opposition by an edition there was healthy rivalry but in all truth not too many of these occasions occurred. On my own particular beat – mostly the courts – there was a certain amount of satisfaction in spotting the 'angle' of a case at an early stage and writing the story (from a shorthand note) on pads of copy-paper we routinely took with us into Guildhall or Shire Hall. The piece was then collected by a copy-boy from the office and taken back to the sub-editors. If we could get a 'good' case into the *Evening News* one edition before it appeared in the *Evening Post* we enjoyed a faint glow of satisfaction. But on the piffling little affairs, which occupied most of our time in the evening, we adopted a policy of total cooperation. Three of four reporters would be regularly employed to go around a series of meetings, lectures and talks to 'pick up' the details and there was absolutely no point in two of us ploughing identical furrows. Thus, Margaret, custodian of the men's bar at the Welbeck Hotel, kept a sort of news editor's diary and knew, on any given evening, which stories were being covered by which reporters. It was there that we met, swopped notes, wrote out our pieces and slipped them back to the office. It was an entirely painless way of dealing with the trivia which had absolutely no news value but was concerned only with people who liked to see their names in the paper.

Thus the days passed by pleasantly, if uninspiringly. The first major upheaval in the life of my wife and I came with the arrival of our son. Our tenancy agreement, like most others, specified 'No children, no pets.' I had managed to smuggle in a stray cat, a handsome creature we named Cleopatra because of the regal way she took possession, and she remained undetected for several months, but concealing the arrival of a new-born baby with very healthy lungs was more difficult.

Consequently, while Jo was spending her three months in God's Own Country ensuring that our son was born on cricket-hallowed ground, I was searching for alternative accommodation. Finally, I spotted an advertisement announcing that a country cottage was available at a reasonable rental in the village of Caythorpe, about ten miles east of the city in the Trent Valley. It was far from palatial and the sanitary arrangements were slightly better than primitive but I fell in love with the village at first sight and for once the old instincts were absolutely right. Caythorpe today has become something of a dormitory for the Nottingham business fraternity, with old, tiled-roof cottages knocked inside out and everything modernized. In 1951 it had its indigenous population of around 120, with one shop and one pub – the superb Black Horse (complete with priest-hole and skittle table) where the landlady's family had dispensed ale since the days of the first Queen Elizabeth. As it was Festival of Britain Year, with its strong bucolic links with Merry England, it seemed the ideal spot to settle, for the time being, with wife and son. The villagers adopted us immediately as part of the community, something which could never have happened in our own part of the world and for the next two-and-a-half years I was back in the life of a small community which I had loved so much in my boyhood.

Television had not yet spread its clammy tentacles across the country and rural folk still created their own fun, taking their pleasures from their environment. They were simple pleasures but they were real ones . . . the annual gala, picnics by the river, on Boxing Day the

Married Men v Single football match for a barrel of beer donated by Mrs Branston at the Black Horse, and skittles matches and children's sports.

Our milk was delivered to the doorstep, morning and evening, still warm from Farmer John Brisland's herd, and the postmistress (or Mrs Branston) knew at any given moment where every resident could be found. It was small community life at its very best and in some ways I would have been happy to stay there for ever. Caythorpe Cricket Club barely existed, fulfilling a few friendly fixtures and taking part in a cup competition against other Trent Valley villages. Today, Caythorpe Cricket Club covers acres of territory, has a splendid modern clubhouse and dressing-rooms, runs three very successful sides as well as three sets of juniors, stages Notts II team matches and coaches something like 100 youngsters who include the sons of Eddie Hemmings and Derek Randall, both Notts and England players. None of this seemed even remotely possible in my days in the village but the present officials have been kind enough to dub me 'Honorary non-playing Member' and I am proud of my association with such a progressive and ambitious club.

And so the next two-and-a-half years were spent in similar circumstances to those I had enjoyed in Eastburn as a teenager. At times I felt that professionally I was drifting rather aimlessly but if the newspaper standards were poor, the social life was good. One after another, colleagues left for better things but I was becoming dangerously content with my life in Caythorpe/Nottingham. Three murders in the year of 1951 kept me busily employed and if contact with the national newspaper boys who descended upon us occasionally made me restive I consoled myself that I had my cricket and my rugby to keep me entertained in the off-duty moments, that my neighbours were warm and hospitable folk, and that my wife and I could look with joy and pride upon our baby son. There was more to life than Fleet Street. Occasional days when I was confined to the office were irksome but even then there were moments of delight, as when a call came from the 'front office' to say that a couple of chaps were asking to see a reporter. This usually meant embarrassing contact with a crank or – even more awkward – having to explain to someone who had just appeared in court that, 'No, we were sorry but we couldn't keep his (or her) name out of the paper.' I walked downstairs, mentally rehearsing the stock answers and excuses, to find two middle-aged gentlemen smiling pleasantly at me. This looked more promising.

'Good morning,' said one of them. 'My name is Coates. This is my brother. We wondered if we might give you some details of a musical weekend at our church in Hucknall to see if you thought it worthy of a mention in your newspaper.'

Somewhere in the back of my mind a bell rang, faintly. Coates? Hucknall? It couldn't be. The visitor went on to describe the planned festivities and mentioned, with the utmost diffidence, that he would be conducting the choir. The ringing of bells became louder and more insistent. Coates? Hucknall? The name had not appeared on Miss Riley's wall charts of great composers at Ingrow Council School and yet I had a vague feeling that a rather distinguished English composer of light music came from the town of Hucknall, in Nottinghamshire. It was worth a try.

'Excuse me, Sir,' I interrupted. 'Are you by any chance *Eric* Coates, the composer?'

He actually blushed, then replied, 'How very kind of you to mention that – and to have heard of me.'

And the composer of the 'London Day by Day suite' and a hundred other popular and tuneful pieces went on quietly to talk about the weekend at his church in Hucknall. I spent the remainder of the day in a sort of glow that I had actually met a composer and that I had found him such a modest and utterly charming man.

Politics rarely reared its ugly head in my life except at election time when we were all required to attend meetings and report the same dreary catalogue of promises and denunciations. I had actually looked forward to elections in my earliest childhood when a car would arrive, belonging to one of the more affluent supporters of the Conservative party, to drive my folks to the voting point. This meant a ride for me and as it never for one moment occurred to me that they (much less I) would ever own a car it was an experience to be relished. Through the 1930s the country had been 'safely' Tory and even the shock of the immediate post-war landslide in Labour's favour was (I trusted most sincerely) only a temporary moment of national madness. So it came as a bit of a shock when I was 'sent to Coventry' by a group of my colleagues in the *Journal* and *Evening News* office – led by a redoubtable lady named Carole Findlater – for writing up an election meeting in what I fondly imagined was a light-hearted way but which, on reflection, was not entirely unbiased. The candidate was William Rees-Davies whose election address indicated that he had won a cricket Blue at, I think, Cambridge. So when he was persistently heckled at one meeting by a rather scruffy individual in the front row I used a cricket analogy to describe the entire proceedings. The heckler was, in my piece, placed 'in the Sidney Barnes position at forward short-leg' and, according to the following morning's *Journal*, had been struck hard several times when he tried to catch out the candidate.

I was smugly self-satisfied with my report and a bit shaken to be vitriolically attacked for Tory bias by La Findlater and her small, but intelligent, band of supporters in the office. It had never occurred to me that they might be of a different persuasion or that they might take politics seriously. Just how naive can one get? But what really upset me about that election was a stream of 'phone calls during the campaign from a lone Communist candidate who always announced himself, 'This is John Peck, DFC. I have a story for you.' It seemed that I always was the one to take his calls and as Communists to me were people who wanted to turn my country into a Russian colony I bristled at the sound of his voice. And it seemed utterly incredible that a wartime pilot should be asking the electorate to return him to Parliament on a Communist ticket. I found it extremely difficult to be civil to the man, quite apart from the fact that his 'story' was quite simply an account of his address at the previous night's meeting. It was, therefore, with some interest that I read in 1990 a piece in the *Daily Telegraph*'s Peterborough column: 'There is a distinctly *fin de siècle* atmosphere at the Communist party's headquarters near London's Smithfield Market where the comrades are attempting to play down the sudden defection to the Greens of the party's most powerful member, John Peck, England's only Communist councillor, who holds the balance of power on Nottingham City Council.

'After forty-five years in the party – several of them spent as its national election candidate – Peck has stunned colleagues by calling it a day. "The project which began in 1917 is over as far as I am concerned. We've got to save the world now, not change it," he tells me bluntly.

'Even the party's imminent change of name, it seems, does not cut any ice with the former wartime pilot, holder of the DFC and a veteran of the Aldermaston marches. "Communism is now so tarnished by what has happened in East Europe that I don't want anything more to do with it," he says.

'Until recently, anyone who left the party could expect to be denounced as a revisionist traitor. In these unhappy times, however, there is no room for public bickering. "John was an outstanding party member," says CPGB development officer Gerry Pocock resignedly. "We're very sad about it." '

Forty years later it gave me a small smile to learn that Mr Peck was still soldiering on, that he had at last seen the light, and that the distinguished Peterborough columnist felt approximately, if less ingenuously, as I had done.

Just one other episode in my 'political' career prompts a personal smile. I had been at a meeting in the wilds of a huge housing estate at Broxtowe, west of the city, and my suggestion to the opposition reporter that we adjourn to the nearest pub to compare our notes met with a blank refusal. This startled me. Possibly there *were* teetotal newspapermen around the country but it had never occurred to me that I would have the misfortune to meet one. Now this new arrival on the *Evening Post and Guardian* (let's call him Watson) was seeking to reject all the accepted canons of reporting procedure. I resolved to blacken his character utterly on the morrow when I once again met up with the more civilized majority. In the meantime, what was to be done? There appeared to be a marked absence of cafés on the Broxtowe Estate and it was unlikely in any case that we would find one operating at half-past nine at night. Checking the note – to establish that we had both got the same set of platitudes, clichés and solecisms – was normal practice but how were we going to do it? Rescue came from the most unlikely quarter, Watson himself. It was a cold night and he suggested archly, 'Now if pubs sold hot beer it would be a different matter. . . .'

Inspiration! 'If I can provide you with a glass of hot beer, will you swop notes?' I countered. 'Oh yes,' he replied, now smiling broadly, secure in his limited knowledge of Nottingham's pubs. We took a bus into the city centre; I led the way to Dabell's wine-lodge, near the Black Boy Hotel, and there, steaming merrily away on a gas-ring was the pride and joy of the house: fettled porter. Over two glasses of this we fended off the cold night, exchanged notes on the candidate's dissertation and I poured Watson into a taxi with a benign, if slightly stupid grin on his face. Nine months later his wife presented him with their first offspring. Good stuff, that fettled porter.

In 1952 the BBC decided to open a 'remote' studio in Nottingham which was, after all, the second biggest city in its Midland Region. It was to be a self-operated studio so that reporters working in the area who had not time to get back to headquarters in Birmingham could record, or broadcast live, their pieces. By sheer chance, I was sent along to cover the opening. One of my questions for Gerald Nethercott, the BBC's Midlands representative, was: 'Will you have a reporter permanently based in Nottingham?' I was motivated to ask the question only by the need for an extra line in my story but it was to have the most profound effect on my working life. Gerry replied, 'No, but I'd like to talk to you about it later.'

With the formalities over, he then asked me if I would like to supply items for the daily Midlands News programmes on a regular basis. It would not affect my duties at the *Evening News*; they would not ask for exclusives that had not already appeared in my own paper. Now at this time there was not a single freelance journalist operating in a city of

300,000 people, nor did any national paper retain a staff reporter there. This meant there was a flourishing trade amongst journalists on both sides of the street in telephoning reports to national papers on a linage basis (i.e. payment by results). Suddenly I had the best linage in Nottingham because the BBC's Midlands News took at least one, and quite often two or three, paragraphs a night and quite quickly I supplemented my weekly wage of £14 a week by fifty per cent. By the time I had been doing this for a year or so I was asked by Peter Hardiman Scott, the Deputy News Editor in Birmingham, if I would like to have a go at actually broadcasting a report myself. This was very nearly the equivalent of being asked if I would like to play cricket for Yorkshire. Broadcasting in 1953 was still a pretty formal affair; the slapdash nonsense which is put out today in some areas of the Corporation would not then have been tolerated for a second, and indeed I was not allowed anywhere near a microphone until Peter Scott was satisfied it would sound at least a little better than dire. Accordingly, he asked me to make a trip to Birmingham with a script already written – about the discovery of a new cave in the rock on which Nottingham Castle stood – which he then dissected, severely but helpfully. I then re-wrote the piece a further eight times before it was accepted as being remotely satisfactory and after that I recorded it thirteen times, during which Peter must have repeatedly asked himself why he had embarked on the creation of this particular new broadcaster. Finally he sent the tape to London, to be broadcast in a programme called 'The Eye Witness' which went out on Wednesday lunchtimes in the old Home Service, the forerunner of Radio 4. I sometimes wake up at night screaming at the thought of how awful it was but Peter, bless him, persevered, and my subsequent broadcasts ranged from feature-like material such as the award of the freedom of the city to the Sherwood Foresters Regiment to more immediate news items dealing with the East Lincolnshire coastal flooding of 1953. Slowly I began to realize the difference between the broadcast *spoken* word and the reading of a newspaper-type report. The knack is, of course, to write yourself a script couched in such terms that it *sounds* like conversational English even though you are reading it. There is a little more to it than that but that is the basic requirement. It was different from writing a good newspaper article, but I enjoyed it.

Still, however, my first love remained court-reporting. I remained in awe of the majesty of The Law, continued to admire the spoken English of the barristers and enjoyed the company of many police officers who had become personal friends. For Assizes at the Shire Hall we set up a sort of base camp in the pub across the road in the congenial company of the landlord, 'Lucky' Wright, who had been pilot of the aircraft that ferried Winston Churchill on many of his wartime flights. It was in his back bar one lunchtime that I received a 'phone call from Michael Parkin, a reporter on the *Yorkshire Evening Post* in Leeds: 'There will be a job going here shortly. Do you want me to mention your name to the Editor?'

Mike Parkin, who for the past thirty years has been a *Guardian* reporter in the North of England, was a friend whom I had met during his regular visits to Nottingham where he had spent his formative years. I knew the *Yorkshire Evening Post* to be one of the best papers in the country; a move nearer 'home' would give me a lot of pleasure in many ways and it would place my wife, who had been an only child, much nearer to her mother who had been widowed early in life. There was a lot to be said for the move. I had been in Nottingham for four-and-a-half years and had enjoyed so much of our time there that there was a serious danger of settling into a rut and spending the rest of my working life there. That was not what I wanted; Fleet Street ambitions might have been set aside but that was no reason for abandoning all journalistic ambitions. My problem was, though I refused at the time to acknowledge it, that I liked the ever-changing scene too much – meeting new people, looking forward to something different developing every day – to aim my sights at an indoor job like News Editor, aiming ultimately at an editorship. I simply could not see myself as a desk man. So it did not take long for me to say, 'Yes please,' to Mike and to bung off a letter to Alan Woodward, the Editor of the *Yorkshire Evening Post*. I got the job; a new chapter opened.

5 *Meeting A Murderer*

Towards the end of summer 1951, I had fixed up a new 'contact' within the Central Police Station in Nottingham. Our arrangement was the usual one of those eminently civilized days: he would provide me with tip-offs and other useful information providing it did not prejudice police work in any way; I would respect his confidence, handle his information in a responsible way and do anything I could to help my informant. No money was promised or expected; every 'transaction' would be on a basis of friendship and mutual trust. This was just as well since cheque-book journalism was in its infancy as far as 'hard news' stories were concerned, and in any case the editorial executives of the Nottingham *Journal and Evening News* would (a) have reeled at the sight of an expense sheet which indicated a reporter had paid for information, and (b) had a heart attack at the thought that payment was being made to anyone connected with the police force. I did not expect the fruits of the new liaison to be as quick or as dramatically harvested as they were.

It was, as I recall, a Friday morning when one of my colleagues, with a quizzical smile, reported a 'phone call from 'someone who won't speak to anyone except you.' It was my contact who said, 'We've had a strange sort of call which might be something or nothing. A reporter on the *News of the World* has called to say they had, on another line, a bloke who claims to have found a body in a wood in Sherwood. They have kept him talking while we send someone out to check. Got to go now.'

This was a bit of a shaker to put to dear old Bob Bowley. By Nottingham journalism standards it belonged more to Hollywood, and a fairly fanciful piece of script-writing at that. A wood in Sherwood? Well, that particular area of the city, fringing on the Mansfield Road, was a pretty well-built-up area. A check of the street map revealed small patches of green here and there, but a wood – nothing like it. I began to wonder if someone in

London had heard the word 'Sherwood' and started immediately thinking in terms of Robin Hood and his merry men. The marvellous insularity of Fleet Street was a standing joke amongst provincial reporters; their geographical knowledge was something less than abysmal once they were outside the metropolis. When you have seen the West Riding mining town of Castleford described (*Daily Express*) as being located 'on the bleak Yorkshire moors on the fringe of the Brontë country' you quickly realize that you are in national newspaper cliché territory. Everything has to be pigeon-holed, Castleford is in Yorkshire, therefore it must be somewhere *near* the Brontë moors. Was this what had happened in the case of Sherwood?

I decided to take a chance, reported to Mr Bowley that a normal check call on the police rounds had revealed a search of some sort was taking place in the Sherwood area. Could I take 'the' car and investigate? Priorities were important to Bob, especially when looking after his Staff. 'But you are off at one o'clock, Mr Mosey,' he replied. 'Will it take long?'

My assurance that I could do the job, take my afternoon off and still report for the evening shift at six seemed to satisfy Bob and permission was given to telephone 'our Mr Sanderson,' a taximan who worked for us on a contract-hire basis. We were in Sherwood within fifteen minutes, and Sandy, sensing something a bit different from the usual routine of taking a reporter to a garden party which was not on a bus route, started looking round for signs of police activity. He spotted a patrol car, fell into line behind it, turned right off the Mansfield Road, executed a couple of turns and we found ourselves in the middle of a pretty substantial police presence beside a sort of orchard which seemed to have been abandoned to nature. A uniformed officer halted us peremptorily, recognized me (long service at the Guildhall and Shire Hall had its compensations) and demanded, 'What the hell are you doing here? The Chief Super has only just got here himself.'

'Oh, we were coming back from a job, spotted a police car and followed it,' I lied. 'What's going on?'

The officer glanced over his shoulder. 'I'm saying nothing and you'd better get out of here sharpish before the superintendent starts asking questions.'

But there was no way the *Evening Post* were going to find out just yet about the police search in Sherwood. I hung about until I could get the barest possible statement of an official nature: the body of a woman, middle-aged and as yet unidentified, had been found. Inquiries were continuing.

By building up the background a bit with a description of the scene, the number of police present, the names of the senior CID officers in charge and a bit of waffle I was able to get a story on to Page One of the main edition of the *Evening News* and our rivals had not even a smell of the story. It took a good deal of persuasion, however, to get myself switched from my evening engagement of covering a lecture on a subject like 'the use of pre-stressed concrete in marine engineering' to be allowed to haunt the Police Headquarters for a more detailed statement.

And that is how I came to make the acquaintance of, to the best of my knowledge, the only murderer I have ever known. Nearly fifty years later it still provides a strange sort of tingle to recall talking at length to a man who was subsequently hanged.

Herbert Leonard Mills, a nineteen-year-old dispatch clerk and amateur poet, was described at his trial in November by Mr Justice Byrne as 'an unlovable man, an exhibitionist and a gambler.' He was all that. He gambled with his own life in the most astonishing way. And he lost. Mills was the man who had telephoned the *News of the World* to say he had found a woman's body, hoping as it turned out, to be paid for his information. By keeping him waiting at the call box from which he had 'phoned the newspaper, the police were able to get there before Mills left and he then showed them where he had 'found' the body when he went to the orchard – known locally as 'The Jungle' – to read poetry. Mills made a statement that evening, provided samples for forensic examination and was released. By now the big guns of the London Press had trundled to the East Midlands in force, headed by Norman Rae, Chief Crime Reporter of the *News of the World* together with reporters from each of the 'nationals.' Even so, the local lads were able to enjoy the privilege of a few minutes of conversation each day with Herbert Leonard Mills who now courted publicity with all the zeal of a lovesick swain. At each meeting the conversation – usually with half-a-dozen or more reporters – took the same tack: 'I've remembered something else. Is it worth a fiver if I tell you?' That ruled out the representatives of the *Evening News* and *Evening Post* who were, of course, also the representatives of the *Journal* and the *Guardian*.

Under normal circumstances this representation would have varied each day, depending upon who was available in either of the two offices, but now two particular reporters were involved who were not going to be prised loose from this story under any circumstances. My good friend and deadly rival Jack Reed (who was later to become Rugby correspondent of the *Sunday Express*) and myself were both 'national-minded', both ambitious, both desperately anxious to stick close to the drama of Herbert

Leonard Mills. Jack and I played cricket together, were both keen Rugby men and drank a lot of beer in each other's company – but would move heaven and earth to beat each other to a story. Every major city in the country at that time had rival evening papers and most of them produced personal competition of that sort. Competition was very much the name of the newspaper game. But shelling out money for information – that was strictly for the national boys. I remember looking at men like Donald Seaman of the *Daily Express*, Ned Conolly (*Daily Graphic*) and Vic Roberts (*Daily Mirror*), watching the way they doled out fivers and smiling at the thought of the reaction that would provoke in my (or Jack's) office. Press conferences meant very little to the national boys; they merely meant that the same set of facts offered by the police were available to everyone present. For the national papers, a *different* story was essential, otherwise news editors would be thundering down the telephone and so the London reporters had to resort to 'think pieces'. These generally took fairly predictable lines: (1) Was it a moon-mad maniac who killed . . . ? or (2) Police were looking for a man with a limp who had been seen hurrying away from the scene of the crime. It was only a matter of time before one of the nationals introduced one of these fictional elements and Mills himself now knocked one of them on the head by volunteering the information that *he* suddenly remembered seeing a limping man as he went to the orchard. It was occasionally possible to work out which reporter was going to follow a certain line in the following day's edition from the questions asked at press conferences: 'Superintendent, have you considered . . . ?' 'No. It's a load of cobblers but if you want to use it it won't do any harm.' Thus originated some of the stories which the great British public read at the nation's breakfast tables.

But in those first few days after the discovery of the body of Mrs Mabel Tattershaw, a forty-eight-year-old woman who probably never did any harm to anyone in her life, we were all positively encouraged by the police to talk to Herbert Leonard Mills. It did not require any deductive genius to work out that he was the prime suspect – indeed, the only suspect remotely on the horizon – and the police were waiting for him to commit the ultimate indiscretion. And then something very strange happened. Herbert Leonard Mills disappeared. We had known where to find him each morning and now he was no longer around to offer pathetic new scraps of information – the position of the body, the limping man, the broken necklace he had seen near the lifeless Mrs Tattershaw – and to hold out his hand for another £5 note. Even stranger, the police did not seem unduly perturbed by Mills' disappearance. Jack Reed and I knew the local CID very much better than the national reporters; many of them were good friends and congenial drinking companions. It was curious that they were infinitely less concerned when the prime suspect vanished than were the boys from the *Daily Express*, *Mirror*, *Herald*, *Mail* and the rest. And in due course one of the detectives tipped us the wink: Mills was in London as the guest of the *News of the World*!

He was accommodated in a West End hotel, quartered with Norman Rae, entertained to trips to the South Bank Exhibition (part of the Festival of Britain entertainment) and it was in a hotel room that he wrote out a confession to the murder of Mrs Tattershaw. The *News of the World* paid him £80; Norman Rae took him, with the statement he had made in his own hand, to Det. Supt. Percy Ellington, head of Nottingham CID, and the nineteen-year-old Mills was charged. With their Saturday deadline for Sunday's publication approaching, the paper had decided Mills had done enough talking to the dailies and the time had come to preserve what was left of his revelations for themselves.

A large number of reporters were warned to stand by to give evidence at his trial and I was very glad indeed not to be called as one of them, first because it enabled me to report the whole of the hearing from the Press Box and secondly, because I discovered I was not as tough as I thought I was and it was a most profound relief not to have been instrumental, no matter how insignificantly, in sending a man to his death, whether he deserved to be hanged or not. My reporting adventures seemed glamorous and exciting at the time; they seemed infinitely less so as I sat in the Press Box of the Shire Hall and heard Mr Richard Elwes, KC (who so brilliantly tried to make bricks without straw in defending Mills) tell the jury: 'just as flies cluster around a garden pot, so crime reporters cluster round when a sordid crime has been committed, as they clustered round this unfortunate young man.' Crime reporting didn't seem *quite* such a good way of life at that moment. Mr Elwes' words, uttered without any particular emphasis other than his personal, clearly expressed air of well-bred revulsion, were positively lacerating.

If there is such a thing as a criminal type, then Herbert Leonard Mills could scarcely be said to fit the pattern. I recall him as a pasty-faced nondescript sort of individual and there was something a bit pathetic in watching him bargaining with the pretty sharp boys from the national papers. He confided in Norman Rae more than once that 'the Press were fools' and 'the police were fools, too,' but we all knew who the fool was as the squalid charade was acted out. Mills had met Mrs Tattershaw in a cinema, arranged to meet her the following day, gone with her to The Jungle and strangled her. There were sexual overtones in the claim by Mills that Mrs Tattershaw had struck up a conversation with him and that she was the one who suggested a meeting the following day, but given the fact that she was so much older than him and far from attractive in appearance they really could have no credibility. What kept the newspapers interested in the story was that here was a man who had rung up one of them to report the discovery of the body and who was, all too clearly, the police's 'favourite' for a murder charge. My personal conversations with Mills did not last long once he realized there would be no money for him but I was present on at least half a dozen occasions when he trotted out pitiful additions to his story in his quest for an extra £5. There was a terrible fascination in watching the way he dragged the noose ever more tightly about him, an awful inevitability in his walk to the scaffold. It is one thing to sit through a murder trial, watching with detached and professional interest the efforts of the Crown to get a conviction with the defence seeking to avoid it. I had been in that situation many times and would be in it many more times in the future. But it was something else altogether to see a man with whom I had been personally involved sitting in the dock on a capital charge.

Each time I saw a judge don the black cap (around twenty times in all) a small shudder shook me. Strangely enough it did not mean that I could put up a convincing argument against capital punishment, nor did I ever seek to do so. I saw too many men sentenced who all too clearly were killers without pity or remorse and it would have been difficult to make out a case for clemency under the law as it then stood. But often I asked myself: if I sat on a jury in a murder trial how would I feel about saying whether a fellow human should live or die? The glib answer is: 'Not very comfortable', but that, of course, begs the question. Mercifully I have never had to answer myself. I have never in forty-odd years as a ratepayer been asked to serve on a jury and I am grateful for it. Even so, I have seen juries bring in verdicts which caused the whole Assize Court to catch its collective breath in astonishment and wondered whether it was fair to put huge responsibilities on the shoulders of many good men and true who were plainly not equipped to handle them. Similarly with lay magistrates . . . there must be few motorists in the country who have not experienced crass idiocy in local petty sessional courts and in particular the it's-your-word-against-his-and-we-must-believe-our-policemen attitude.

An equally spectacular murder case in Nottinghamshire that year involved the discovery of the body of a pretty young mother of twins in a ditch near Mansfield. No one was ever charged with that crime but it provided me with three educational weeks of contact with national newspaper reporters. On one occasion the lights failed in The Swan (which had become the unofficial Press Room) where about a dozen of us were sitting, yarning, and thus it was by appropriate flickering candlelight that we drank our beer and listened to Stanley Bishop (*Daily Herald* and doyen of Fleet Street crime reporters) tell how he covered the arrest of Dr Crippen!

And on a particularly unnewsworthy day the *Daily Express* representative produced a highly colourful 'think-piece' which began, 'The town hall clock struck twelve, the Salvation Army band in the market square played, "O Rest in the Lord", and old Bill Bloggs talked about the twelve unsolved murders of Nottinghamshire.' *Twelve*? The rest of us looked at this and blinked. Twelve? It was then discovered that the *Express* had delved into history and gone back to the death of a servant-girl, a murder of the 'Oh-Sir Jasper' type – in the eighteenth century. The reigning chief constable of the county was not amused by this slur on his force's detection rate!

But it was interesting to learn a little more about writing styles, about national paper requirements, about some of the personalities of Fleet Street. It might all be useful some day. . . .

6 *Back to Yorkshire*

One of the saddest features of provincial journalism in the past twenty-five years has been the loss of so many evening newspapers in major cities like Manchester, Liverpool, Birmingham, Bristol, Leicester and Nottingham, to name but half-a-dozen. The death of many regional *morning* papers was probably inevitable because they could not hope to compete with the 'nationals' but local 'evenings' have always had a strong commercial and sentimental pull on the purse and heartstrings of their own communities. Saddest of all, from the journalist's point of view, has been the disappearance of *opposition* papers in those cities. Free from competition, the need to get editions on to the street quickly and efficiently has gone and the papers which remain have, in many ways, lost their journalistic souls. The inevitable consequence has been that editorial policy is now dictated largely by accountants rather than by newspapermen and news takes a back seat to advertising. This effectively cuts off the lifeblood of a newspaper.

I was distinctly lucky to join the *Yorkshire Evening Post* at a time when it had excellent opposition in the *Yorkshire Evening News*. Both papers had absolutely first-class staffs of reporters, feature-writers and sub-editors; both were brilliantly edited; both were heavily geared towards beating the opposition, not just within the city of Leeds but over most of the heavily populated areas of the West Riding where there was competition as well from papers in Bradford, Halifax, Huddersfield, and Sheffield. My experience of more than four years in Nottingham now seemed to have moved at a funeral pace compared with the high-speed operation in Leeds and I had not been there a week before I realized I had to sharpen up my work in every conceivable way. The Assize Court judges sat in Leeds for something like six months of the year and, once again, I had opted for this side of reporting as my specialist interest. Now I found myself up against a man called Harold Vaughan of the *Evening News*, older and more experienced than me, with a better shorthand note and a 'contact' in every nook and cranny of the police as well as amongst the senior members of the Bar. Harold was a magnificent court reporter and an absolutely 'straight' man. If he said he was not going to touch a particular case I knew with complete certainty that I need not fear a furious 'phone call from the News Editor, Ken Lemmon: 'The *News* are leading Page 3 with this case from Halifax. We haven't got a bloody line. WHY?' With four courts going on in various parts of the Town Hall one could not be everywhere at once. One never knew when a seemingly unimportant case would yield a superb 'line' which could be built up. To trust the opposition was essential; then it became a straightforward matter of one's ability against the next man's – the speed with which one decided upon the point of the story, the ability to conjure it up into an eye-catching 'intro', and above all the adeptness at dictating the story straight from one's shorthand note to a copy-taker in the office building. You won some, you lost some. If you lost a lot you expected to be moved out of court to less demanding pastures and if you didn't do your stuff there then you expected to be asked to look for another job. No good newspaperman would have wanted it any other way.

These were undoubtedly some of the best days of my newspaper career. One had to be on one's toes every minute of every working day, and yet while this meant maintaining a professional awareness of, it seemed, ten thousand different things going on round about, there was always time for a beer and a laugh. The Town Hall Tavern, run by Kath and Paddy Moran, took on every lunchtime the role of the Bar Mess, the CID office and the Press Club. For every detail of every case we reported across the road in the Town Hall there were a dozen which never came out. These were the background stories, the unchronicled details of the lives of a thousand malefactors, the murky character and antecedents to which juries were not privy and there was much vicarious pleasure to be derived from sitting through a trial, knowing what we knew (nudge-nudge, wink-wink) while the twelve good men (and women) and true tried to unravel a particularly tangled tale. We could admire the way a gifted barrister could paint a picture of his client which showed him to be purer than the driven snow, more sinned against than sinning, an innocent victim of circumstances, while we in the Press Box knew him to be a double-dyed villain of the deepest hue. And there *were* brilliant barristers in substantial numbers. In those days (the mid-fifties) many of our Sunday newspapers were fond of recalling in serial form the more celebrated cases of leading advocates such as F. E. Smith, Norman

Birkett and Patrick Hastings, which showed these undoubtedly great lawyers to be men whose achievements could never be equalled. Yet every day it was our privilege to sit there and watch similar miracles being wrought by the pleadings of Rudolph Lyons, Henry Scott and Raymond Hinchcliffe, and the up-and-coming 'youngsters' such as Gilbert Gray and Raymond Dean (probably the best mitigation pleader I ever heard). Inevitably, whenever I heard Ray Dean speak highly of a black-hearted crook who had pleaded 'Guilty', I thought of W. S. Gilbert's line in *Trial by Jury*: 'And many a burglar I've restored to his friends and his relations.'

We learned which judges had the confidence and respect of barristers, those who were regarded as unpredictable, those who were irritating 'interruptors', those who would not stand any nonsense, and those with whom counsel would occasionally take a chance. Muttered asides like, 'Oh well, it was worth a try,' were often audible in the Press seats. Once I was invited to take sherry with their Lordships – all four of them in their full pomp and majesty – after organizing a general expression of good wishes from the Press to Mr Justice Cassells on his birthday. On the strength of a brief joust with writing in his extreme youth the learned judge was often referred to as the 'journalist-judge' so, under the influence of an extended lunchtime in the Town Hall Tavern, a few of us thought the greeting would be in order. I must say His Lordship was extremely civil about it all even though his sherry did not sit too well on top of the Tetley's bitter! And always there was the language and the wit and, just occasionally, a shaft that transgressed the boundaries of propriety:

Mr Justice Hallet (interrupting for the umpteenth time): 'Mr X, am I to understand that at the tender age of twenty years your client is in receipt of the handsome remuneration of £20 per week?'

Mr X: 'Me Lord, yes. It is only at the Bar that the plums are restricted to the elderly and decrepit.'

Judicial reproof was swift and appropriately outraged but by that time I was outside the courtroom, shaking with hysterical laughter.

Proof – if any were needed – that truth is very much stranger than fiction came during a divorce action to which my attention was called by a police officer friend who was acting as an orderly in that particular court.

The petitioner was a husband who found himself worn to a shadow by the excessive demands of his wife, which was not bad for starters, was it? He was not only required to perform his marital duties on a regular nightly basis but had to return from work at lunchtimes as well! The wear and tear on his particularly personal equipment was such that he was forced to employ an artificial aid and as this was long before the days when sex shops existed on the streets of Britain the husband crafted his own device from wood and rubber. And what was the occupation of this long-suffering creature? He was a toolmaker by trade.

In return for taking Saturdays off in summer to continue playing cricket I worked on Saturdays throughout the winter (playing my rugby in mid-week) but this was very much a pleasure, too, since I was borrowed by the sports department to report the matches of one of the city's three Rugby League clubs, Hunslet. Here again I was joined by Harold Vaughan, my Assize Court sparring partner, who was a lifelong supporter of the South Leeds side. Like most Union men in Yorkshire (and in Lancashire and parts of Cumberland as well), I had grown up in fairly close contact with the professional game and admired the strength, speed and handling dexterity of its players. The Hunslet players were a great bunch of lads and it was good to spend every Saturday with them, home and away. I was not similarly enthusiastic about all the directors since some of them seemed to think that in return for the hospitality of transport in the team coach I was required to be totally uncritical of everything within the club. Happily, 'the lads' did not share this view. If League at that time lacked the *bonhomie* of a Union clubhouse, I still shared several Saturday evening pints with the Hunslet players, men like Arthur Clues, the big Australian second-row forward, Don Hatfield, an eighteen-stone prop, Alf ('Ginger') Burnell, the scrum half and Ted Carroll, a loose forward whose grotesquely bent and twisted nose not only bore testimony to many a close-quarter combat but was to give him a whole series of parts as a TV heavy in later years.

Through a mutual friend, Jack Wainwright (a good Bradford League cricketer) I had come to know Brian Close well in those years in Leeds. Closey was a soccer man, having spent much of his youth playing for Arsenal, Leeds United and Bradford City, but he was a gifted sportsman in other fields – and a natural *competitor*. Thus, when Jack and I coaxed him one day to watch a local 'Derby' between Hunslet and Bramley, Brian was highly critical of the goal-kicking shortcomings that day of Bramley's Maori full-back, John Wilson. Not unnaturally, this goaded Bramley's supporters to fury. 'We'd like ter see wot thar can do,' was the taunt. At the end of the game Closey borrowed a pair of boots from the Hunslet dressing-room, took out a ball (shaped like no other he had ever handled) and proceeded to kick goals from all angles, with both left and right feet! No challenge could ever deter D. B. Close.

But it was not all courts and sports. The Editor, Alan Woodward, used to send me off into the countryside when the Assize Courts were not sitting, with a photographer, Harry Fletcher, with the simple instruction: 'Get me some picture-features for the leader page.' These were not projects which found favour with the News Editor, Ken Lemmon, who saw these excursions as an excuse for holing up in a country pub for two or three days before returning to submit expense sheets heavily endorsed with large amounts for 'reciprocal hospitality'. He was quite right in his suspicions, of course, because setting up base camp in a rural hostelry was precisely what we did. But we never came back withour three, four, five or more features. There is a great deal of glorious countryside in the Yorkshire Ridings and a large number of superb village pubs. Happenings which seemed commonplace to the villagers, characters who were regarded locally as unremarkable, provided excellent material for readers whose lives were spent largely amongst the dark satanic mills of the industrial areas.

In the Cleveland Hills, for instance, we discovered a postman whose round was so extensive that he had bought himself a horse and rode round his delivery area. He was at first reluctant to be interviewed because he felt his masters in the GPO would disapprove of his not making the rounds on foot but the villagers of Commondale talked him into cooperating and my colleague shot a series of splendid pictures of him on mounted patrol in settings of high scenic beauty. Not only did the Post Office approve but they asked permission to reproduce the *Evening Post* feature in their own house magazine.

In Wensleydale we found a pub where a tame fox ran with the landlord's dogs in a pen at the back of the hostelry; we found a pig which drank pints of beer from its personal trough in the bar; a duck which waddled along the top of the serving-bar and would drink only *bottled* beer. In Wharfedale we discovered one of the Duke of Devonshire's gamekeepers who had a grouse as a family pet. On 12 August it was taken indoors as a precaution against falling prey to guns of His Grace's guests and Fletch got some magnificent pictures of this shyest of birds perching contentedly on the wrist of the keeper.

All these bucolic ramblings induced another of the EP's photographers, Ted Winpenny, to invite me to join him on a trip rather close to his heart. Ted, who sported a quite magnificent handlebar moustache, was a keen potholer. I had dabbled with this pastime in my youth but discarded it as being rather too uncomfortable for my tastes. However, the promise of a sail across a subterranean lake in a 'tin' bath fired a certain enthusiasm and off we went – to explore the parts of the White Scar Caves at Ingleton where the paying tourist public are not allowed, at midnight. This first involved wading, thigh-deep, for what seemed miles, then twisting and squeezing our bodies through impossibly narrow crevices for something like an hour. I remarked to our professional guide that this part of our exploration seemed in marked contrast to the natural cave in which we had started. He replied, airily, that The Crawl was necessitated by a rock-fall which had occurred possibly 25,000 years earlier and I could not dismiss the thought that we might be overdue for the next one! However, The Crawl ended in another huge cave, and the stream we had left behind now reappeared in the form of a long, underground lake and there, sure enough, was a long zinc bath with oil-drums strapped to its side to provide buoyancy – our craft for the midnight sail. The light from the carbide lamps fixed in the front of our helmets was now supplemented by the flash of Ted's camera as he snapped joyously away at the small party of half-soaked figures, and their transport. The fleeting thought that pressing down from above was the 2,200-foot peak of Ingleborough was more than enough to summon up an attack of screaming claustrophobia so it had to be firmly dismissed. But it was with infinite relief that I finally emerged from the caves into the chill of a winter night.

One of the quintessential appeals of speleology is, of course, the knowledge that one is probing the last unexplored parts of the planet but it most definitely is not a hobby to be pursued without expert knowledge and guidance. Nevertheless, I was lured into one final experience by the enthusiastic Mr Winpenny – the Whit weekend camp arranged by Bradford Pothole Club at Gaping Gill, another cavernous opening under Ingleborough but one reputed to be large enough to accommodate York Minster. I did not pause to measure it but I have to say the experience was an interesting one. The descent into the Gill was by bosun's chair which was rather like dropping in a lift which was out of control. It took at least half an hour to recover from that. At length, curiosity took over from terror as I sought from some of the fifty or sixty souls who had chosen to spend the weekend underground an explanation for their choice of a troglodytic holiday. They were scattered not only about the main cavern but in many of the passages that branched off it and, unless they chose to provide their own illumination, it was an existence in Stygian darkness. It wasn't, for instance, the sort of break on which one took a good book to read. But the worst experience was yet to come – the ascent in that bosun's chair. It was, of course, a very much slower process than the descent and I made the mistakes of glancing up at the trapdoor of light 360 feet above, then down to see how much progress I had made. Acrophobia took over and in a complete, gibbering stupor of abject terror I clung to the ropes attached to the sides of the chair. When I finally surfaced, Mr Winpenny deeply regretted having only monochrome film in his camera – he swore I was quite literally green with fear. I would not for one second dispute the contention. I *felt* green.

A more pleasant memory of those three-and-a-half years on the *Evening Post* was provided by a mixture of cricket and hypnotism. A certain disciple of Hypnos claimed he could influence the ability of sportsmen so I was deputed to undergo a spot of treatment with a view to improving my personal weekend performance on the cricket field. This took place in Polly's Bar, across the road from the paper's offices at that time in Albion Street, Leeds, and since I had a certain reputation as the finest No. 11 batsman in the North of England it was decided that it would be a fair test if my ability in this branch of the game could be improved.

There was an audience of my colleagues present and I cannot recall any moment when I felt under any influence other than that of my own faculties. It seemed an unreal experience as I listened to the hypnotist telling me that I would bat on the morrow with a complete faith in my own ability to do well. Whether I was under his influence at any time is difficult to say; most certainly I didn't *feel* as though I was. However, in the interests of journalism I persuaded an incredulous captain to let me open the innings the following day. I hit the first ball of the innings back over the bowler's head for six; the next delivery bowled me. It is for others to judge whether the experiment was a success or not.

In July 1957 I received a note from the Northern News Editor of the *Daily Express* asking if I would like to go over to Manchester for a chat with a view to joining that paper. On the one hand I was flattered by the invitation because it indicated someone outside the EP thought my work had some merit; on the other I was very happy indeed in Leeds. I found my job satisfying and professionally rewarding. Merit was recognized in the form of bonuses and regular reviews of the salary scale; there was an excellent pensions scheme, good friends amongst my colleagues; and in every way it was an extremely good paper to work for. Our second son Andrew had been born two-and-a-half years earlier and the family home was back in Eastburn where I had been brought up in my teens. I had my rugby and my cricket and life seemed pretty good. But still a faint flicker of ambition told me I should not pass up the opportunity to join a national paper, especially as it would not mean having to move the family to London. At least I ought to see what the *Express* had to offer, which turned out to be £7 a week more than my *Evening Post* wage.

I had told my News Editor that I was going for an interview, then I spoke to the Editor, a man I liked and respected. Alan Woodward offered me an extra £4, regretted that he could not match the *Express* offer, most generously stressed that he did not want to lose me but said at the same time he would understand if I went to Manchester. It took four days to make up my mind.

The *Daily Express* was very much *the* newspaperman's newspaper, at that time under the Editorship of Arthur Christiansen. It was brilliantly 'subbed', bright and attractive in appearance and was known to recruit its staff in the North only from the outstanding papers in Manchester, Leeds, Liverpool and Sheffield. It was something of a distinction to be head-hunted and the money was attractive. Alongside that, my wife and I had boys of six and two-and-a-half for whom we wanted a good future. Also, the younger of my two brothers had just won a scholarship to Cambridge, and, if he required any help I did not want my parents to have to make yet more sacrifices. Not without reservations and some soul-searching, I decided to take the plunge and go into national newspapers at the ripe old age of thirty-two. But it had been the best of possible working lives so far – I could not remember a day, apart from a handful in Derby, when I had not looked forward each morning to going to the office – and there seemed no reason why it should not continue, perhaps even with enhanced excitement.

7 *The World's Greatest*

The vast modern building that was the Northern headquarters of Beaverbrook Newspapers seemed to have acres of glass as its outside walls. The public could stop in Ancoats Street and watch the great presses start to roll about eight o'clock in the evening, turning out the Irish, then the Scottish editions, followed by the thousands of copies to be whipped off to the railway stations by a fleet of trucks for distribution around the North and the North Midlands. On the next floor was the huge open-plan area that housed editorial, advertising and circulation staffs. At one end was the Newsroom, at the other the photographic department known as the Art Room. Sub-editors worked on the Ancoats Street side, sports subs on the opposite flank, and right in the middle of it all was a single, immense desk and a great padded chair. This was the domain (when he was in residence) of Henry Rose, the best-known sports writer in the country. He was to have many impersonators in the years that followed his death in the Munich air disaster of 1958 (which wiped out so many superb Manchester United footballers and a large number of football writers) but none has achieved his stature or his eminence. He was 'bigger' by far than any writer in London yet insisted on remaining in Manchester. His seemed a reasonable example to follow, even for the newest and most insignificant recruit to the reporting staff.

Henry Rose was quite simply a legend in his own lifetime and it pains one deeply to have to use such an overworked cliché to describe so distinguished a newspaperman. Beaverbrook heaped riches and lavish gifts upon him, once sending a telephone message requesting him to look out of his window. There in the street was a gleaming new Jaguar car. Aware of my sporting interests, the News Editor, Keith Howard, suggested shortly after I joined the *Express* that it would be an interesting experience for me to accompany Henry to a Saturday match. On Saturday mornings the back page of the *Express* carried a little 'panel' which announced: 'The match Henry Rose will see today will be . . .' And that day it was to be a game at Anfield. Henry, one of the most courteous and gentlemanly journalists I have ever known, drove me to Liverpool, introduced me around as if I had been a visiting VIP, and, precisely five minutes before the kick-off, lit a fresh cigar, adjusted his black Homburg and the belt of his teddy-bear coat, and went up the steps that led to the Press Box.

The roar that greeted his emergence into the stand was, I swear, louder than that for the players who appeared a minute later. Every pair of eyes in the ground, as far as one could judge, was turned to the Press Box; every set of lungs strained to make individual voices heard in the floodtide of shouted comment directed at the one individual. It was not all complimentary, by any means. Indeed, some of the vehemence shook me. Henry smiled, removed his cigar, raised his hat and took his seat. Only once was I ever to witness public reaction to a man of the media which was even remotely similar to that. When John Arlott retired from cricket commentary at Lord's in 1980 the crowd and the players rose in affectionate tribute to a great broadcaster and writer. For Henry Rose, the crowd rose *every week* not so much in affection on every side but in acknowledgement of the man's stature. His *modus operandi* was simple: if you write something pointed and/or controversial enough, people will react. In those few brief months that I knew him I listened once as he told a famed Manchester United player in the City's Cromford Club, with an engaging twinkle in his eye, 'Tomorrow I shall say that if you are an England centre-forward, I am Father Christmas.' The player grinned, 'Fair enough, Mr Rose.' *Mister* Rose! Does any football writer today rate that note of respect? Has any football writer since Henry Rose ever received it?

It is a privilege to have known a great journalist in the days when writers were the important men and women on newspapers, instead of those sub-editors who can dream up the most outrageously eye-catching headlines. His name was not on the first list of casualties reported from Munich . . . the terrible news filtered through slowly. But every 'phone in the building was jammed with calls from the footballing public asking for news of Henry. And when finally his death was confirmed, that great football pitch of an office was awash with telegrams and letters. He might well have been, in his lifetime, 'the man you love to hate.' In the end, everybody loved him. And, indeed, those who knew him found so much to love. He was gentle, generous and kind. A thousand good deeds for which he was responsible went unpublicized – at his insistence. His public persona was another matter. It was simply his way of making himself the most talked-about man in the game. As a Liverpool director said after my visit with him to Anfield, 'All we need is that little bit in the morning paper to say he will be here and we know there will be 10,000 more people in the ground. Most of those extra 10,000, to be sure, would read his Monday morning report with pen and paper by their side, ready to write, 'You saw a different game from me.' But it was a reaction no one before, and no one since, has been able to induce to anything like the same degree.

I was now in a completely different newspaper world from anything I had known so far. There had been competition in Leeds, but there were now multiple competitions from the many national papers based in Manchester – *Daily Mail, Daily Mirror, News Chronicle, Daily Graphic, Daily Dispatch, Daily Herald* and, of course, the *Manchester Guardian* as it then was. Similarly, there was a weekend multiplicity – *Sunday Express, Sunday Dispatch, Sunday Chronicle, Empire News, The People, Reynolds News, Sunday Pictorial* and *News of the World*. There were plenty of excellent journalists who preferred to stay on provincial papers, to be sure, but all these nationals and Sundays were staffed by bright, young and ambitious chaps. It was dog-eat-dog on every story, every day of every week. With six or seven opposition reporters ranged against one on every assignment, *Daily Express* reporters were nevertheless required to hold their own (at worst) against them all, and failure to turn in a story that was at least a little bit different meant an inquest the following morning in the News Room. It was hammered into us all, day after day, that the *Express* was 'the world's greatest newspaper', a pretension that was patently absurd but was believed implicitly by a fair proportion of my colleagues. It was certainly a very good paper indeed at that time but 'the world's greatest'? How did anyone start to measure greatness?

My 'own' newspaper, in fact – the one I had had delivered to my home since demobilization – was the *Daily Mail*. Its reporting standards seemed just as high as those of the *Express* and it did not indulge in the eternal trumpeting of its own 'greatness' as the *Express* did. I walked into the News Room one morning actually carrying my copy of the *Mail*. An icy curtain descended as Keith Howard asked, 'What is *that*?' His tone gave the impression that I had brought in a carton of bubonic plague germs. 'Keith,' I replied, 'I know what is in the *Express*. I want to see what the opposition have done with the story I covered yesterday.' That seemed to take him by surprise and nothing more was said. But I operated more discreetly after that.

From time to time it was necessary to endure, and if possible circumvent, a headlong plunge into bad taste. Some months after the Munich air crash I was working in the Newcastle area for a couple of weeks and Bobby Charlton, who had survived the disaster, was due to fly into Europe with Manchester United for the first time since the loss of so many of his team-mates. I was instructed by the News Room to go to Ashington and ask his mother if she had any sort of premonition of another disaster! I had been given some strange instructions in my time but this one topped the lot. In fact it was difficult to credit that I had heard the briefing aright. Thoughtfully I drove northwards, asked my way to the Charlton family home and was re-directed to the town's football ground where Mrs Cissy Charlton was watching the East Northumberland Cup Final. There were two or three thousand people in the ground but every one of them, it seemed, knew exactly where Mrs C was standing. I introduced myself, asked if I might talk to her about her two footballing sons when the game was over, went home with her and over a cup of tea enjoyed the most delightful chat. Munich, needless to say, was not mentioned by either of us. But the end-product was a story so wholesome and so pleasant that I feared it would never see the light of day. It was telephoned through to Manchester too late for the following morning's north-east edition so the *Express* held it over for a day, then used it as a news-feature with an excellent display. I got a 'Well done' for totally ignoring my instructions. But what was best of all was the meeting with a wonderful lady who absolutely adored football and was so touchingly, but understandably, proud of Jack and Bobby.

Not every assignment could be turned, or channelled. An awful lot of time was spent trafficking in human misery, on intrusions into private grief, in joining groups of colleagues and rivals besieging the homes of people trying to hide their distress. From time to time I was able to get into an Assize Court or Quarter Sessions but only to await the outcome and then try to buy up one of the principals in the case. No one seemed interested in the factual details of the dirty deed. I was once accused by the Deputy News Editor: 'The trouble with you, mate, is you've got ethics.' He made it sound exactly like an infectious disease.

There was fierce competition within the office to move to headquarters in London. Everyone seemed to have an idea of the approximate pecking order in which Manchester staff would get 'the call' but no one was taking any chances. It was another aspect of keeping everyone on his or her toes. In many ways there was more journalistic satisfaction in working in Manchester where far more off-the-cuff stories occurred, while in London there were obviously many more routine assignments to be covered which 'might' yield a story. But it was always going to be head office that provided the 'plums' – the special, and foreign, correspondents' roles, the glamorous trips abroad, the shoulder rubbing with personalities on the world's stage. When it became known that I had asked for a contract that did not require me to work in London I achieved a certain popularity. This was enhanced when I declined to work on Saturdays for the *Sunday Express*, which employed only a small permanent staff and relied for its immediate (Saturday) news coverage on reporters from the daily. The fact that I preferred to return to Yorkshire to play cricket in summer and either to play or watch rugby in winter rather than work a £10 shift (plus expenses!) for the SE stamped me as something of an eccentric.

My first morning on the *Daily Express* was spent in fixing myself up with a bachelor flat, leaving my wife to travel over later in search of a house to buy. I rented a place over the telephone, dropped my suitcase in it just after noon – and saw it again a week later! In the meantime I had been despatched to chase a story in Cheshire, another in North Wales, one in Preston and I fetched up on the Friday night at Eskdale in the Lake District. The young Marquis of Londonderry had been causing a bit of anxiety in his family with his youthful capers and had been enrolled in the Outward Bound School in the hope that some of his excess energy might be worked off in expeditions over the Lakeland Fells. No one had so far succeeded in getting His Lordship's views on his new, and excessively physical, lifestyle but with a bit of patience, a lot of luck and the expert assistance of my photographic colleague Eddie Rawlinson, I managed to get a dozen 'quotes' from the young peer. The following morning at breakfast in our country pub Eddie greeted me with a big smile and one word, 'Congratulations'. A few minutes later the landlord brought in a note of a telegram, the contents of which had been 'phoned the last five miles from the nearest post office: 'Congratulations'. That was from the Northern Editor and News Editor.

Mystified (because the daily papers did not reach that remote part of Cumberland until noon, or mid-afternoon) I asked Eddie what it was all about. 'I've been on to the office,' he said, 'and you've got the lead Hickey both in Manchester and London. No one has ever done that before in his first week.' The lead Hickey meant the top story in the William Hickey column. Up to that point I had filed eight stories without getting a line in the paper. I had been introduced to the abominable practice of cheque-book journalism – trying to buy up people for personal stories (something I detested). I had been in courts; knocking on the doors of people who did not want to talk to me; listening to people I did not want to talk to; I had travelled something like 400 miles without getting a line of copy printed, and now I was wallowing in an avalanche of bull. I returned to Eastburn for a day and a night with my family.

'What is it like?' asked my wife. 'A sort of mixture of being a private eye and a money-lender,' I replied wearily.

The next year was spent in getting used to the *Daily Express*'s particular brand of bull, its almost frenzied attempts to brainwash all its employees into believing they were something very special. It governed every moment of our working lives and spilled over into the pub when a shift was finished and even into parties, which were regularly held in one or other of our homes. We were simply expected to accept that we were indeed 'the world's greatest'. In fact I found the *Express* the most difficult paper to write for that I had so far encountered or was to find in the future. One of Christiansen's edicts – they hung in a great sheaf outside the News Room – was that no sentence should contain more than ten words, no paragraph more than two sentences. Words of French origin were shunned in favour of Anglo-Saxon. Thus, no one ever 'arrived' in the *Daily Express*; they 'got there'. This made the *Express* the easiest paper to read by people with a basic vocabulary and had to be one of the secrets of its success at that time. But the finest example of *Express* exclusivity I encountered had nothing to do with the written word. . . .

In July 1958 I was spending a week in Belfast, working with our two regular staff men based there. The troubles had not then fully descended upon the six counties but I found it a sad, depressing and unhappy part of the world and I was looking forward to flying home for a weekend's cricket. On the day I had started work in Manchester we had been joined by a chap from the London sports department called John Thicknesse who had been posted to the provinces to get a bit of experience in all-round newspaper work before returning to pursue his ambition to be a cricket writer (John is now the longest-serving, London-based cricket correspondent in the country, with the *Evening Standard*). With a background of Harrow School and Oxford University his role as a Northern news reporter with the *Express* seemed a trifle anachronistic to me but I had learned that as a cricketer he was a talented batsman and slow left-arm bowler. Now, in Belfast, I got a 'phone call from Manchester: 'Book yourself a flight to London tomorrow. You are required to play for the *Daily Express* against the *Daily Mail*.' This was an annual fixture about which I had vaguely heard but it meant nothing to me.

'Hold on a minute,' I replied, 'I have commitments of my own tomorrow in Yorkshire. I'm certainly not going off to London to play in some comic-opera game.'

'Oh yes you are,' came the terse reply. 'This is an Editor's "must". Thicknesse is not available and you have to take his place.'

77

Bull again. Thick and heavy. With the additional outrage of being required to 'substitute' in comic cricket for a man I regarded as 'amateur' in every sense of the word. It just wasn't on. But further protests were simply swept aside. The *Express* would organize my kit from Manchester to London; accommodation would be arranged for me. But I *would* be on parade at the *Daily Mail* sports ground, out in Surrey at 2 p.m. I resigned myself to doing as I was told, 'phoned to cancel my own cricket at home and flew to London. Presenting myself to the captain, I was told to put on my pads and open the innings. This was madness.

'I'm the best No. 11 in the North of England,' I protested, 'not an opener.' The reply was imbecilic in its simplicity: 'You are substituting for Thicknesse. He would have opened the innings.'

There was really no arguing with that sort of mentality. I put on the pads, trudged out to the middle, scratched around for most of the afternoon and amassed thirteen singles. My return was marked by an uncomfortable silence in the dressing-room. I was not specifically 'sent to Coventry' during the tea interval but no one was anxious to chat.

We took the field and I started to mark out a run at the top end of a fairly pronounced slope. The captain hurried over to inquire, 'What are you doing?' Yorkshire pride (or arrogance, depending upon where you come from) could take no more. 'I know,' I exploded, 'I am substituting for Thicknesse but if you expect me to bowl slow left-arm spinners you are dafter than I thought. Now will you please set the bloody field . . . as follows.'

Morley Richards, the great News Editor of the *Express* in its best years, now, like Christiansen, retired, was the umpire at my end. He greeted the fall of the first three wickets with jigs of not entirely impartial delight. In came Arthur Wareham, Editor of the *Daily Mail*. 'What happens now?' I asked Morley. 'Do I give him one off the mark?' 'Certainly not,' was the reply. 'But I might want a job from him some day,' I countered. 'Don't worry about that,' replied Morley and turned to his duties. Disregarding instructions, I bowled a slow dolly to Arthur who had completed an agricultural mow and was facing mid-wicket when the ball arrived. 'Brilliant,' chortled the umpire. 'Deceived him completely.'

It was now getting to an 'England, their England' state of partisanship. The innings ended fairly shortly. I had taken seven for 22, 20 of which had gone through the slips. My second return to the dressing-room was somewhat different from the first. The Editor of the *Daily Express*, Pickering by name, greeted me with the affection of a Biblical father for his prodigal son. 'I understand it has been a bit inconvenient for you to come here and play,' he said. 'When you put your expenses together, be generous to yourself, then double the amount and mark it "personal" to me. And, by the way, you will *never* leave the *Daily Express.*'

The following summer I played *for* the *Mail* against the *Express.*

If I had not been thirty-two years old when I went to Ancoats, if I had not been around a bit, I might well have become a victim of this concentrated barrage of bull, for it was all about us. When I once suggested, in the office pub, that we ought to start each day by singing, in chorus, 'We are the world's greatest little girls and boys' to the tune of The Ovaltinies programme on Radio Luxemburg, it was received in shocked silence. It was possible to enjoy a laugh at some of our worst excesses, as when Big Jim Smith, our senior man in Newcastle-upon-Tyne, mentioned at an office party that he had never worked in Dublin. 'You shall, dear boy, you shall,' replied the Northern Editor, Roger Wood. 'Off you go – at once.' And Jim, fortified by a couple of hours at the party and editorial sanction, went off to the airport and flew to Eire. He surfaced a week later, filed a story that began, 'The only place in Ireland where you can't get a drink on Sunday is Dublin airport,' and flew home.

But (and I was probably the only member of the staff who took such a prissy view) I found this nonsense more of an embarrassment than a joke. I liked to fraternize with the opposition once we had all telephoned our stories and this was officially frowned upon. We of the *Express* had to be aloof, exclusive. Ignoring this, I spent each evening during a rare breach-of-promise action at Stafford Assizes enjoying a jar-or-several with half-a-dozen rivals plus the lady who was the plaintiff in the action. A genial soul, she dispensed 'background' information liberally to all of us so that by the final day there was not one single detail of any kind that was not known to every reporter involved in the hearing. Yet my News Room absolutely insisted that I 'buy up' the lady for a story to be written by me but printed under *her* by-line. The piece did not, unsurprisingly, contain a single fact or comment that did not appear in every other national but we had shelled out £100 to have the lady's name at the head of it. The economics of newspapers was absolutely lunatic, for this was by no means an isolated instance, nor were we the only paper to pursue the practice.

But it was what is known today as the 'hype' and 'razzmatazz' that bored me most of all. While I was spending a weekend off in Yorkshire a story broke twenty-five miles away in Kettlewell, at the head of Wharfedale, concerning six potholers who were trapped underground, fairly high up on the slopes of Great Whernside. As soon as I heard this news I telephoned Manchester to say I was pretty close to the scene, that I knew the area and had some (slight) experience of potholing. 'It's all right,' said Keith Howard. 'We've got a team on the way from here.' Every instinct told me to go to Kettlewell but the News Editor's word was law. I stayed put. The following evening Keith telephoned me, drama exuding from every syllable, to instruct me to proceed with all speed to Kettlewell. 'We're sending in a new team,' he boomed. 'Some of the boys up there are flakers. They've had no sleep for forty-eight hours.'

As it was barely thirty-six hours since the story had broken, this seemed a little improbable but by then I knew the ropes. It was not done to spoil the histrionics. I arrived in Kettlewell to find one of my colleagues, a London-born 'townie' who barely recognized a field, returning to base camp (the Bluebell Hotel) from 'up the mountain', swearing by all he held dear that he had been pursued by a wolf! All the rooms in the hotel had been booked by the *Daily Express* to prevent any rival finding a bed there and the landlord had been heavily bribed to refuse anyone from any other paper access to his telephone. Not only that but a team of four reporters were being employed solely to carry out a fillibuster on the public 'phone outside in the street to prevent any alien use of that. I suddenly felt very old-fashioned in my attitude to journalism.

In Spring 1959 I received a 'phone call at home from Ken Donlan, the Northern News Editor of the *Daily Mail*: 'Would you like to come and have a chat over a spot of lunch next week?' I replied immediately, 'I'll come for the same money as I am getting at the *Express*.' 'Don't make it too easy for me,' laughed Ken. The sense of outrage in the office when I offered a month's notice was something that could be physically felt. Word travels quickly in newspaper circles and it was already known where I was going. One simply did not leave the *Daily Express* in Manchester for any destination other than the *Daily Express* in London. But to have a reporter leaving for the *Mail* . . . this was treason of the highest order. The *Mail* was regarded by the *Express* as its chief competitor. The *Mirror* might have the larger circulation but it was not regarded as a threat in terms of readership amongst the bourgeoisie. The *Sun* and the *Daily Star* had not yet been spawned. It was *Mail* v *Express* at every turn and I had gone over to the enemy.

The *Mail* was an infinitely more wholesome camp in every way. There was the same keenness to get a beat on the *Express* as there was in the opposite direction but without the sounding of trumpets and beating of drums when it happened. Life on the *Express* had been exciting with a hint of madness; life on the *Mail* now proved exciting in an atmosphere of sanity. In Harold Pendlebury the *Mail* had the best reporter I have ever known. He looked like a favourite uncle, with an approach which could persuade anyone to talk to him on any subject.

He could keep people talking on the 'phone for a full hour after they would have hung up on anyone else. On virtually every assignment with the *Express* one was asked (when making a check-call to the News Room): 'Who's there from the *Mail*?' If the answer was 'Pendle' two extra reporters were despatched from Ancoats Street immediately. Harold was now on my side and I was very glad. I liked Ken Donlan from the first, and his deputy, Bill Dickson, together with the Night News Editor, Jimmy Lewthwaite, completed a trio of fine journalists without that touch of hysteria which was never very far away at the *Express*.

One tradition which I had enjoyed at the *Express* was now introduced to the *Mail* – the Maunday Thursday outing, which was descended from the age-old printers' wayzgoose. Good Friday and Boxing Day were the only days England, at that time, was without newspapers, and the preceding days were holidays for the majority of the editorial and printing staffs. Individual newspapers had their own way of celebrating this occasion. The *Mirror*, for instance, went off *en masse* to Southwell Races but on the *Express* a different venture was tried each Maundy Thursday. One piece of mild madness was when we took a coach to Liverpool and sailed to the Isle of Man ('for a drink') but as the timetable allowed just one hour on the island and the party was about forty-strong there was time, literally, for just *a* drink before we re-embarked. It was a bit of a surprise to discover the *Mail* did not mark Maunday Thursday in any corporate way but my Editor, Harry Myers, was enthusiastic when I suggested we do something about this. We went off on a reconnaissance together to seek out a series of suitable hostelries including the all-important one which would stay open all afternoon and a new tradition was started in the Deansgate office. They were good days because they brought together, for the only time in the year in a social context, something like ninety-nine per cent of the editorial staff. We discovered that the most improbable candidates had unsuspected talents in the field of impromptu entertainment but above all we laughed together for something like twelve hours which made them, surely, the most therapeutic of all office outings?

There was a tremendously good atmosphere in the office and the years 1959-64 were among the happiest I can remember. It was little short of tragic that they should end on a sour note but that was some time in the future. Towards the end of 1959, I wrote a series of articles on 'shamateurism' in sport, which involved a certain amount of liaison with the sports department. Soon afterwards I wrote another series, this time a really tough job of reporting the 'fixing' of League football matches for betting purposes, which I undertook in partnership with Bob Greaves who later became a popular news editor, then programme presenter with

Granada Television. We uncovered a whole series of particularly nasty cans of worms; spent long hours persuading players to sign affidavits and even longer hours arguing with the paper's lawyers whose job it was to protect the *Mail* from libel actions. The result of these investigations made me just about as sceptical when I looked at some Saturday results as I was about dog pedigrees after my stay in Derby, ten years earlier.

I was still travelling to Yorkshire each Saturday in summer for my cricket. This, plus my interest in rugby of both amateur and professional codes, drew me closer, in social terms, to the Sports staff and when I was in town I often enjoyed a lunchtime drink with John Trickett, the Sports Editor, and columnist Jack Wood. They were entertaining, one day in March 1960, the London Sports Editor, J. L. Manning, and invited me to join the party. Jim Manning was one of the most respected journalists in the country, a crusading type of writer who campaigned long and hard (but unavailingly) against the practice of printing 'ghosted' columns that were ostensibly the work of professional sportsmen. As the maximum wage for a League footballer at that time was £24 a week it was perhaps a little hard to condemn hugely talented players from earning a few quid more in this way but Jim was ever a man of principle and he was vehemently against the system, which was mainly followed by Sunday and provincial evening papers. Indeed, the two Manchester 'evenings' – the *News* and the *Chronicle* – were instrumental in helping both United and City to induce players to join the clubs. The clubs might be able to offer no more than a £24 wage packet but an extra £20 for putting a name to a ghosted column in the local paper was a powerful persuader and the practice was followed, to greater or lesser degrees, in other parts of the country.

Now, as the four of us were taking the waters in the Manchester Chop House, Jim's thoughts turned to other matters and he mentioned the experimental short tour which was due to take the Scottish Rugby Football Union to South Africa shortly. The riots and bloodshed in Sharpeville had occurred only recently and Jim mused, 'Suppose something like that happens while the Scots are there? We ought to cover the tour but it needs a news reporter who also knows rugby union so that if there is trouble we have a man on the spot but if not the games can be reported in the normal way. Where do I find a man who can do that?'

Jack Wood grinned at him: 'You've got one standing next to you.' Jim turned to me, checked my qualifications and asked, 'Would you like a trip to South Africa?' 'Delighted,' said I, 'if you can clear it with the News Editor.' He could and did and off I went in April for a quite superb three weeks amongst men who, thirty years later, are still my good friends.

There were no problems and I was able to concentrate exclusively on the rugby, though I wrote a series of features on other matters to justify my existence. There was one Test, the first international match to be played on the newly built Boet Erasmus Stadium in Port Elizabeth, and two provincial matches in Kimberley and Springs (Transvaal). There was no other pressman covering the tour and the Scottish party made me immediately and most cordially welcome. Special friendships were struck up with Charlie Drummond, the assistant manager but still a marvellously extrovert, ex-centre threequarter from the Borders; with Tom McClung, an Edinburgh Academical and superb practical joker; and with Arthur Smith, the great wing threequarter who came from Kirkcudbright. But in all truth, by the time we returned home, I loved them all, each and every member of the party, which was skippered by Gordon Waddell and managed by Wilson Shaw. It was a truly wonderful three weeks. In the years that have followed I have kept in touch with many of them – Charlie and Arthur until their deaths, with Tom and with Dave Rollo, the immensely strong prop from Howe of Fife, a wonderful, soft-spoken Samson of a man, who farmed for much of his life near St. Andrews. When my elder son embarked on a career in golf and played in his first Open Championship as a seventeen-year-old amateur it was with the Rollos that he stayed, and he immediately developed the same admiration and affection for Dave, and his wife, Jean, that his father cherished. And when in 1975 those who remained from that South African tour decided to stage a 25th anniversary party it was a magnificently sentimental reunion of old friends. It was just one more manifestation of the unique camaraderie of rugby football. I have never found anything to match it in any other sport.

On my return I learned that Gerald Williams (later to become the BBC's tennis correspondent) was leaving Manchester to join the *Mail*'s London staff. He had been used in the North, necessarily, as an all-round sports writer and there was little opportunity for him to develop his special skills and use his contacts as a tennis man. He could clearly be of greater value to the paper in the metropolis. That meant a vacancy on our sports staff but I was astonished when John Trickett and Jack Wood approached me to ask if I would like to fill it. Up until then, sport had simply been a hobby and an outside interest to me. I was a News man and proud of it. Had my News Editor approved this approach? He had. That, in a way, dismayed me. Ken Donlan had thought me a good enough reporter to 'buy me out' from the *Express*. Had he changed his view of my capabilities? Ken quietly reassured me. If he hadn't thought a move would be useful to the paper he would not have agreed to the approach. There was a feeling that we could sell a lot more papers in the North by having a specialist cricket writer, especially if we concentrated heavily on *Yorkshire* cricket. It was felt that after twenty-five years in the leagues I had the right sort of background and contacts. It was known that several of the Yorkshire team were my friends, that on the other side of the Pennines Brian Statham had been my neighbour and that I had a couple of mates in the Derbyshire team as well. At thirty-five, wasn't I getting ready to retire from playing, particularly as I was a bowler? There would be an increase in salary and I would have a guarantee that my expenses would never fall below a certain level.

A whole series of conferences took place and gradually it came to me that the main stumbling block was my pride. There was a tendency for news men to look down on sports writers as cliché-merchants; there was certainly not the same opportunity for good *writing* on the sports pages and I still shuddered slightly at the memory of those 'end-to-end-play-ensued' days in Nottingham. But wasn't cricket different from football in terms of writing? I was never going to be a Cardus or Robertson-Glasgow by any stretch of imagination but I did *care* for cricket and I hated to see it described in the crash-bang-wallop terms employed by many of the popular national papers. Would I be allowed to write about *the cricket* and not just the personalities? I would.

Before giving my decision I took myself off to Cambridge where Yorkshire were opening their new season against the University. I had visited the place while brother Stuart was 'up' in 1957-9 and thought once again how I would have loved to spend three years there instead of slogging away for a correspondence course degree. But the purpose of my visit was to talk to Brian Close, Ray Illingworth and the new captain, Vic Wilson, about what life would be like on the cricket-writing circuit. At the same time I looked up Gordon Waddell, with whom I had recently toured South Africa, who was at Peterhouse, and from him I learned that the Irish RFU were going to make a similar tour to that of the Scots, in 1961. So on my return to Manchester I agreed to become a sports writer and dropped a very heavy hint that I would like to visit South Africa again the following year! And so, in my thirty-sixth year, my career took off in another new direction. The next five cricket seasons were sheer joy . . . at least after the first week!

8 *And So To Cricket*

With a lot of competitive cricket behind me, with the people I knew in the
game and with a fair amount of experience *watching* it at county and Test
level I felt I had at least got some of the basic qualifications. Nevertheless,
a low-key approach was essential and in less than a week the realization
came that watching first-class cricket is entirely different from playing it;
taking part in league cricket is a different matter from the three- or five-
day game. It was going to be necessary to learn my trade all over again. I
was fortunate in my tutors. . . .

The Yorkshire team – and, in a less intense way, those of other counties
– ate, drank and breathed the game. For the most part I stayed with
Yorkshire, though when they were in the south, and some of their games
were reported by colleagues from the London office, I spent time with
Lancashire and with Derbyshire. Otherwise my summers were spent with
my fellow countrymen, travelling around the country in convoy every
Tuesday and Friday night, in pre-motorway days, with journeys taking
anything up to eight hours – Bradford to Swansea, Manchester to
Gravesend, Clacton to Scarborough, Bournemouth to Middlesborough.
From and to almost everywhere, it seemed, we had to pass through
Birmingham and that, in the early sixties, was a nightmare. Indeed, the
story went around of meeting motorists on Birmingham's so-called ring-
road, who had been trying to get *off* it since the end of the war! But to the
players, who might be called upon to field all day after a 2 a.m. arrival at
their hotel, the problem of travel were simply something that went with
the job. There was a natural amount of good-natured grumbling but only
once an outbreak of full-scale revolt – when the Yorkshire secretary,
attracted by what appeared to be a generously reduced tariff, booked the
team into a temperance hotel!

The great thing from my point of view was that during the games there was 'cricket talk' of the very highest quality every evening in the hotel bar or lounge. Close and Illingworth were respected throughout cricket as the best brains in the game. Both became, and still are, my very good friends and to listen to their analyses of each day's play was as splendid an education as any a cricket writer could hope to enjoy.

There was something to be learned from every session with these two and I neglected no opportunity: the different techniques required for batting on different pitches, against different types of bowling; field-placings for individual batsmen (both mentors had a card-index in their minds with the strengths and weaknesses of every man in the game stored away); which bowlers were specially respected and how they might be countered. If a Yorkshire batsman had recently shown a noticeable technical deficiency he was (quite informally) introduced into the discussion and invited to consider an absolutely constructive criticism, delivered with a professional skill that demanded respect. I was privileged to sit in on all these debates. Then there were the breakfast-table previews of the day ahead. I listened to the plotted downfall of some of the game's outstanding players. Nothing could have been more valuable than the Close-Illingworth plans for the destruction of Colin Cowdrey. The measure of their success was that although 'Kipper' scored 107 centuries I never saw one of them! Probably I missed a lot in pure cricketing terms but as far as learning my new trade was concerned it taught me a great deal more to hear his dismissal fashioned over breakfast, or the previous evening, then see it accomplished a few hours later in the pre-ordained manner.

Occasionally, of course, things did not work out as planned and then there was a certain amusement in having a fairly good idea what was being said out in the middle! There was also a good deal to be learned from talking to the players of other counties and getting an objective view of the Yorkshiremen. More than twenty years have now passed since their days of supremacy so it is important to remember just how Yorkshire were regarded in the 1960s – and in countless years before that. Every other county wanted to beat them oh-so-badly; victory meant far more than against any other opponents. No one made quixotic or 'sporting' declarations against the Yorkies; no one gave them an inch. Every advantage had to be earned by skill, by honest toil, by out-thinking the opposition and, it has to be said, by sheer gamesmanship. And I sat and watched, and lived through so many hours of this.

It was not all grim intensity, by any means. After two or three hours of cricket talk an evening might develop into a singing night, especially in Scarborough, or in South Wales where we rashly claimed to be able to out-sing the Welsh. There was fun and laughter throughout the season, and through the long months of winter we met frequently for more laughter and song – and more cricket talk. There were the weddings as the years went by . . . of Close, Wilson, Nicholson and Sharpe . . . there were christenings, Christmas and New Year parties, golf days, benefit functions and, quite simply, meeting-for-fun days. And in all of these, at some stage, there would be cricket talk. It was a good time to learn.

After five seasons of this intensive study I knew every man in the game personally and, thanks to my tutors, something about each of them as a player. It was rather like a budding artist being able to take master-classes with Michelangelo, Rembrandt and Gaugin; a music student working alongside Haydn, Mozart and Beethoven. And I was grateful for it all. There were times when space restrictions on the *Mail* limited one's opportunities to express the magic of Yorkshire cricket in particular at that time (and a more general affection for the game as well) so it was difficult to resist a yearning to be writing for the *Daily Telegraph*, with a chance to spread oneself. But I made no move to change; the *Mail* was a good outfit to work for and I was, in the main, content. For most of the time I was following a winning team and that always makes life easier for the correspondent. Yorkshire won the county championship in 1960, were runners-up in 1961 (and I was asked for 1,000 words to explain this fall from grace!); and winners again in 1962 and 1963. They were good days, happy days, wonderful days.

Professional contacts blossomed into personal friendships and much time was now spent swopping visits between my home and those of a number of players; the annual dinner season brought invitations to speak; there were cricket societies to be addressed; throughout the winter there was always the opportunity for an exchange of views, most of which were helpful and instructive. But winter raised one particular problem – what was I to do for the *Daily Mail*? As everyone knew, my winter game was Rugby Union and the main coverage of that game was carried out from London. In the North, Frank Davies (the chief sports sub-editor) was deskbound throughout the week and rewarded by a visit to a rugger match on Saturday. That was the only work available to a northern rugby correspondent following the amateur code. How was I to be employed for the next six or seven months?

'No problem – football,' I was told. 'But I don't know anything about soccer,' I protested, but the reply was that *that* was no problem, either! I had once been to watch a match between Burnley and Blackpool some years earlier, in the hope of seeing Stanley Matthews play, but the team-news announcement before the kick-off intimated just one change in the published programme: someone-or-other in place of Matthews at No. 7 for Blackpool. My interest evaporated at once. I didn't even know the rules of the game so I borrowed a book and learned something about them. But the most important factor was that I had no *feeling* for the game. This didn't seem to matter, either. What really seemed to be required was for me to put myself about and make the acquaintance of club managers so that when I rang them during the week they would have some idea who was calling to ask if they were interested in signing so-and-so or if they were really 'poised to make a £50,000 bid' for what's-his-name? For most of the time, it seemed to me, we wrote stories one day so that we could knock them down the next. It was boring and most of it was futile.

I was never able to develop any affection for the game and there was much about it that I disliked intensely. For instance, if one went to Liverpool or Everton, in particular, cars had to be parked in the streets near the Anfield or Goodison Park grounds and a horde of boys would appear the moment one stepped out and locked up, to inquire: 'Watch your car?' It was more of a threat than an offer. To refuse was to invite deflated tyres, scratched paintwork, snapped aerials or even broken headlights. The going rate was sixpence or a bob (depending upon the size and cupidity of the 'guard') but it was really advisable to pick out the biggest and/or oldest in the group, give him two bob and offer a bit of flattery, such as: 'You look like the boss of this lot.'

Liverpool is, of course, a city of great individuality. It has its own accent (which has nothing at all to do with Lancashire), its own humour, its own pop-music sound, its own rich tradition of producing showbusiness personalities, its own political persuasion and probably lots of other things as well. And the most distinctive of these characteristics, I have always felt, is the Liverpool humour. In an age when the music hall has, so regrettably, been killed off by television, the incomparable Ken Dodd alone is able to fill the London Palladium and be given critical acclaim as a stand-up comic. And the spontaneous wit of the Anfield Kop is something which is probably unsurpassed anywhere in the world.

I shall always be sorry that I was not present on that football ground for an occasion described to me by a member of the folk-music group, The Spinners. In the massed ranks of The Kop one Cup-tie Saturday a man fainted and the body was passed, in time-honoured fashion, over thousands of heads until it was placed, gently, on the turf behind one of the goals. For once, no St. John Ambulance Brigade representative was immediately available, and the only man in sight who might possibly provide rudimentary treatment was a policeman on horseback. As he dismounted and leaned over the patient the whole Kop, with that telepathic insight no one has ever been able to explain, struck up a swelling chorus of the current No. 1 in the charts: Rolf Harris's version of 'Do you think I would leave you dying when there's room on my horse for two?' That was spontaneous wit that surely can never be surpassed.

On the other hand, the first outbreak of crowd violence I ever saw was at the Baseball Ground, Derby, when Liverpool were the visitors in an FA cup-tie. Not only was there a pitch-invasion – something relatively unknown at that time – but after the game hordes of Liverpool supporters rampaged through the middle of Derby terrorizing the Saturday shoppers. It horrified me to such an extent that I wrote a piece for Monday's *Daily Mail*, which was featured as the back-page lead and headlined, in very large type, 'The Scourge of Soccer.' By chance I went to a game at Bury that evening, and amongst the visiting dignitaries was Bill Shankly, the one-and-only Shanks, manager of Liverpool in all his glory. Over a cup of tea after the game he approached me and demanded: 'What's this in the *Mail*, calling MY supporters "The Scrooge of Soccer?"'

I replied in terms that I felt The Kop might have appreciated but which Bill most certainly didn't: 'I don't know what the Dickens you are talking about.'

Judicial humour, which I had so enjoyed in my High Court years, ventured into the world of soccer in 1990 when Paul Gascoigne, a Tottenham Hotspur player, sought an injunction preventing the publication of a book called *Gazza*, the name by which he was popularly known. Opening the plaintiff's case, Mr Michael Silverleaf informed the judge: 'Paul Gascoigne is a very well-known footballer.'

'Rugby or association football?' inquired Mr Justice Harman with a fine show of what was, one imagines, false ignorance of this everyday story of sporting folk.

When Mr Silverleaf had satisfied the judge's curiosity, his Lordship commented, 'Isn't there an operetta called *La Gazza Ladra*? It means the Sicilian Ladder.'

Alas, to give judicial humour its most telling impact, you (judge or not) have to get your facts right. *La Gazza Ladra* is an opera by Rossini but in translation it is *The Thievish* (or 'Thieving' – depending upon who has carried out the translation) *Magpie*. There is indeed another Rossini opera called, in English, *The Silken* (not 'Sicilian') *Ladder* but the Italian title is *La Scala di Seta*.

Nice try, judge. But he got his headlines, just the same. A combination of modern English soccer and nineteenth-century Italian opera was always going to be a winner.

Conversation in football circles thirty years ago seemed as limited as the literature on the game and if it had not been for the forays into Europe from time to time what little appeal football had for me would have palled rapidly. I snatched at every opportunity to see new countries and cities, especially when a fixture provided an opportunity to visit one of the countries behind the Iron Curtain. Life could obviously be rather tough there. In Budapest I saw a radio commentator – whom I came to know quite well in later years – operating in a mobile role, standing on the touchline in a snowstorm. It kept him in pretty close touch with the players and the game but the quality of the transmission must have been a bit rough and I can't think of many British commentators who would have been willing to work in such conditions.

Occasionally the media party played a silly game of ordering three dishes 'blind' from a menu in the vernacular, the main proviso being that all three had to be served on the same plate. This caused some concern (and even one or two flat refusals) in countries where their sense of humour was a little different from ours. But it gave the rest of us a childish cause for amusement when one of our number ordered, and was served with, goose's barnacles (whatever they may be), strawberries and ice cream, and a thick brown sauce. It was, needless to say, a point of honour that the whole mess had to be eaten. In some countries the game was not possible because most of us had a smattering of schoolboy French, a few knew a bit of German and the earlier pioneers of holidays in Spain had a certain advantage on games in the Iberian peninsula. But in Slavic countries all things were possible and there was a fair amount of entertainment to be found in Greece, Turkey and Scandinavia as the scope of the European competitions widened.

My first glimpse of the Danube was a disappointment since the river, which in Strauss's Vienna might well have been the 'schöne, blaue Donau', had become a dirty stream of grey sludge by the time it reached Hungary. Prague, on the other hand, was fascinating and I spent a good deal more time exploring the castle and the museums than checking the latest team news. Liverpool, Manchester United, Burnley and Leeds United were some of the clubs involved in Europe during my soccer-writing period, but while we were able to join the official party on their charter aircraft and in their hotels with other clubs, Burnley (through their all-powerful chairman Bob Lord) had put a complete block on any form of co-operation with the *Daily Mail*. This stemmed from something that had been written by one of my colleagues before my transfer to the sports staff, but Bob was not a man for compromise – the ban applied to any and every *Mail* man for evermore! As the club fielded one of the most successful and attractive teams in the First Division at that time we were unable to follow a reciprocal policy of ignoring Burnley. Bob refused us Press Box and telephone facilities during home games at Turf Moor, and we could not enjoy refreshments in the Board Room (more importantly, we could not talk to managers and directors there) after the game. But with a nice touch of sardonic humour, the Chairman *did* allow the paper to buy season tickets for a couple of seats adjoining the Press Box on condition that no one passed a telephone over the barriers to us. We had to improvise by paying a shopkeeper near the ground for the use of his telephone to send through our reports from night matches, all of which occasioned a lot of good-natured leg-pulling from our rivals and from the Burnley supporters who sat about us. Opportunities for retaliation did not arise very often but one chance came on the day before Hamburg were due to play at Turf Moor. In a fairly heated exchange, which required an interpreter, Bob Lord refused Hamburg's request to practise under the club's footlights. On the fringe of these deliberations I heard the German centre-forward, Uwe Seeler, remark sarcastically, 'Tell him we'll pay for the electricity if that's the problem.' The interpreter diplomatically omitted to pass on this barb to the volatile Burnley Chairman but I passed it on to *Daily Mail* readers in a back-page lead that no one else had got. It was the first practical use I had ever found for my Keighley Grammar School German and it earned me a nice little exclusive – and a new, *personal* ban from Mr Lord.

A lot of money flew about in the form of chequebook journalism in sports circles, especially when noted players found themselves in dispute with their clubs for whatever reason. At Middlesbrough, in those early sixties, a large section of the players took exception to the appointment, as their captain, of Brian Clough and I went off to Teeside to see what it was about. I arrived to find loudspeaker-vans patrolling the streets and announcing: 'Read Brian Clough's exclusive story in the *Daily Express* tomorrow – only in the *Daily Express*.' And in the wake of the vans came Len Shackleton, that marvellous innovative footballer with Bradford, Newcastle United and Sunderland – a man twenty-five years ahead of his time in the matter of being financially rewarded for outstanding entertainment value – and now the *Express*'s man in the north east. Shack was my good friend; we had covered Yorkshire cricket together (he was an extremely good cricketer apart from his God-given talent as a footballer) and we spent many long and laughter-filled hours together. He now grinned, and said, 'We've got him (Clough) completely sewn up. Face it. Let's have a beer and a round of golf.'

'I can't do that, Len,' I replied. 'I've got to give it a go, at least. See you in an hour's time for that beer.'

So off I went to knock on the door of Mr Clough. Half-an-hour later I came away. Brian had in no way breached his contract with the *Daily Express*. He had not been offered any money. But the *Daily Mail* the following morning carried as good a story, I felt, as any that could have been contrived without a Brian Clough by-line on it. And I like to think a certain mutual respect has existed between us since that day although we have met rarely. We have watched a bit of cricket together at Scarborough, and once at Derby, and really that's all. But fifteen years or so later I wrote (as a BBC producer) to him to ask if he would take part in a 'Sports Forum' recording for Radio 2, cautioning that the fee would not exactly inspire thoughts of early retirement. He replied agreeing to join the programme and adding, 'About the fee, I thought it was bad manners to talk about money between friends.' I liked that.

Don Revie became a chum in not entirely dissimilar circumstances. Leeds United were setting off to a game in Spain (Zaragossa) and at the airport the manager started a distribution of 500-peseta notes, one to every member of the accompanying media party. I refused to accept one. Don said, 'There are no strings attached. It's just a little gesture from the directors to the fellows who write about us – a thank you, if you like. It's all part of our public relations.'

'It's very kind,' I replied. 'and I appreciate the offer, but I absolutely cannot accept it.'

We had a very good relationship during the rest of Don's life.

Although I had quit the *Express* partly to get away from all the 'bull', I still had to endure one of the most distasteful things about football reporting, which was to see one's picture on hoardings, outside newsagents' shops and attached to lampposts around football grounds, with quite idiotic claims about one's ability as 'The North's No. 1' and rubbish of that sort. Some of my colleagues actually believed this nonsense; I have known one of them to put in a fierce complaint that there were more posters advertising a rival than there were for him! A sense of humour enabled one to retain a sense of proportion but once anyone started to believe his own publicity he was on an ego-trip with no return ticket. Mercifully no one in the circulation department insisted on following the same policy at cricket matches, because I think I would have resigned at once. It has come in more recent years, sadly, and it is difficult to repress a shudder to see a 'bill' announcing as 'Cricket's No. 1 writer' an individual whose knowledge of the difference between an off-spinner and a scrum-half is slight and whose grasp of the English language is dodgy.

But it didn't happen in the 1960s and we were grateful for it. The howls of derision from cricket's dressing-rooms would have been deafening. As it was, every word in every paper was considered and analysed with great care every morning of the summer. Not that the players ordered copies of all the papers, certainly not a body of good Yorkshiremen, careful with their brass. They simply stretched out a hand for the Pressmen's personal copies with the courteous request, 'Let's see what sort of crap you've written today then.' Any slips, whether on the part of the writer or in the printing process, were vigorously condemned.

The essays of J. M. Kilburn in the *Yorkshire Post* were read with respect, as were Bill Bowes's reports and weekend reflections in the *Evening Post*, and the *Daily Telegraph* columns were searched for news of rivals' progress. The rest of us had to endure more critical scrutiny. By 1961 every 'popular' national paper had followed the *Mail*'s lead in covering cricket more regularly and in greater depth than had previously been the case, and by and large we co-existed peacefully and happily. By 1962 Len Shackleton was no longer with us, having taken up an appointment with the *People* as its north-east man, an existence so blissful that once when I 'phoned him to say I was going to be in his parish and how about a round of golf, he replied: 'Thursday. No, I can't play on Thursday. It's my day off.'

'Surely,' I protested, 'that makes it exactly the right day to play?'

'Oh, no,' he replied. 'I play golf on the other six days. Thursday is my day off.'

It was precisely that touch of humour that moved him to startle the football world when he included in his autobiography one blank page with a chapter heading: 'What the average director knows about football.' Shack was a genius with a football at his feet, or so I have been told by experts, and after seeing him conjure with a rubber ball or a tennis ball, and once even a beer bottle, I do not doubt the claim. He was also a delightful companion and good colleague. We missed him sorely. But with a reporter from the *Mail*, *Express*, *Herald*, *Telegraph*, and *Mirror* joining the representatives of five Yorkshire papers, the county team found its reputation in championship cricket circles enhanced to a certain degree. Not only did Yorkshire play a more uncompromising game than anyone else, with no favours expected or bestowed, but they carried around their own private Press Corps – almost all of them Yorkshire-born. Other counties could not be blamed for feeling that public opinion was being professionally marshalled against them as well as having to contend with the most powerful team in the country.

This was the Yorkshire squad of Close, Illingworth, Trueman, Binks, Sharpe, Bolus, Padgett, Taylor, Stott, Platt, Ryan, Cowan and Wilson, with Birkenshaw and Balderstone as senior Colts-in-waiting, and Hampshire making his first appearance in 1961, Boycott in 1962. They played marvellous cricket, positive and dynamic. There was individual ability in abundance but in 1958 and 1959 Ronnie Burnet had created a spirit of togetherness that the county had probably never known before, certainly not to the same extent. There might have been arguments from time to time between the bigger personalities in the ranks – there certainly were – but from the captain to the newest recruit there was an awareness that transcended all others: no one was bigger than the side, no one was bigger than Yorkshire cricket. There was a metaphysical quality about it, which defied definition. Who could explain how Mel Ryan was able to bowl out Lancashire when Freddie Trueman couldn't? Or how FST could be the first and warmest in his congratulations instead of slinking off into a corner (as might well have been expected of such a towering personality) to wrap himself in a cocoon of self-analysis? One felt that each member of that Yorkshire team would willingly have died for each other on the field. And at the end of the day they would drag themselves out of the trance and become separate entities, different individuals with contrasting characters, interests and pastimes. Simply being a peripheral part of this unit was an extra educational experience that was invaluable.

During those four summer months of the year I was conscious of undergoing a complete personality change. All the unfulfilled childhood dreams of being a part of Yorkshire CCC myself (which I nurtured like all those of my age) were now, albeit obliquely, somehow being realized. There was never a thought, forward or backward, of winter sporting activity. I neglected my family through lack of care and concern as well as by my absence. I rarely went near the office. I was utterly and completely a slave to the game of cricket. When, ultimately, I emerged from the trance I might have been a more knowledgeable cricket correspondent but I had deteriorated profoundly as a husband and father. I later realized just how much precious time I had lost when I should have been loving and understanding my two boys. Thank God they had a wonderful mother.

My second visit to South Africa came in 1961 and it was as enjoyable as my tour with the Scots the previous year. Ronnie Dawson was the Irish Captain and the party was managed by Noel Murphy, as lovely a man as ever downed a pint of Guinness. As his son, also Noel, was one of the wing forwards they were known as 'Big' Noel and 'Young' Noel and in 1989/90 it was good to see the third generation of the family playing in Ireland's colours. One Test was played in the magnificent setting of Newlands,

Cape Town, and there were provincial games in Mossel Bay, Potchefstroom and Salisbury (Rhodesia). The final part of the trip, in the land of Cecil Rhodes, was enlivened by an overnight stay at Victoria Falls and a morning cruise on the Zambezi amongst the frolicking hippopotami. This produced the best 'Irishism' of the tour. Some of us watched a trifle warily as a launch approached unnervingly close to the Falls, with scrum-half Andy Mulligan dangling his feet over the sharp end of the craft. He was hailed from the stern – as far back as he could possibly get – by the No. 8 forward Tim McGrath: 'Mulligan, I hope yez in a State of Grace 'cos if the brakes fail you'll be the first to go over.'

They were a wonderful bunch of chaps, and looking back sadly on the past twenty years of problems in Ireland I cannot help reflecting that there was not one second's suggestion of any difficulties of either a religious or political nature between any members of the party who were, of course, drawn from clubs in both Eire and Ulster. If only all Irishmen north and south of the border could be drawn together in the same spirit of camaraderie. As with the Scots, some of those friendships have endured for many years, and though the players of 1960 and 1961 have long since gone into retirement the annual international between Scotland and Ireland is always an occasion of fond nostalgia for me.

Ironically, it was through association football that I returned to broadcasting. My winter writing was carried out almost exclusively with tongue in cheek. Since I was woefully ignorant of, and indifferent to, the pursuit of association football it was difficult to take that season seriously. Probably I was lucky in my colleagues at the *Daily Mail*. John Trickett, the Sports Editor, was more of a friend and drinking companion than a boss. Our columnist Jack Wood was a highly intelligent chap with a philosophy of enjoying life to the full and realizing he could do it with all expenses paid. Don Hardisty was the best soccer writer in Manchester and enjoyed the respect not only of his rivals but of club managers and directors for his honesty and integrity. But some of our opposition took themselves very seriously indeed and the more pompous they became, the more I laughed. Indeed, during the period when the Players' Union (now the P. F. A.) were holding a series of meetings in Manchester with a view to shaking off the maximum-wage restrictions (and the *Mail* misguidedly sent me along to report what Jimmy Hill, as Chairman of the Union, had to say afterwards) I listened with amazement as Mr Hill trotted out what I thought was a great deal of arrant nonsense while the various 'No. 1' football writers listened with respectful attention. Finally I complained that he was seeking to insult our intelligence. But he did not have to defend himself – my fellow scribes rounded on me! No, I can in no way claim to have been anything but an abject failure as a soccer man. It has caused me no sleepless nights.

During this 1960-64 period the *News Chronicle* ceased publication and a number of their staff were absorbed by the *Daily Mail*, the most notable being a promising young writer called Ian Wooldridge. Some were with us briefly, others on a more permanent basis. For a few months Frank Taylor (another survivor of the Munich crash) was with us in Manchester and each Wednesday evening he and Don Hardisty went off to take part in a North Regional BBC radio programme. On one occasion Frank was unavailable and asked if I would like to take his place. I had not broadcast for nearly ten years and in all truth this had not disturbed me unduly because my earlier efforts had by no means suggested to me that I was a 'natural' in this branch of communications. It had been an interesting exercise but I had felt a bit out of my depth. However, thinking it might be helpful to Frank if I maintained the continuity of the *Daily Mail*/BBC connection, I agreed.

Don Hardisty and I were required to forecast possible draws in the following Saturday's League programme for the benefit of pools punters, DH on the First and Second Divisions, DM on the Third and Fourth. The fact was that I barely knew which teams operated in those two divisions, much less having any idea which games might be drawn, but bearing in mind the lessons in scripting the spoken word that Peter Scott had taught me a decade earlier I put together a piece and duly delivered it. At the end of the programme, the producer, Jack Harrison, took me on one side with the comment, 'You've broadcast before, haven't you?' I admitted my guilt and a few weeks later received a 'phone call asking me to contribute a piece on a subject other than pools forecasting. And with the arrival of the new cricket season I began to provide a weekly report on cricket in the three northernmost counties in the championship. When the next winter came round I was asked to take out a tape recorder – a big, bulky EMI machine – and interview a prominent figure in the football or rugby scene for another sports programme, broadcast on Friday night. It was interesting to note how my inexpert efforts seemed so much tidier and comprehensible when the tape was played into the programme so I asked to be allowed to watch Jack carrying out the editing, and I learned something completely new about a different form of communication. In Nottingham my stuff had always been recorded 'down the line', thirty or forty miles away in Birmingham and I had not had much chance to see how the transformation was effected. Now I became very much more interested. I began to contribute match reports to the Saturday (North Regional) programme 'Sport Spotlight', and then to the London-based

'Sports Report'. Whenever possible I watched Jack Harrison putting together the fabric of 'Sport Spotlight' before it was ready to go on the air and gradually I became fascinated by the whole framework of programme production. Up to that point I had no idea what a producer actually did; now I came to see how he conceived the whole content and shaped the style of a programme, appointed his contributors, 'balanced' the mix of voices and subject matter, timed everything to a split second and, finally, stood or fell by the performances of his actors. This was something *completely* different and it interested me.

There was still no thought, however, of making any more than my two or three pieces of broadcasting a week, which were a pleasant diversion, and a pleasantly profitable one, too. I had enjoyed most of my newspaper life so far and I saw no reason why that should change. Sensing my distaste for soccer (though I tended more to laugh at my winter activities than get cross about them), John Trickett gave me a weekly column, 'Man to Man'. This took the form of a question-and-answer interview, reported verbatim, with a well-known sporting personality. Because it involved amateurs as well as professionals we settled on a standard reward for each participant: everyone would receive a gold Schaeffer pen – a valuable item most people would be glad to have – but cash was never involved. In two years of meeting people, only once did a candidate refuse to be interviewed unless a cash payment was made. It staggered me that this was Frank Woolley, the great Kent cricketer between 1902 and 1938, a man I had only once seen play but who was indeed a legend. Not only did he insist on cash but he was pretty shirty about it as well. I shook my head sadly as I told him, 'I am very sorry, Mr Woolley, but we shall just have to forget all about it. But may I say you have destroyed an illusion for me?'

The series helped to make the winter months more pleasant and to widen the rather limited scope of my sporting knowledge since our subjects ranged from boxers to motorcycle scramble riders. One interview was with an American expert in the art of staunching cuts sustained in the boxing ring, a colourful character called Whitey Bimpson, who was accompanied by an even more colourful personality, Mickey Duff, today an even more substantial figure in boxing promotion and a vastly entertaining man with a pungent East End humour.

But times were a-changing on the *Mail* in Manchester. John Trickett had gone to London, along with Jack Wood, and with them a lot of laughter and good fellowship went out of my working life. The new Sports Editor was an entirely different type, one with whom I had absolutely nothing in common and I did not like the way he worked. In the summer of 1964, while I was away with Yorkshire on a southern tour, he

97

perpetrated what seemed to me unacceptable behaviour. I could have coped with that but he must have been aided and abetted by the Northern editor, a man I regarded as a personal friend. The details are not important now but at the time I felt betrayed. Honesty and straight dealing had always been essential in my relationships and to my mind they had gone out of the window. On 15 August 1964 I sent two telegrams from the county ground at Hove. One was to my friend Freddie Trueman congratulating him on his 300th Test wicket at The Oval, the other to the London Editor of the *Daily Mail* to say I resigned with effect from the end of the current match between Sussex and Yorkshire. The following Tuesday night I drove back North, told my wife of my intentions and next morning I went to the office, cleared my desk drawers, placed a note of resignation on the Northern Editor's desk and walked out. I had no job in mind and no savings but I had a mortgage, a wife and two boys aged thirteen and ten. The outlook was bleak but selfishly I felt my principles were intact.

It was not too difficult to keep the wolf from the door by freelancing. Other papers were generous in giving me match reports to do and I started to contribute one or two items a week to BBC radio news programmes in the North in addition to my sports work. Unfortunately, this meant some form of book-keeping and I had neither the inclination nor the capacity to do this properly. I was heading for future problems with the tax inspector! But salvation came from a quarter I least expected. Over a lunchtime beer Jack Harrison mentioned that he was moving to television and asked, 'Why don't you apply for my job?' For the very first time I considered the field of broadcasting as a new career – and liked the idea. This might be rather different and I was already intrigued by the production work I had seen. I went with Jack to his office, asked him a lot of questions, emphasized my limited experience in his branch of the media and listened carefully to everything he had to say. In the end I completed an application form (a trifle late, as it happened) but Jack put it through the necessary channels and in due course I was invited to appear before a selection board.

9 *Life with 'Auntie'*

BBC Appointments Boards provide an interesting experience to the uninitiated. A fair percentage are fixed before they start (i.e. the successful candidate has been pre-selected for one reason or another). In the next twenty years I was to sit as a member of enough Boards to convince me that we could all have saved ourselves a lot of time. But the democratic process demanded that justice, on these occasions, must at least appear to have been done and so one went through the motions. However, my first encounter with the system was as an applicant sitting *before* a Board.

My c.v. listed a fair measure of experience in communications and a smattering of knowledge in sporting areas. My two outside 'referees' were Brian Close, Captain of Yorkshire CCC, and Dr W. A. Mulcahy, Captain of the Ireland RFU side. One way and another I felt the paperwork put up a fairly good case. Consequently, I was not prepared for the opening gambit of Henry Riddell, Assistant Head of Outside Broadcasts: 'You don't mention rowing. Do you have any experience of rowing?' With at least a passing acquaintance with cricket, football, rugby of both codes, golf, athletics, tennis and ice hockey, all indicated on the papers before Henry, this seemed to me to be a rather provocative probe and no doubt my reply – 'None whatsoever. Is it a vital matter?' – sounded a trifle testy. It brought an immediate question from another member of the Board (Neville Stiff, ex-Army major, currently Assistant Head of Administration, North Region): 'Would you describe yourself as an abrasive personality?' Aha! I began to appreciate the value of a five-man board. Nevertheless, to thine own self be true. . . .

'If you mean do I suffer fools gladly, then the answer is "No, I don't."' I replied, and left thinking I had not done myself any favours at all. I went home in a distinctly well-sod-you-then frame of mind and did not expect to hear anything more from the Corporation. They let me stew for something like eight or ten weeks, by which time my bank manager was sending out distress calls, and then informed me that I had been appointed a general programme producer (outside broadcasts) at a salary of £1,300 per annum. This was a drop of £700 from my *Daily Mail* pay and I would now lose two or three broadcasts a week at five guineas a time.

Even my non-mathematical brain could tell me that the family income had, almost overnight, been halved at a rather important time in our sons' education. One was in a private, fee-paying school learning, as far as one could judge, exactly nothing; the other was approaching his 11-plus examinations. Once again I was not making a very good job of being a husband and father.

The Outside Broadcasts Department in the North consisted of two producers and three secretaries. As Jack Harrison moved to television his colleague Alan Clarke was redesignated a staff commentator, concerned mainly with association football and motor-racing, though he was a good all-rounder who had, in his time, turned his hand (or rather his voice) to a wide variety of broadcasting.

That meant a double change in Manchester and shortly after moving in I was joined by Tony Preston, a former regular Army officer, who had spent a short time in the London OB Department after leaving the Service. He was the new senior producer and thus my head of department, which seemed to me to be the wrong way round since his experience of communications in any form was sketchy in the extreme, and the only sport with which he was familiar was horse-racing. Furthermore he had only the barest grasp of the geography of the North and he certainly didn't understand northern people. However, like a good newsman I had arranged sources of information in our London bureau and they now advised me that Captain A. C. N. Preston was a favourite protégé of Charles Max-Muller, the BBC's Old-Etonian Head of Outside Broadcasts (Radio). I should tread warily.

So for the next three-and-a-half years I played sergeant major to Tony's company commander and it proved an interesting experience as I was given a quite dazzling illustration of the old Service axiom: 'Bullshit baffles brains.' The first thing Tony did was throw out his (Alan Clarke's) old desk and requisition a new (and much larger) one. The second thing he did was produce a master plan for the amalgamation of Radio and Television OBs in the North – with himself in charge. As the senior TV producer was a close personal friend of the Controller, the idea was knocked down and Tony had made a rather powerful enemy! His third move was to organize a search (to be conducted through our Northern

TV News programme, in which he wangled a three-minute spot every Friday evening) for a shot-putter good enough to make the Olympics team. This was a good idea. Unfortunately Tony decided that he would direct this part of the programme himself though he had no idea how to 'drive' a television studio and he refused professional guidance from the 'Look North' team. The result was that because of the most elementary error of faulty timing his final programme (when the winner was to be announced) was faded out before the name could be revealed! For once the favourite newspaper cliché about the BBC's switchboard being jammed with calls of complaint was correct.

But gradually Tony settled down and we made a good team. He loved to attend meetings – something I hated – and the BBC cannot feel it has had a good day unless at least half its personnel have been involved in some sort of meeting, seminar, talk-in or symposium. Our 'empire' covered the area between the Solway Firth and The Wash, Berwick-on-Tweed and North Wales and Tony absolutely loved visiting its farthest-flung outposts to rally the troops. He was a chum of Peter Bromley, Radio's brilliant racing commentator, and spent a lot of time at our many northern courses – York, Chester, Haydock Park, Thirsk, Newcastle, Redcar, Beverley, Catterick Bridge and, once a year, Aintree. He was a splendid organizer and when the World Cup came to England in 1966 he really came into his own. The setting up of facilities in Manchester, Liverpool, Sheffield and the north-east for scores of overseas commentators was an enormous undertaking; there were more than fifty broadcasters from Brazil alone and others from places like Portugal, Hungary and North Korea, to name but three, all requiring commentary facilities in grounds that were not really equipped, technically, to accommodate such numbers.

While all sports broadcasting in the vast area of the North Region was our responsibility we were by no means concerned with sport alone. 'Have a Go' (of Wilfred Pickles fame), 'Down Your Way', and Royal visits came under the umbrella of Outside Broadcasts, as did the recording of the Christmas Bells for transmission on the morning of 25 December. We had three regular weekly programmes to be put together for Friday and Saturday evenings. The first of these was a preview of the weekend sport, the second was a full coverage of the day's sport on Saturday, 'Sport Spotlight', and the third was a short fifteen-minute programme for anglers on Friday evening called 'Fisherman's Inn'. While I could handle the other two without problems, it came as a bit of a shock to have the third dumped on me as well, especially as I knew nothing whatsoever about the gentle art. But one of the great advantages of having a sound newspaper training and background is that if there is something you don't know, you usually know someone who does. As Tony knew virtually no one my local knowledge seemed impressive enough for him to call me 'The Oracle'. Finding the right man to present 'Fisherman's Inn', with a budget of five pounds, was a task at which my Delphic ancestor might have jibbed.

After an initial disaster, I was saved by a genius who wrote and volunteered his services. He was called Hal Mount and already he contributed an angling column to the *Daily Mirror* accompanied by illustrations which he drew himself. He now proceeded to display a third form of artistic expression – acting. Each Friday morning he sent me a script describing a search for trout, roach or tench – whatever he felt like 'catching' that week – in the river, or lake, and off I went to the Effects library in Broadcasting House, overlooking Piccadilly (Manchester), to dig out the recorded sound of gently lapping or fast-flowing water, seasonal bird-song and the distant lowing of cattle or the bleating of sheep. At six o'clock Hal arrived, reel in hand, and with only a brief rehearsal we spent fifteen minutes chasing the fish of the week to a background of appropriate rural effects. Hal grunted and groaned as he spoke his lines, reeled in, gasped in disappointment, cast again, got a bite and finally collapsed over the table, exhausted but triumphant. Olivier himself could not have surpassed the performance.

Gradually I began to get a bit carried away and elaborated with the effects ever more ambitiously until I slipped up by using a record (these were on disc at the time, not tape as in later days) labelled 'Mixed bird-song in a woodland environment'. As the script said we were fishing that October evening in a small stream that passed a heavy clump of trees, this seemed the right illustration. But in the chorus of blackbirds, finches, tits, buntings and the rest came one solitary cry of 'Cuck-oo, cuck-oo'. Only the most conscientious ornithologist could have identified it; only the most fastidious listener would have written to point out that cuckoos are not normally heard in October.

Inevitably the letter – addressed simply to 'The BBC, Manchester' – fell into the wrong hands. Instead of landing on my desk it was delivered to the Assistant Head of Programmes, an academically gifted young man. Instead of having a quiet word with me over a beer he began an investigation. Now it was no secret amongst producers that 'Fisherman's Inn' came out of Studio 5 in Broadcasting House and not from the river bank. No one had attempted to hush up production methods; indeed it would have been impossible to do so.

But it was news to the Assistant Head of Programmes, in all his glory. He sent me a memo, a deeply pained memo, saying it had come to his notice that I had been deceiving the public with my Friday masterpieces and demanding an explanation. I seemed to remember that his string of qualifications included one in Law so I replied – formally, as required, though he lived one floor apart – confessing all but claiming that I was merely attempting to give 'a touch of artistic verisimilitude to an otherwise bald and unconvincing narrative.' Clearly, W. S. Gilbert was not his kind of barrister for a thunderous response bounced on to my desk: I was debasing the coinage of broadcasting and the practice must cease forthwith.

So, on its budget of £5, 'Fisherman's Inn' now moved out into the countryside, taking anything up to a day to record and with far less satisfactory results. We didn't catch as many fish and there were even more serious setbacks. Out-of-doors recording was not easy on the pretty crude portable equipment we used at that time, and one breath of wind, one gentle zephyr, across the head of a microphone sounded like a clap of thunder on the tape. But just before waving my flag of surrender I fired one parting shot by asking my leader, 'Have you ever heard of a programme called 'Out with Romany'?' This was one of the best-loved features of Children's Hour, which in turn was one of the most popular of all Radio programmes. But he hadn't. It was a studio production about walks in the country.

What delighted me most about the move from newspapers to Radio was that I now had opportunities – almost unlimited because there were literally hours of air-time to be filled in the Regional programme schedules – to give expression to my own ideas. One could sit down with a pen, a piece of paper, and an idea, and *create* a radio programme, or a series of six or more. If the effort was successful the programme could be offered to Network and, once accepted, it would be broadcast to the wider, national listening audience. Once I had realized this, programme ideas began to stream out of the Outside Broadcast Department, and not simply on sport. One's whole range of interests could be reflected. You put up an idea to the planners, asked for budget if they liked it and away you went. It was only the outline which had to be accepted; the exact content of the programme was entirely the producer's responsibility.

It was like being given a blank cheque, and I filled in mine for huge amounts of job satisfaction. Nothing like this had been possible in newspapers; I now lay in the Elysian fields of communication and the sun was always shining. I was totally in love with this job, besotted by it and I worked at it for seven days a week. When studio programmes or outside broadcasts were not being put on the air, new thoughts were being put down on my pad and typed out to be sent to the planners. When I left the

BBC I had 504 days off owing to me and I don't think I ever took my full four-weeks' holiday entitlement in twenty years. It was, of course, achieved at the expense of family life, which was not as important to me as it should have been at the time, and much have I regretted this in later years.

One of the first features I produced was called 'Portrait of a Test Cricketer', and its star was Geoffrey Boycott. Another one-off was 'A Day in the Life of a Country Village', and while researching it I was able to recapture my boyhood and the days when I cycled round every inch of the Yorkshire Dales. The idea was to show how a small community can be self-sufficient in terms of entertaining itself when it is far from a big town, cinema, or major football club. In Austwick, just inside the Dales National Park, we recorded twenty-seven different kinds of community activity, ranging from a traditional-type blacksmith to a choral-music class and the guarding of a rare orchid that can only be found on the limestone fells surrounding the village. My secretary, a complete 'townie', complained at breakfast that she had not been able to sleep in the village pub 'because it was *too quiet* – until the birds started singing in the middle of the night.'

Tony Preston conceived a series on sailing, which covered the whole of the British Isles, not simply the North of England, and I countered with a series of six on steam railways which, in the early sixties, were beginning to be revived by groups of men and women who bought up stretches of track, miraculously found the money to buy locomotives and rolling-stock, and so preserved something of a way of life that was fast disappearing. Six more programmes followed, then another six, by which time we had exhausted all the little private companies which then existed. The idea for these programmes came when I heard a broadcast – it was probably 'Desert Island Discs' – in which a guest requested nothing but records of engines steaming along certain bits of track. I like to think my series might, in some way, have inspired 'Great Train Journeys', which was produced in the North twenty years later. The format was simple. First I took a ride along lines like the Severn Valley, the Festiniog, the Dart Valley or the Bluebell, recording nothing but the sound of the engine and the train as it puffed its way along ten miles or so of track. Next I recorded the people who ran the operation telling their own stories. And finally, editing the tapes in Broadcasting House, I 'fed' the effects behind the voices to produce the impression of chat as we cruised along. This meant that when the programme was complete I still had separate recordings of the transport and the people, which was just as well because requests now came flooding in for copies of the tape – from as far away as South Africa and Australia – with the sound of the trains.

Once again I found myself getting carried away . . . the excellent people who ran the Severn Valley Line (from Bridgnorth to Bewdley) allowed me to travel on the footplate of one of their locos and, with my secretary (in a nice, clean summer dress) working the recording equipment, I carried out a commentary while stoking the boiler-fire. Little did I realize what hard work that is. The result of this ambitious enterprise was one bad back and one ruined dress.

Next came a series on Inland Waterways at a time when the IWA was trying to stimulate interest in restoring some of our canals. It would be nice to think we played a small part in creating an awareness of this part of our heritage as we chugged up and down the Leeds and Liverpool, the Llangollen and the Grand Central talking to everyone from lock-keepers and holiday makers to the more traditional families who lived on the canals.

Meanwhile, all the regular programmes continued and there was a never-ending call from London for the setting-up of facilities for events ranging from football matches to the Royal Maundy Service. The OB Department in London was entirely separate from Sport (which was a small sub-division of News), run by Angus Mackay, often referred to in BBC circles as 'the legendary . . .'. Angus did not speak to me because I was the junior of the two Manchester producers! On the day I was appointed Senior OB Producer in the North, Tony Preston having moved on to higher things, Angus came on the 'phone in the first hour of the day: 'Don, old boy. How are you? and many congratulations.' They were the first words he had spoken to me in three-and-a-half years.

It seemed an amusing touch of snobbery. On the other hand, I had given him little cause to love me. Calls from his department were almost inevitably to ask for an interview with a footballer – my idea of hell! On one occasion, after recording Nobby Stiles (at that time Manchester United and England wing-half) I persuaded the technician working with me, who had the same twisted sense of humour as myself, to cut out of the tape every one of Nobby's 'You knows' then string them all together. They totalled seventy-nine, from a recording of two minutes' duration. There was not, therefore, much substance left, but I sent both tapes to London, thinking to give a smile to some of my more congenial colleagues there. Unfortunately, Angus heard the wrong tape first . . . seventy-nine 'You knows'. He was not amused.

A footballing encounter of a different kind came when the Sports Room asked for George Best to be invited into a studio to be interviewed 'down the line' by someone in London. This was not the easiest thing in the world to set up. Matt Busby was often difficult to track down during the day and his permission was, of course, necessary. Then came the even more acute problem of getting hold of the eighteen-year-old star and inducing him to visit Broadcasting House. A studio had to be booked in Manchester and one in London, together with technicians. And Mr Best then failed to turn up. Half-a-dozen people were left kicking their heels for an hour while we telephoned Old Trafford in a search for the missing hero. In the end the whole operation had to be abandoned and re-arranged for the following day. This time I asked Alan Clarke to go to Old Trafford and physically transport George into the city centre. Through no fault of Alan's they arrived an hour late, when both studios and technicians had to be re-booked, not the easiest of tasks when all studios were in constant use all day long. Eventually the recording was completed and I escorted George out of Broadcasting House to find his blood-red car parked diagonally across the busiest corner in the city. 'Good Lord,' I exclaimed, 'you'll get life imprisonment if the police spot that. You'd better scarper as quickly as you can.' 'Sure, there's no need to get excited,' replied the young man nonchalantly. 'They all know George Best's car and they won't knock me off. And if they do, what's a £10 fine?' As he drove away I remarked to Alan Clarke, 'There goes a youngster who could well grow up to be anti-social.' I recalled those words when I saw George in September 1990 on the Terry Wogan TV Show.

When I became head of department I made very sure that my colleague was always a man who could handle all our football commitments. There were only two of them in the seventeen years of my incumbency – Arthur Appleton, a grand Wearsider with much of his heart in Roker Park, and when Arthur retired, Ron Gubba who was not only a soccer enthusiast but a racing specialist as well. They were good colleagues and good friends.

I played one other practical joke on London but revealed it to only a tiny handful of people in my twenty years on staff. Part of our duties, as OB producers, was to find new broadcasters. Aspiring commentators were recorded and the tapes sent to headquarters to be played to a listening panel of specialists in a particular sport, and broadcasting executives. Very few auditions were successful the first time and usually a tape came back with a list of points to pass on to the aspirant. In my earliest days I recorded myself doing a *football* commentary. I did it 'straight' but with entirely mischievous intent for nothing was further from my mind than getting closer than I needed to association football. The tape then went to London with an explanatory note that it was the work of 'Arthur Harris', who had requested an audition. Back, with indecent haste, came a thumbs-up and a request to give Mr Harris as much experience as possible in the shortest space of time! I put away the tape, and the verdict,

Riding shotgun on a steam-driven car past Walmsgate Bar, York, *en route* to Castle Museum.

Derby Borough Police XV, 1949–50.

Keighley Boys' Grammar School XI v. Old Boys, Founder's Day, 1956. The author stands second left, and his brother, Stuart (School Captain) is in the centre of the picture.

An underground sail in an old zinc bath!

Golfing with York-shire, 1964; partners Don Wilson, Ted Lester, Brian Bolus.

Chatting to Ken Dodd for a *Daily Mail* 'Man-to-Man' column.

Judging a Miss Great Britain Beauty Contest.

Above left Judging Dairy Board Awards, Yorkshire v. New Zealand, 1969. *Left to right* Graham Downing (NZ Captain), the author, 'Dairy Queen', Brian Close, Richard Hutton.

Left Famous faces at Denton Golf Club, Manchester, including Joe Corrigan (Manchester City), Alex Stepney (Manchester United), Freddie Trueman and Geoff Boycott (Yorkshire), David Lloyd and Brian Statham (Lancashire).

Commentating in Pakistan, 1977.

Brian Johnston

Cliff Morgan

John Arlott

In memory of Dylan Thomas died Nov 9th 1953 RIP

Wynford Vaughan-Thomas at Dylan Thomas' graveside.

The author and his wife with 'Neighbours' stars Ian Smith (Harold Bishop) and Anne Charleston (Madge).

'Test Match Special' 1990. *Left to right* (*standing*) Peter Baxter (Producer), Bill Frindall, Farokh Engineer, Henry Blofeld, David Lloyd, Mike Selvey; (*seated*) Christopher Martin-Jenkins, Freddie Trueman, Brian Johnston, The Alderman.

in the only drawer in my desk that was kept locked. For the remainder of that football season inquiries came at fairly regular intervals: 'What about Harris? When are you going to put him on a match?' Mr Harris was unavailable for a surprising variety of reasons and, mercifully, by the following season London had forgotten about him.

We had our moments of drama on the weekly 'Sport Spotlight', as when Roger Moffat, a staff announcer who was well ahead of his time in versatility and twisted skills, read (for a bet in Mrs Mac's, the pub at the back of 'old' Broadcasting House in Piccadilly) the League football results, all with the wrong inflection. As he lowered his voice, usually indicative of a defeat for the away team, he suddenly announced an away *win*, and so on, through the whole set of results in England and Scotland. Thousands of people across the North, pens poised to check their football coupons, were thrown into utter confusion and, once again, the old switchboard was flooded with complaints. It is not the easiest thing in the world to read all the results with the *correct* inflection; to read them all with a wrong one takes a particular kind of genius.

In the late sixties Orrell RUFC (today the biggest and most successful side in the North) were a junior club overshadowed by the mighty Wigan Rugby League Club on their doorstep. Then they started a run of success, which I first noticed in the columns of the *Sunday Express*, and I began to take a sharper interest. When the unbeaten run topped the thirty mark it seemed a good time to start a little feature spot in 'Spotlight' so we began saving Orrell's score until the end of our rugby results sequence with 'and, wait for it, Orrell 24 pts, Someone-else nil. That's thirty-three successive wins.' It went on for an astonishingly long time over a couple of seasons and feedback told us that in other clubs throughout our area there was a lot of interest being shown in Orrell's run. When most of the sport was frozen out one January Saturday we invited in Eric Smith, the Chairman, and Des Seabrook, the Captain, to talk about their club, and a month later we went one better. We took the programme out of the studio and produced it as an outside broadcast from a rugby match: Kendal v Orrell. And in London the nationally networked 'Sports Service' decided to cash in on the facilities we had set up on the edge of Lakeland and came over in the half-time interval of England v Ireland at Twickenham. Thus the whole of the British Isles learned that this junior club from south-central Lancashire were now heading for yet another victory. By the time the winning sequence came to an end a lot more people knew about Orrell than when it began. The players and the club organization had done it all, of course, but it was nice to feel our programme had been involved in a peripheral way.

Meanwhile I was getting a great deal of practice as a cricket and rugby commentator. It might be thought that any sane person would have been content with the work involved in producing our regular weekly programmes, organizing a multitude of outside broadcasts for London, dreaming up and producing things like the railway and canal series plus a mountainous amount of paperwork. Every programme required about a hundredweight. But the North Region regularly offered our department forty-minute and twenty-minute 'slots' which it was sensible to fill with county cricket and county rugby. It was even more sensible to avoid spending money on fees and expenses for London-based, non-staff commentators. And since I had been broadcasting for a year or two before joining the staff it seemed most sensible of all, to our Head of Programmes, for me to be used. Accordingly, I spent hours gaining priceless experience at Headingley and Old Trafford, Bramall Lane and Southport, Bradford and Chesterfield. Once, at Southport, I had a forty-minute spell (Lancashire v Derbyshire) of commentary in which not a wicket fell and not a single run was scored. There was no other way in which I could gain experience like that. Even though I was praying at the time for a train to pass on the Liverpool line, I reflected on the way home that if I could talk my way through forty long minutes of inactivity I ought to be able to cope with most situations in live broadcasting.

There were some areas of the BBC which I regarded with grave suspicion and one of these was the Audience Research Department. I had never met anyone who had ever been asked to express a view to this mysterious body until I found one of their researchers gravely noting viewing and listening habits from people emerging from . . . the BBC car park in Lower Mosley Street, Manchester! So I was naturally incensed when an AR report gravely issued figures showing that my commentary on Yorkshire v Leicestershire at Harrogate had been heard by more people during Friday than on the previous day. The match had, in fact, finished on Thursday evening when Yorkshire claimed the extra half hour and there had, in consequence, been no commentary on the Friday. I showed the report to Tony Preston, heavily sardonic in my fury, and Tony – who generally adopted a strictly defensive stance during my outbursts – finally was moved to send a polite note of inquiry to AR asking how they arrived at their figures. They took a little time to reply, then sent a most erudite study proving conclusively that if there *had been* commentary on Friday it would have had a bigger audience than Thursday. I looked at them with a new respect after that.

When Test Matches were played at Headingley and Old Trafford I acted as on-site producer and liaison man with Michael Tuke-Hastings, the BBC's cricket producer, in London – he sat all day in the 'Test Match Special' studio in Broadcasting House. Here was another essential part of my education, listening all day long to Arlott and Johnston, various permutations of Robert Hudson, Alan Gibson, Peter Cranmer and, at the end of the day, the summaries of E. W. Swanton. Here was the richest of harvests to reap, and a lesson to be picked up almost every minute of the day. It seemed almost heretical to feel the programme was less than perfect yet it seemed to me that, splendid though it was as a piece of radio, it was just a bit too solemn for what was, after all, a description of a game. The occasional *bon mot* from John Arlott or Alan Gibson pierced the cloud cover once or twice but rarely if ever was there laughter of a hearty nature. We had a smile at the well-turned phrase or perhaps a touch of classical wit but it was a humour of the Brains Trust rather than the Crazy Gang. A touch of the latter, it seemed, at least to my producer's ear, would not be too far out of character once in a while. The nearest we came to this was when Alan Gibson, a classicist of renown, and Pearson Surita, a commentator from India who was more British than the British, embarked on the declension of a non-existent Latin verb! There was a hold-up in play at the time and most of us found the exercise quite diverting but not Charles Max-Muller, sitting in his office two hundred miles away from Headingley. He stormed into the TMS studio, screaming shrilly at Michael Tuke-Hastings: 'What's this nonsense? Stop it at once. Stop it at once.'

Down my cans (earphones) in the commentary box came the weary, quasi-long-suffering voice of 'Tuke': 'Don Mosey to the telephone.' Out I went to speak to Michael on the control line in the engineering box: 'What's going on, old man? Whatever it is, Charlie doesn't like it.' So ended an attempt to lighten the atmosphere of 'Test Match Special' in the 1960s. Not many others were attempted during the Max-Muller regime.

I don't think Charles knew much about programme-making but he did listen to the department's output and he had very clear ideas on what he did *not* like. The only conversation I ever had with him during his period in charge was one in which he informed me very clearly indeed that I could abandon any hope of being invited to commentate on cricket outside my own Region. My voice, and my accent, he said, were 'not suitable' for a cricket audience outside the North. This rocked me a little until I realized that John Arlott was already an established international voice of cricket, Hampshire burr and all, before Charles came to power. By the 1960s John's was the best-known voice of cricket in the world and there was nothing to be done about that. But with that notable exception, Charles was determined that no voice from outside the public school network would ever be heard delivering Test Match commentary. It was after noting the arrival in the TMS box of a man whose knowledge of the game and its players was so sketchy that he should not have been allowed within a hundred miles of the operation that I had sent my own audition tape to London. It had been 'cleared' for use in the provinces; now it had been made clear to me that I would progress no further along that road.

It seemed unfair to me that an arbitrary decision of that nature could be made on unworthy grounds but clearly there was nothing I could do about it. Tony Preston had also been told, and on our return to Manchester he spelled it out for me, that I had absolutely no chance at all of being used as a commentator outside our own parish. I adopted what I hoped was the realistic attitude to this news. In terms of knowing what was happening out in the middle I felt I could hold my own; when it came to sheer broadcasting ability, use of language, 'colouring' the commentary to invest the duller passages with something to entertain the listener and to develop a distinct style of my own, I knew I was light-years behind Arlott, Johnston and Gibson. It was only when a new voice was introduced which I knew, both as a producer and a broadcaster, was inadequate in every way that I could feel resentful with any justification. I set out to remedy my deficiencies as quickly as I could.

It was, therefore, a surprise when Brian Johnston telephoned one day in 1968 to say my name had been put into the schedules to commentate for Network (i.e. to the whole country) on a match in Yorkshire. 'But I thought I wasn't allowed to do this,' I replied. 'Don't know anything about that, old man,' said BJ. 'Your audition tape has been passed, hasn't it? You'll be happy about doing the game, won't you?' And that was the start of cricket broadcasting on a wider scale. If things were not moving as quickly as I would have liked, now in my forties, at least they were moving.

Meanwhile I was still churning out programmes of all sorts. I started a series of conversation-pieces between sporting personalities who had never previously met each other. The first two candidates were F. S. Trueman and Harvey Smith and they provided a rip-roaring overture. From there I moved on to six programmes on 'The Humour of Sport' with three guests swopping yarns that formed much of the folklore of their respective games. Two on cricket, two on rugby, one on golf and one on rallying turned out rather well and all were accepted by Network Radio 4. Disappointments there might have been on the commentary front but when it came to opportunities to express my own ideas through programmes there could be no complaint at all. I absolutely loved my job and I was only going to kick over the traces when it seemed to me that someone was able to jump the gun (as in TMS commentary) through being in closer touch with, and having the ear of, London-based executives. The disadvantages of my reluctance to move to London became clearer every day. All sorts of things happened which could, and sometimes did, affect me but I only learned of them when it was too late. It was necessary to devise a method of letting OBs in London know that some of us in the Regions were experienced, and now senior, members of staff and we were not always happy with what happened without consultation.

BBC Radio did not (and does not) like confrontation. In television, everything works on a larger scale. Swords and axes are used for stabs-in-the-back; there is widespread blood-letting. In radio we have always used the poisoned dagger. Open, face-to-face argument is always discouraged because it makes people feel uncomfortable. My personal preference – for saying what I have to say, getting everything out in the open, then going for a friendly beer with the argument settled – has always been anathema to most of my metropolitan colleagues. Very few have been able to cope with eyeball-to-eyeball encounters. Additionally, the Corporation is riddled with gossips. It was time to put this to use. When potholers are trying to map a new cave system they put dye in the stream, which flows through most of the limestone fissures, and note where it re-appears. I now pinpointed the chief tittle-tattlers in London and 'fed' them with apparently irrelevant asides and off-the-cuff comments during tele-phone discussions, then waited to see what happened. Almost invariably my remarks were passed on and in due course a call would come from someone higher up the ladder, referring only obliquely to the topic I had so 'innocently' raised. It amounted to the establishment that he-knew-I-knew and I-knew-he-knew-I-knew. It was all very petty and childish but since everyone at headquarters in any position of authority recoiled in horror from discussion of controversial matters it was the only way to make a point. It became an important, if unorthodox, means of internal communication.

We moved on into the 1970s amidst rumblings of massive changes to take place in radio broadcasting. The Regions were to disappear and be replaced by a network of local radio stations which would provide a service of community broadcasting. Our hours of Regional opt-out broadcasting would be lost and we would work more closely to our masters in London. It was not a prospect which appealed to most of us in the provinces. There was a transitional period during which we, in Manchester, retained our Saturday 'Sport Spotlight' for a time, together with a Sunday morning programme called 'Talkabout', which still gave us the scope to create our own programmes but their days were known to be numbered. I had one last fling at creativity with my most ambitious project so far – a journey through the Dales in music, verse and prose, which required recording the sound of Aysgarth Falls and curlews on the Brontë Moors as well as hiring people to read poetry.

In London, Charles Max-Muller had retired and plans were afoot for the merger of the Outside Broadcasts Department and Sport. This seemed an entirely sensible move. Many of us had long regarded it as a bit of a nonsense that OBs put on the air every Saturday afternoon a four-hour programme of sport around the country and at 5 p.m. Angus Mackay's boys staged their 'Sports Report'. There were various manifestations of bitchiness about these two separate operations, with Angus refusing to use for his one-minute reports some of the commentators who had been working all afternoon for the OB Department. He probably had his own good reasons for this and one accepted that any producer's right to appoint his own contributors was sacrosanct. But it did seem a bit wasteful in terms of manpower and money. However, Angus was due to retire in a few years and the amalgamation was not scheduled as an immediate move.

In the meantime, his Sports Room had a new recruit, Christopher Dennis Alexander Martin-Jenkins, son of the Chairman of the Ellerman Shipping Lines. He had joined the BBC from Marlborough and Cambridge University via three years as Deputy Editor of *The Cricketer*. Brian Johnston was due to retire shortly as the Corporation's Cricket Correspondent; Jim Swanton was the *éminence grise* at *The Cricketer* and I was sure he had a great deal of influence with Bob Hudson who had succeeded Charles Max-Muller as Head of Outside Broadcasts. It did not take a genius, then, to work out the likely course of events. And Chris had very quickly nettled me by making mock – unforgivably, *on the air* – of my north-country accenting of his name when I was 'handing over' to him from one cricket match to another. I made a note to watch this particular situation rather closely.

In early 1973 the 'phone lines between London and the Regional OB producers in Birmingham, Bristol and Manchester – where Richard Maddock, Tony Smith and I were now pretty senior in the OB hierarchy – were red-hot with excited discussion. The amalgamation of the two departments was indeed due to take place but instead of the experienced staff of the OB department being given precedence over the bright young things of Sport, it really boiled down to a take-over of Outside Broadcasts by Sport! It was unbelievable.

And since it was known that Bob Hudson was to take early retirement, the burning question was: Who would head the new department of Sport and Outside Broadcasts? Everyone, but everyone, now started floating opinions and ideas around. Almost without exception, the OB staff let it be known they would be unhappy to be led by Bob Burrows who was the longest-serving member of the Sports Department but hopelessly inexperienced beside most of OBs. The sports boys, on the other hand, made it quite clear they would not like Jacob de Vries (Chief Producer, OBs, and next-senior after Bob Hudson) as their leader. This seemed to me a pity because I liked and respected Jacob as a very good producer, organizer and ideas-man. Bob Burrows, in contrast, was dismissed in my mind in good West Riding terms as 'nobbut a lad'.

Someone within the Corporation now produced a stroke of genius by appointing to the post an outsider, Cliff Morgan, the former Welsh international fly-half and an experienced freelance broadcaster. He would not take over until the Hudson retirement took effect, later in the year, and that in itself was a pragmatic move, allowing the dust to settle while everyone sorted out his reaction to, and anticipation of, the Morgan era. As I saw it, it was a brilliant appointment and I hoped my colleagues would see it in the same light. Not all of them did, but then that was too much to expect perhaps. My mind was exercised by weightier matters . . .

I received an extraordinary letter from Bob Hudson to say that the BBC was planning to resurrect the title of Cricket Correspondent, a post which had not been filled since Brian Johnston's retirement – compulsorily at the age of 60 – in 1972. As I knew, continued Bob, Chris Martin-Jenkins had, in effect, been carrying out the duties for the past year. He knew that I valued my 'autonomy' in the North and felt sure I would not be interested in moving to London but at the same time it seemed right to him that the matter should be 'mentioned' to me. If I *should* be interested, then a Board would be necessary to select the candidate, but if not, then Chris seemed the logical choice.

Now I felt really, steamingly, furiously angry for the first time since I had joined the BBC. I actually wrote down on paper CMJ's qualifications alongside mine and decided it was no contest.

It was the sort of letter which could only have originated within the BBC – You are obviously well qualified for this job but you don't want it, do you? In all truth I had never thought about it. There had been only one BBC Cricket Correspondent and Brian had done it so well that I thought the Corporation had regarded him as an impossible act to follow. I was a very happy fellow indeed in my own job in all respects but one – I badly wanted to be a 'Test Match Special' commentator. I didn't want to make cricket broadcasting my life's work and I wanted to continue creating programmes of my own as well as running my department in my part of the world. But if I had specialized in any particular field it was in cricket and I had not yet reached the pinnacle of achievement in this respect – the

'Test Match Special' operation. The job of cricket correspondent gave automatic entrée to this exclusive circle and that I *did* want.

So I began to examine all aspects of this intriguing situation. It would mean moving to London, something I had hitherto shunned utterly. But with our elder son now embarking on a career as a tour-professional golfer and the younger boy safely ensconsed in Loughborough College of Physical Education, it might not be such a bad thing after all. A lot of work had gone into making myself a reasonably competent communicator on the game. It would mean a good deal of travel to places I had never visited but my wife could join me at times on tour. Should I then mildly stand aside and see an absolutely plum job go to a young man who seemed to have been rather fortunate in life so far. I had heard of children being born with a silver spoon in the mouth but for Chris to walk so easily into the cricket correspondent's post with relatively little experience smacked of being born with a diamond-encrusted golden spoon thrust well down the throat! He had a beautiful speaking voice, a fine, confident, natural delivery. But what depth of technical knowledge of the game had he? How well did he understand the mind of a professional cricketer?

And in the last analysis I admitted to myself that my thinking was coloured by a resentment. I had had to work hard for every modest advancement I had achieved; the BBC cricket correspondent's position looked to me like the best job in the cricketing world – had I not done more to earn it than Chris?

I decided to try a little experiment. I wrote to Bob to say, 'Yes, I *am* interested in the job. I think I have the necessary qualifications. What I would like from you is an assurance that they will be considered, dispassionately, when compared with Chris's. In short, I want to know that the Board is not fixed.'

Quite clearly, this caused a major panic in London. Back came the most astonishing letter I have ever received in which the Head of Outside Broadcasts devoted a page of single-space typescript to listing all the reasons why I would *not* like the job! These ranged from 'surrendering the autonomy' I enjoyed in Manchester to a warning that the cricket correspondent's duties would not be the same as when BJ held the post. He would now have to carry out normal departmental duties as a sports assistant. But if I insisted on applying there would have to be a Board and – of course – he could say it would not be fixed. (As a celebrated lady witness in a court case once said, 'Well, he would, wouldn't he?') Then came the sting in the tail: 'Chris is already going to cover the winter tour. The arrangements have been made.' I showed the letter to John Arlott. He whistled. 'Never seen anything like it,' he said.

No one had to spell it out for me. I could understand Bob's dilemma. A fundamentally straight and decent man, he knew of my ambitions and of my frustrations but he had not for one second considered that I might regard what was so clearly going on in London as *unfair*. I did not know whether Bob's predecessor or someone else altogether in high places was behind it all but whoever it was, I could not let him get away without at least a bit of a struggle. I wrote to some of my cricketing friends and as a result I soon had in my hands testimonials to my suitability for the cricket correspondent's job from two England captains, four county captains and five England players! Then I gently filtered this down my private grapevine to London with *my* sting in the tail. These letters would be placed before the Board, along with my paper qualifications, and if I *then* was passed over I would drop the story to Michael Parkinson, whose *Sunday Times* column just occasionally referred to the North-South divide.

There was, naturally, no official response. There couldn't be. But my 'sources' in London reported panic on a now monumental scale. A few days later one of our Northern executives, normally never seen in the BBC Club, just happened to join me at the bar. With the most elaborately casual air he steered the conversation round to contractual obligations which prohibited unauthorized writing for the Press. As a former newspaperman, did this not present problems for me occasionally? If it had not involved a principle which was important to me I would have found it amusing. As it was, I replied, 'If I felt strongly enough that an injustice was being committed I would not let the contract bother me.'

And then something happened which changed everything. I became ill. Not to put too fine a point on it I had a complete nervous breakdown and spent most of the summer of 1973 in hospital or convalescing. Bob Hudson made no reference to my threatened, breach-of-contract course of action. He referred only to the Board, saying it could be postponed until I was fit again. Meanwhile, I was to take as long as was necessary to recover and I was not to think of returning for duty until I was a hundred percent.

Skullduggery I could fight; decency and concern I couldn't. I withdrew my candidature for the cricket correspondent's job. Chris was appointed at the age of twenty-eight. Twenty years older and, in my subjective view, about fifty years more experienced, I wondered if principles were much help in life.

10 *A New Department*

Under Cliff Morgan, the new combined department got away to a flying start. I had admired him on the rugby field, liked him as a broadcaster and now came to have a great respect for him as a departmental head. Middle management was always a weak link in the BBC's chain of command, in my view. Gifted programme makers tended to continue making programmes (a) because that is what gave them the greatest sense of fulfilment and (b) because that is where they were always going to be most valuable to the Corporation. Less talented people were shifted sideways with great regularity; an administrative role always seemed to be available and, if not . . . well, it was easy enough to create a new one. A secretary was necessary, of course, and shortly after that an assistant, also with a secretary. There was an enormous amount of dead wood within the organization because no one, however incompetent, was ever dismissed. Making a complete cod's head of one's job was deemed far less reprehensible than making waves. It simply could not have happened in newspapers and I marvelled at a tolerance that I never expected to see in any form of employment.

To the Sport and Outside Broadcasts Department Cliff brought a startling new approach. He identified very quickly indeed the 'dead wood' areas and sealed them off in corners where they could do no harm until such time as he was able to dispose of them. He took advice from people he respected professionally, irrespective of whether he had any personal liking for them. His main concern was getting the best programmes possible out of his staff. Like most of his countrymen he had music and poetry in his soul and he had a brilliantly perceptive 'feel' for the spoken word. He had a natural affection for good radio and an enthusiasm for his new department which was infectious. Hours before any other member of the staff arrived in the morning he could be found in the Sports Room,

3090 in Broadcasting House, listening to dozens of tapes which accumulated in the course of a day, sifting the wheat from the chaff, bringing new and fresh ideas to the output. He disliked the endless round of meetings, which seemed to go on interminably, and delegated this side of the routine to Bob Burrows, who had become his first lieutenant. Bob was a good organizer and 'admin' man and together they fused the two departments of OBs and Sport into a more streamlined unit, immeasurably more efficient than either had been individually.

Cliff, above all, had a contempt for cant and hypocrisy and back-biting. The twice-yearly meetings, which, in my ten years' experience had been a mixture of waffle and mealy-mouthed platitudes, now became occasions for an exchange of very frank opinions. If you were offended by something a colleague had done you were encouraged to get it off your chest in as clear and concise language as you liked. But – and this was the vital part – having said your piece you were expected to have a beer with the bloke you had criticized and start with a clean sheet. Whispered rumours and stabs in the back no longer had a major part in the Sport and OB set-up. This was a revolutionary concept of life in the BBC; we must have been the only department within the entire Corporation where the personnel knew exactly where they stood and what was expected. There were, as far as one could see, no favourites and no one who could expect preferential treatment.

Once, wearing my senior producer's hat in Manchester, I sent a tart note to London about something that had upset me, then departed to do golf commentary on the Benson and Hedges International tournament at York. At the farthest end of the course, following Tony Jacklin, I received a message that Cliff wanted to speak to me on the 'phone – urgently. I trecked back to the Press marquee, rang London, and was given a blast by Cliff for my note sent the previous day. I exploded, 'Have you dragged me two miles across a golf course to tell me that? Surely it could have waited until I had finished this round with Jacklin. You will be wanting a report on him in the 6.45 Sports Desk.' Cliff paused for a second or two, then explained that he had *not* expected me to come in from the course and the call *could* have waited until the end of the Jacklin round. *But* – since I was now there, my note had been offensive and he was giving me a bollocking for it. Right? Oh yes indeed. I could work with a man like that, *very* happily.

What Cliff would not tolerate was laziness or slipshod work and he had no time for those who did not share his enthusiasm for the job. He made the important decisions but at the same time he laboured at shop-floor level like the most junior recruit. He 'voiced' programmes, edited tapes, and rang round his wide range of contacts to persuade people to come in and take part in programmes. He worked longer hours than anyone else without ever losing a buoyant air of enthusiastic pleasure in what he was doing. He had an eye for talent, too. From an obscure corner of local radio he took on a young ex-Wren officer as an administrative assistant. Less than ten years after Cliff's departure his protégée had risen to be Head of Outside Broadcasts and then to become the first Controller of the new channel, Radio 5 – Pat Ewing.

Since I had first joined the BBC there had been a meeting every March to decide on our radio coverage of cricket in the following summer. This was chaired by Michael Tuke-Hastings, the man who 'invented' the ball-by-ball coverage of 'Test Match Special' and who was the cricket producer. It was attended by the three English Regional producers, Tony Smith (West), Dick Maddock (Midlands) and myself, and a certain amount of horse trading took place so that each Region got its share of coverage in the commentary matches. There was also a discussion on the men to be used as commentators, and though Tony, Dick and myself had no final 'say' in these matters, our opinions could be voiced and our views were sometimes accepted. Cliff attended the first of these meetings to be held under his leadership and asked me to have a private word with him during the day. He asked, 'What would *you* do to improve 'Test Match Special'? They were words I had waited a long time to hear.

'First of all, I would like Freddie Trueman to be given a chance as a summarizer,' I said. We had had a whole succession of men, sensible and respected ex-players, doing the inter-overs comments but they all seemed to me to lack a spark of natural broadcasting ability until the arrival of Trevor Bailey in the late sixties. Trevor was different, right from his first Test – intelligent, informed, authoritative, but with a touch of impish humour of the type I had longed to hear in the programme. It seemed to me that he and FST would make a splendidly contrasting pair of summarizers and that Fred would be invaluable in the other change I had, as a producer, in mind. 'Right,' said Cliff. 'What else?'

'It makes me weep when we slavishly go back to the studio for music the minute rain stops play,' I went on. 'People love to talk cricket so it's reasonable to suppose listeners would enjoy cricket talk when we have rain. With Fred and Trevor in the box, along with John Arlott and Brian Johnston we have the most enormous, untapped store of cricket-lore and anecdote it is possible to gather in one room. Let's use it.'

Now a lot of nonsense has been written in recent years and a lot of mis-information has been fed to journalists who have come to write features about the unit that became cult broadcasting in the following years. It happened quite simply as I have described and it is to Cliff that the credit must go for the creation of 'TMS' in the form it now followed. As Cricket Correspondent, Chris Martin-Jenkins was now added to the commentary team, and Henry Blofeld was a new candidate knocking on the door. Cliff had not the special fondness for public school products which his predecessors had shown. 'What do you think of Henry?' he asked. 'He knows his cricket and he has a good sense of fun,' I replied.

So two new names were added to the list of TMS personnel when the 1974 list was promulgated. To my great delight, Freddie Trueman was to be a summarizer, along with Trevor, and to my complete astonishment (because I had now written off my chances of joining the team) my name appeared, too. Tones of ripest West Riding accentation now joined the smoother and more polished public school mellifluence of Brian, Chris, Henry and Trevor, together with the most easily recognized voice in the cricketing world, that of John Arlott. We still had Alan Gibson, whom I admired greatly but who had angered Cliff by making a deprecating response to the studio presenter of 'Sport on Two' when he cued him in for a rugby report during the winter. At the start of the 1975 cricket season Cliff wanted to drop Alan; Tony Smith and I pleaded for his retention on the grounds that, on his day, he was as polished a commentator as any in the business. Reluctantly, Cliff agreed; Alan was assigned to the Third Test, England v Australia, at Headingley and I was given a grim warning: 'He's your responsibility, bach.'

Alan did not – shall we say? – do himself any favours. By the end of the fourth day orders came from Cliff, in London: 'Tell him not to bother to turn up tomorrow.' A tricky situation was avoided by the sheerest chance – on the fifth morning the pitch had been dug up by the friends and supporters of a convicted criminal, George Davis. Further play was abandoned, the match declared a draw and a matter of acute embarrassment had been avoided. But Alan did no more Test commentary.

It was an odd sort of life for me at this time. Sometimes I was a commentator on Tests, sometimes the producer and sometimes both! In the meantime I was also being used as a commentator at golf tournaments and I now auditioned, at Trooping the Colour, as a commentator on State and Ceremonial occasions. This was successful and I went on to describe such events as the Lord Mayor's Banquet, the opening of Liverpool Cathedral by the Queen, and part of the 1977 Royal Jubilee celebrations. The North Region had disappeared altogether, leaving a lot of creative people with fewer opportunities to put programmes on the air. There was no noticeable reduction in staff, however, and I marvelled at one post occupied by a colleague who produced two TV programmes a year, one of which was broadcast, the other consigned to the dustbin.

This inevitably gave him a lot of spare time, which he occupied by writing plays and short stories which he *sold* to the BBC! The economics of it all seemed to border on lunacy.

However, the opportunity to make programmes for Network Radio had by no means disappeared and there was a yearly tour of the Regions by the Controller of Radio 4, who would consider 'offers' of ideas from individual producers. I was keenly interested in these visits and usually managed to 'sell' one or two programmes, one of which gave me particular pleasure. I called it 'Christmas is for Children' and it was unashamedly based on the absolute broadcasting certainty of kids' uninhibited chatter. Groups of them were interviewed in such contrasting settings as the rougher end of Belfast and Manchester, a tiny village school in one of the most remote parts of Wales, and a class at a US Army Air Force base in Suffolk. It produced some magic touches of radio and it was delightfully linked and presented by that eternally lovely lady Nanette Newman.

Organizing all the outside broadcasts in the North was in itself a full-time job for the two of us but first Arthur Appleton, then Ron Gubba and myself regarded it as a challenge to get other things on the air. During the reign of Robert Hudson as Head of Outside Broadcasts, the producer of 'The Countryside' (Arthur Phillips) had retired and I made formal application to take over that seasonal programme, produced four times a year. London were reluctant to allow it to go completely to a Region and the good old compromise was reached by which I produced two programmes and the other two were put together by John Haslam, a senior member of the 'old' Outside Broadcasts Department. This became one of the great delights of my working life. 'The Countryside' was known as the best-loved programme on radio. It had not the biggest audience by any means but almost unfailingly it gained a reaction index (the yardstick by which listeners' enjoyment of a programme was statistically measured) of 80 upwards, while the general average for Radio 4 programmes was around 64. Once, one of my productions was given a figure of 79 and I spent several sleepless nights and an equal number of days listening over and over again to the tape to see where I had gone wrong. When I inherited my 'share' of the programme it was scripted and presented by C. Gordon Glover, a great broadcasting name. When he died there was much debate about whether the programme could continue with a new voice, and Cliff Morgan sought advice on a possible new presenter. I suggested John Arlott, but the final decision was that it should be taken over by Wynford Vaughan-Thomas and what an inspired choice it proved to be. Wynford was perhaps the most *complete* human being I have ever known. He had been a BBC war correspondent, had flown on bombing raids with the RAF, had been at the invasion of Anzio (he later scripted the film of that epic action); he had been up mountains and down caverns, and had explored the bottom of the ocean with Jacques Cousteau. He had been a close friend of Dylan Thomas and was, in fact, an executor of his estate, and a considerable poet in his own right. He had translated the libretti of operas, loved rugby and was one of the most fascinating conversationalists I had ever known. I had known him in the context of quiz programmes but had never previously had the opportunity of working closely with him.

The format of 'The Countryside' was basically simple. I inherited a company of regular and trusted contributors and was at liberty to find more of my own. Six were commissioned to provide suitable items for each programme and mostly they offered two or three alternative subjects. With twelve to eighteen ideas in front of him, the producer then worked out a balance of subject matter, of voices, of geographical coverage, what sort of sound-effects were desirable and, of course, whether the budget could stand the ultimate 'mix' of contributions. When the final decision had been made, one wrote to Wynford, detailing the 'inserts' and when the tapes came in from the contributors they were all edited to the required length and another note went to Wynford telling him how much time remained for his linking script. His vast experience of life, his travels, his enormous fund of anecdotes and his gift with words then all went into a narrative that was, invariably, broadcasting of the highest order. Very rarely indeed did 'The Countryside' go out on Radio 4 without some pearl from WVT being abstracted for 'Pick of the Week'. Never, before or since, have I been associated with radio work that was more professionally rewarding. Because of Wynford's involvement with so many things it became easier for John Haslam and I to go to Cardiff to record the programme than to have him visit London or Manchester and this in itself provided additional delights. My secretary, Trisha Lowcock, somehow contrived to fix recording dates when the Welsh National Opera were in residence so we enjoyed music on the night before the programme was put together. Then it was up to me to arrange matters so that 'The Countryside' was safely 'in the can' by 12.30 p.m. – when the bar opened in the BBC Club!

It was on one of these occasions that Wynford casually pulled out of his inside pocket a slightly wrinkled sheet of paper. 'Do you remember the leaflets the RAF used to drop in the first few months of the war, exhorting the German people to turn on their masters?' he asked. 'Well, I kept a bundle of them as a bit of a souvenir and the other day I discovered *this* trapped in amongst the leaflets. I had forgotten all about it.'

He passed over the sheet, which was headed, 'Saturday Night in Newport, Cardigan.' It was a handwritten poem, starting firmly enough but with the calligraphy gradually deteriorating in quality and some of the lines running off the edge of the paper, as though the poet was enjoying a few as he wrote.

'I had come back from a raid over Berlin,' explained Wynford, casually, 'and I had done my report in the news the following day when a 'phone call was put through to me. A voice said, "Allo, 'ero. Can you lend me a fiver? I'm in the last pub on the left-'and side down the King's Road in Chelsea." Now Dylan was usually broke and he often borrowed a fiver. I never expected to see them returned but on this occasion I suppose the boy thought he'd provide some sort of *quid pro quo*. This is it and, bless me, I'd forgotten about it.'

'Wait a minute, Wynford,' I said. 'Are you telling me that I am holding an unpublished Dylan Thomas poem, in his own handwriting?'

Thoughtfully, he replied, 'I suppose I ought to do something about it, don't you?' I did. Dashing to the telephone, I called a Radio 3 producer who specialized in poetry programmes and gave him the news. He almost choked. The following week 'Saturday Night. . . .' was reproduced on the front page of the *Sunday Times*. And a right bawdy ode it was, too!

That was but one of the many bonuses that resulted from my association with a dear and wonderful man. He was unbelievably multi-talented; there seemed to be nothing he had not done – with excellence. One day my wife and I, taking a short break in the West Country, made a diversion into Wales on the way home and spent a night at an hotel in Fishguard. I telephoned a greeting to Wynford, in his home high on the cliffs on the other side of the harbour, was rebuked for not having stayed with him and made to promise to call the following morning for coffee. Six hours (and about a dozen bottles of wine) later he was playing the piano while I sang Gilbert and Sullivan – not a pretty sound, but a hugely enjoyable session. I never saw him without a twinkle in his eye or a smile on his lips.

He had an amusing and/or entertaining anecdote to complement every conversational gambit and miraculously could introduce them without giving his companion the impression that a story was being 'capped'. He was, too, a good listener, always courteously attentive and seemingly interested in what others had to say. Brian Johnston recalls seeking his advice at the time he was hoping to go into broadcasting and being told by Wynford, 'Always *listen* to what is being said. Don't let your mind stray to the next question you want to ask. It may not be necessary.' Heeding that advice helped to make Brian the best *pleasant* (as opposed to *probing*) interviewer I have ever heard.

Sadly, Wynford died while I was abroad and I was unable to attend his funeral. I would have wept for the loss of a friend but rejoiced for a life which had been so fruitful, so fulfilled, so complete, one which had contributed so generously to the pleasure and happiness of his fellow creatures. He was one of the great men of broadcasting but he was so much more than that. He could bring the dullest subject to life. He did a superb TV series on Welsh castles, an equally brilliant one on radio in which, in his seventieth year, he explored the mountains of Wales with the same joy and enthusiasm he had experienced on a similar trek in his youth. He could make as brilliant a story out of the call by Llanelli third fifteen for a late drinking session in a village 'local' as he could about the majesty of a Royal Tour of New Zealand. If he had lived a thousand years earlier he would have been the tribal story-teller, the sole entertainer, the man who chronicled fable and folklore for posterity. But then he would have had to be the chief, the elder, and the high priest as well.

My original meeting with Wynford was for recordings of a quiz programme called 'Treble Chance' in which a resident team of broadcasters toured the country competing against regional teams of non-broadcasters. He was joined in the 'BBC' team by names such as Nan Winton, Ted Moult, Brian Johnston and Patrick Moore, and naturally enough the quizzes were not only tests of knowledge and wit but they were occasions of great fun as well. This sometimes took unexpected turns as when I had to leave the transport of the London-based team in the hands of an engaging character from a local radio station who was on a three-month attachment to my department in Manchester. His driving was – whall we say? – a little eccentric. The recording had been at Keighley Golf Club which is reached, from the main road, by a narrow, twisting, unmade-up lane and an even narrower bridge over the River Aire. The journey to the club had been hair-raising enough for the party in daylight; the return trip to their hotel, with a driver as unfamiliar with the route as his passengers, so unnerved Patrick Moore that he leapt out of the car and refused to travel any further in it. And the following morning when the driver presented himself at the hotel entrance he discovered that the entire London party had left early to walk a couple of miles to the station rather than risk any more of his chauffeuring.

The format of the 'Treble Chance' programme was later changed to involve four teams from each of the 'national regions' (i.e. England, Scotland, Wales and Northern Ireland) who first of all competed against each other to provide four semi-finalists, and thus we proceeded to a grand final. I produced this whole series for two or three years in the early eighties, and after the original Chairman, Desmond Lynam, found his television commitments too pressing I invited Nigel Starmer-Smith to act as quiz-master. He was a bit unlucky to find one of his earliest recordings in the far west of Wales, at Haverfordwest, with Wynford Vaughan-Thomas as one of the competing captains. Apart from his many other attributes, Wynford was a serious competitor – and not above manipulating the questionmaster if he was given a chance. His chance came when Nigel ruled that an answer from his team was incorrect. Wynford brushed this aside, assuring Nigel: 'Oh no, my dear chap, I do assure you our answer is quite right.'

Sitting outside in our mobile recording caravan I smiled a trifle wearily, pressed the talk-back key and told my questionmaster, 'Don't take any notice of this flannel. Tell Wynford he's wrong. There's no argument, and get on with it.' Every moment of debate meant more editing to be done at a later date and as I had set the questions and carefully checked all my references I knew that WVT was 'trying it on'. But he was a master at conveying an impression of absolute conviction and as Nigel had already been profoundly impressed by the scope of Wynford's general knowledge, he was now uncertain. And Wynford was *there*, on stage, alongside him and in full view of the audience, as large as life. His producer, on the other hand, was simply a voice in his 'cans'; no one could see *him* and no one could hear what he was saying except the quiz-master. He floundered wildly; Wynford (I could sense) grinned delightedly and pressed home his advantage. The result was a delay of fully eight minutes on my stop watch until I had to emerge on to the stage and chastise Wynford like an errant schoolboy. Finally the recording continued.

Afterwards, over our tea and cakes, 'Starmer' tried to explain his dilemma. I cut him short. 'Until you are more frightened of me than you are of a team captain,' I snarled, 'we are not going to get anywhere.' We had no further problems of a similar nature. But then there were no other Wynford Vaughan-Thomases around.

One of the curiosities of my various BBC roles at this time was manifest a few weeks later. On one particular Monday we were due to record a 'Treble Chance' programme in Northern Ireland. But the previous Saturday, Nigel and I found ourselves in Jesmond (Northumberland) with the two of us commentating on a Rugby Union county championship semi-final. 'Starmer', for television, was accommodated in a nice, comfortable box elevated ten or twelve feet on a scaffolding base to give him an excellent view of the game, while I, for poor old radio, had to operate – standing – at ground level. However, the scaffolding was so close to the field of play that it was cushioned in bales of straw to prevent injury to players who might be hurled into touch and they provided me with a rough sort of desk on which to put my notes and various bits of broadcasting paraphernalia. All was going reasonably well until Nigel flipped a cigarette end out of his window and it lodged, unknown to me, between two of the bales. It lay there smouldering for a while until, caught by a gust of wind, it burst into flames . . . just as the studio cued over to me for a ten-minute period of commentary. It is the only time I have described a rugby match with the microphone clutched in my left hand while the right was busy fighting a fire with a copy of the *Daily Telegraph*! It was not until we met in Ulster forty-eight hours later that I was in a position to administer a proper rebuke to the arsonist.

11 Home and Away

Programmes of all kinds may be put together with an air of clinical detachment and sound like excellent, professional productions. Rightly or wrongly, I believed throughout my production years that programmes that were invested with a touch of personal affection must have a greater, if more sentimental, appeal to the listening public. I felt that a producer had to *care* for his output with a strong, special attachment. 'Test Match Special' had for so many years made its greatest impact upon cricket-lovers in the purist vein; it was accurate and informed and authoritative but to me it lacked something in general appeal. With Fred and myself now giving it a different sort of *sound*, the time had come to give it a different idiom. Within two years of the changes in personnel the sound of laughter, hearty as opposed to polite, was now heard more regularly on Radio 3 in summer, and laughter is not only therapeutic – it is infectious as well. Most of all, when rain stopped play, the 'chat' sessions were being talked about in wider cricket circles and the audience was beginning to develop. It had been impossible, before 1974, to visualize non-cricketing housewives tuning in to the programme; now the postbag indicated that they were switching to TMS in very large numbers.

For the purists the cricket was still, we felt, being quickly and accurately described and, most importantly, the score up-dated at frequent intervals. For this section of the listening public the rain-stops-play periods were not simply occasions for irrelevant chatter. There was an occasion when Brian Johnston 'corpsed' completely and simply could not utter another word because he was laughing so much. This not only affected everyone in the commentary box but the listening public all over the country. It has been fortunate for me that I have always lived amidst the listeners and so been able to feel that I get a good deal of feedback from those who switch on their wireless sets. My London-based colleagues, it has seemed, have always been to some extent distanced from the general public and have had to rely on letters, and Audience Research, to find out what the listeners think. Personally it has always seemed an immeasurable advantage to be able to walk into a pub or a club and be told, first-hand and in no uncertain terms, *exactly* what listeners are thinking and saying. North country bluntness can be useful!

But not everyone was completely delighted with the changes in TMS. At the commentators' dinner (which is held on the Thursday night of each final Test Match of the season) in 1976 John Arlott made an off-the-cuff remark about Charles Max-Muller, which could have been construed as critical. I added to it, 'Hear hear.' The following morning I was taken on one side by Brian Johnston and ticked off. He was sorry to think that I had agreed with criticism of a man who was 'not there to defend himself.' I found it just a little sad that Brian obviously did not recognize that that was precisely what happened within the BBC every day of the week. But by a staggering coincidence on that very same day John Arlott invited me to have a private word with him and told me, 'A friend of mine who has a very high regard for you as a commentator is sorry to note that you seem to be joining the Johnstonian school of broadcasting.' And he went on to explain that my approach was becoming more flippant and frivolous. I made a mental note to change things just a little – not to abandon the emphasis on humour, which I regarded as important, but to tighten up my broadcasting discipline. I respected and admired the expertise, in their different styles, of both men.

In 1977 Chris Martin-Jenkins approached me and asked, 'Would you like to do the tour in Pakistan this winter?' This came as a considerable surprise because that was the job of the cricket correspondent but it would not be his decision if someone else was to undertake the tour. However, surmising that he was testing the temperature of the water – and still yearning to do a little more travelling myself – I said, 'Yes.' and awaited developments. It was not until later that I learned what Chris had in mind was that I should 'do' Pakistan and he would take over in New Zealand! In due course came the word from Bob Burrows, who had taken over from Cliff as Head of Sport and Outside Broadcasts (sadly Cliff was with us barely a couple of years before moving to the corresponding role in television), that I was to go with England to Pakistan and New Zealand from October 1977 to March 1978.

So off I went the following month – to experience at once a nasty shock. We had never before mounted full coverage of a tour in Pakistan and while I would be commentating on the Tests in the normal style of a TMS operation in England, reports on the other matches would be made by telephone calls, reversing the charges, of course, otherwise I would have needed a Pickford truck to carry around the rupees needed to pay for all the calls involved. The first thing I learned in Pakistan was that reversed-charge calls were not possible in that country! A whole schedule of reports for sport and news programmes, running to several pages, was immediately rendered useless. The next discovery was that there was a delay of between three and eight hours on any kind of call from Pakistan to the United Kingdom so that even if I had been in a position to make the calls, a schedule that required reports at hourly intervals (for the Sports Desks and, earlier in the day, for the 'Today' programme) could not have been carried out in any case. The staff work and the organizational back-up to coverage of the tour had collapsed completely within hours of my arrival in the country. I was there as a commentator but my thirteen years' experience as a producer told me there had been a most serious slip-up of an un-BBC-like nature. Whatever the Corporation's shortcomings, the organizational side of setting up broadcasts was usually impeccable.

Responsibility for the organizing of broadcasting in this tour lay with Peter St. J. Baxter, whose appointment as cricket producer after the retirement of Michael Tuke-Hastings, had seemed a strange one to me. I knew that within the OB Department he had not been a producer, and after seventeen years involvement with the county cricket scene I had never heard of him in those circles, either. I did not know whence he came. But I still produced 'Test Match Special' in the North and Dick Maddock still produced the programme in the Midlands so Peter's appointment had not really touched me in any way. Until now. The next nine weeks in Pakistan proved something of a struggle; in terms of communication with the United Kingdom it was often like disappearing round the dark side of the Moon. I was completely out of touch. Nor was it particularly comforting to know only too well that back in London it was a good deal easier to blame the man 6,000 miles away for the shortage of news than to look a little closer to home in seeking the reason for it. I had a card that enabled me to cable messages to London but since no one had yet devised a means of broadcasting a cable that was not too helpful in providing one-minute reports for Radio 2 and Radio 4. And I didn't much like a cutting from the *Daily Mail*'s Nigel Dempster column, sent to me in a letter, which described me with ludicrous inaccuracy as 'one of Chris Martin-Jenkins' minions' and talked of my 'sunning myself in Pakistan.' (In point of fact I was colder at a one-day International in Lahore than I have ever been on any other cricket ground anywhere in the world.) In the meantime I had been tear-gassed during a riot which interrupted a Test Match, watched some of the most unutterably dreary

international cricket I had ever seen, had to struggle with the communications problems in dealing with vital stories like a threatened
strike of the England players (against the possibility of Pakistan fielding
players who had taken part in Kerry Packer's World Series), and the
injury to Mike Brearley, the Captain, which put him out of the tour. It
was quite the most difficult nine weeks of my reporting life. I was more
than ready to fall violently in love at first sight with New Zealand. And
I did.

When I returned home, the administrators in Manchester were
becoming increasingly restive about the 'time-off' that was accumulating
in my account and about which I had always declined to concern myself.
Now I startled them by announcing that I would take my three months'
'Grace Leave' the following English winter, and I went back to New
Zealand, guest-commentating on their Test series with Pakistan, gathering material for a series of one-off feature programmes to offer to
Radio 4, meeting friends from my previous visit and making many new
ones as I travelled from the foot of South Island to the tip of North Island.
I returned in 1984, again touring with England, and since my retirement
in October of that year I have re-visited New Zealand every year. Apart
from the incomparable kindness and hospitality of its people, the country
throws up some new delight on every visit. And the one delight still
untasted is to be in New Zealand during the rugby season. It is good to
leave something yet to be savoured. . . .

Back with 'Test Match Special' but still running my department in
Manchester, it was good to find the programme was now beginning to be
featured by the Sunday supplements and by a number of newspapers in
the provinces. The postbag had grown very heavy indeed and a large
proponderance of letters came from female listeners, housewives who
enjoyed a few friendly voices about the house as they attended to their
duties and who particularly liked it when rain stopped play. For this
popularity we had to thank Brian Johnston far more than anyone else. He
could sustain and unobtrusively direct a conversation (ideally with two
others involved) far better than anyone else and he never failed to come up
with a new topic when one seemed to be fading. Then came his 'View
from the Boundary' series of Saturday lunchtime chats to well-known
personalities in other walks of life who were cricket-lovers. Any aspiring
broadcasters who want to specialize in interviewing should tune in to one
of those sessions. They are enduringly and unfailingly brilliant. Brian has
the sort of warm and seductively friendly charm that induces people to
'open up' to him, and he extracts, with deceptive ease, a flow of revelation
and reminiscence which surprises professional communicators. Above

all, following the precept of Wynford Vaughan-Thomas, he *listens* to what people have to say. And he follows up.

The result is that 'A View from the Boundary' is not so much an interview as a conversation, and more often than not a dazzling one. My favourite for many years was an hilarious half-hour with Michael Bentine, of The Goons, until the arrival of Bill Pertwee, a thoroughly professional actor though perhaps best known as the air raid warden in 'Dad's Army'. Rain prevented a resumption of play after lunch and the show went on for two-and-a-half hours, a supreme *tour de force* by Brian (then in his mid-seventies) and a sublimely versatile performance by Bill. I could have listened until close of play and long after that but one brief, almost imperceptible, pause told me that BJ was exhausted. Sunil Gavaskar, the former Indian captain, appeared in the box and I started a chat with him which went on for nearly an hour. 'Sunnie' talks supremely interesting cricket and in almost any other context I would have felt rather pleased at the way the interview went. But it *was* an interview and not a conversation. It was intelligent cricket talk but it was not entertainment for the wider public. Somehow I sensed nationwide fascination with 'Test Match Special' that day ebbing away. . . .

It is more than ten years since John Arlott retired from the TMS team yet his name is spoken with respect bordering on reverence. Rightly so. He was the great artist of description in terms which no one, before or after, has been able to equal. He had an instinctive feel for the *mot juste*, the most felicitous phrase, the perfect touch of gentle irony and the most telling shaft of wit. He loved his cricket with passion and intensity. He followed the Cardus tradition of investing players of yore with a majesty they did not, perhaps, entirely deserve but so painstakingly delicate was his choice of words to describe them that no one has ever begrudged the licence. He did not entirely approve of Brian's schoolboy-humour style of commentary and though I never heard one word of criticism from him I could never escape a feeling that he actively disapproved of the public school approach generally. His final words to the listeners when he retired in mid-afternoon on 2 September 1980 were deliberately and predictably matter-of-fact: 'A word from Trevor Bailey and then it will be Christopher Martin-Jenkins.' The great professional was going out on a completely professional note, irrespective of the standing ovation from the crowd *and the players*, and his colleagues. But the last words he actually uttered in the box were rather different.

He walked over to the corner where I was sitting and chuckled into my ear: 'That's stuffed Johnston. He won't be able to retire for at least three years now.' So the two great pros had their rivalry – unspoken, never put on public display, never even hinted to the listeners. Probably John's greatest accolade has come in later years, towards the end of the 1980s, when the TMS honeymoon with the columnists had ended and the operation, which once enjoyed such acclaim, was becoming increasingly the subject of media criticism. The most frequently voiced view, even from the best of all columnists, Ian Wooldridge, has been, 'Oh for the measured words of John Arlott.' Some of the criticism has been unfair, some we have brought upon ourselves. There *have* been times when we have failed to up-date the score regularly enough; there *have* been times when we have burbled on about outrageous irrelevancies; there *have* been times when the schoolboy humour has gone unacceptably far over the top. Much of the blame must be laid at our own door for not observing the few but necessary disciplines of the otherwise most pleasant of all ways of making a living. But even more of the responsibility rests with those within the BBC whose duty it is to *listen* to all this and to know when to cry: 'Enough.'

When Bob Burrows left suddenly and unexpectedly in 1980 to join Thames Television, the most surprised person of all was Chris Martin-Jenkins who, only weeks earlier, had given notice of his resignation as cricket correspondent to join *The Cricketer* as the magazine's editor but to continue broadcasting as a freelance in both Radio and Television. He had not enjoyed the Burrows regime but it was too late to change his plans. The new Head, after a seemingly interminable interval, was 'Slim' Wilkinson, a former TV producer, who was about three years away from retirement (which is mandatory for BBC staff at the age of sixty). It was an appointment that ultimately proved to be the worst disaster of my working life though I had no means of knowing it at the time. I had once played golf with him at Turnberry but otherwise our paths had never crossed. However, from our very first meeting in Broadcasting House it was clear that we were not going to be bosom pals. I didn't know why and I have never found out.

Puzzled, I got along with the 'other' side of my job. 'The Countryside' series had given rise to another sequence of programmes for Radio 4, in the meantime. Sitting at my window one day and watching the oyster-catchers and curlews foraging in the muddy wavelets of a new tide in Morecambe Bay, it occurred to me that Britain's coastline is subject to changing seasonal moods no less than the countryside. I put a few thoughts down on paper and at the next 'offers' meeting with the Controller, Radio 4, sold her the idea of a four-times-a-year programme. Finding a suitable signature tune presented a few problems until I remembered that the TV series *The Onedin Line* had solved a similar one by setting aside the more obvious claims of music that had been written with the sea, or sailing ships, in mind and going for a marvellously evocative passage from Khachaturian's ballet 'Spartacus'. I took this up with our Head of Music in Manchester, David Ellis, and he said, 'There's a bit of Vaughan-Williams' "The Wasps" which would probably suit you. Try that.' I dug the record out of the music library and copied a couple of minutes that had probably nothing at all to do with the composer's original intentions but which conjured up an immediate picture of the ocean rolling in to a seashore.

Contributors were now needed and I started writing to freelance broadcasters all over Britain to ask if they were interested. Gradually a repertory company on the lines of 'The Countryside' team was built up. 'The Seaside in Spring/Summer/Autumn/Winter' went on the air and I was tickled pink with it. Once again, a poor thing, but mine own. The second presenter I tried was Ken Blakeson, a Yorkshire journalist who had left newspapers to work as a full-time freelance script-writer. His principal income at that time came from writing episodes of 'Emmerdale Farm' for Yorkshire Television but he was into all kinds of other things and he was a young man with lots of ideas. When we had been working together for a year or so he came up with a proposal for a series on graves. Yes, graves! Few things could have sounded less appealing until we sat down and started looking at this one in detail. Ken felt that a lot of prominent people had been buried in what seemed unlikely, or at any rate unusual, places, and by combining a bit of biographical detail, throwing in a few anecdotes and getting someone who knew the deceased well to talk about him/her we might have something worthwhile.

Monica Simms, Controller, Radio 4, took a good deal of convincing that the idea had possibilities but she gave the go-ahead to produce a 'pilot' programme. If it worked she would consider a series. I was sure I had the right combination for that – the grave of Dylan Thomas, and Wynford Vaughan-Thomas to talk about him. And Ken and I went off to South Wales to record our material. Wynford caught the mood immediately and without over-stepping the boundaries of good taste by as much as a millimetre gave us enough tape to put together six programmes. It broke my heart to discard so much of it, but in the end we had what I thought was a very good programme indeed. So did Monica and she commissioned a series of six programmes. But, while the subject of Dylan appealed to her and Wynford's reminiscence was very much to her taste, she was not too keen on Ken Blakeson's voice or linking-script. She wanted the other programmes presented by different people. But it had been Ken's idea; he didn't want it taken over by others, no matter how expert. And I had to sympathize with him. In the end it was settled by his agent who refused to accept the fee offered for the pilot *and* the idea.

So as a producer, no less than a performer, you can't win 'em all. This had been brought home to me some years earlier when I conceived a series of programmes based on the dreariness (!) of my grammar school Speech Days. It might be fun, I thought, if these solemn occasions could be taken over by someone who would create a glorious send-up of it all and have the boys rolling in the aisles instead of yawning and praying for it all to end. I scrounged the money for a pilot programme and took Ted Ray back to his school in Liverpool where the headmaster cooperated nobly. The best ad-libber in show business put on a tremendous performance but the then-Controller, Radio 2, didn't like the end product. Ten years or so went by and one day, in conversation with the current Controller (David Hatch – now Managing Director, Radio) he mentioned, apropos nothing at all, 'At the back of an old file in my office I found an idea with your name on it. It seemed a good one to me. What became of it?'

But there's one thing about the BBC – they waste a lot of money but they rarely waste an idea. I have no doubt that 'Speech Day' will pop up somewhere, some day . . . as someone else's creation. I hope Ken Blakeson's agent is watching out for 'Graves'.

The first suggestion I made to Slim Wilkinson as Head of Sport and Outside Broadcasts was that as there was now no other cricket specialist within the Department I should be designated cricket correspondent and do the job from my Manchester base. I had discussed this with Cliff Morgan who had said there was no reason at all, other than a certain geographical convenience, why the cricket correspondent had to work out of London. Slim turned it down flat but gave no reason. Nevertheless, it immediately became apparent that I was expected to *do* the job, without the dignity and prestige of the title, as well as my own as senior OB producer in the North. I was involved in all Tests either for Radio 3 (commentary) or Radio 2 (reports and interviews); I wore the medallion which was, at the time, issued by Lord's only to the bona fide front-line representatives of the media; I went on tours to the West Indies (1981) and India/Sri Lanka (1981-82), and I shuttled up and down the country between Manchester and London to attend meetings of the TCCB and MCC. At the same time I was expected to run my department in the North with a great deal of organization and administration involved and to produce two (sometimes three) 'Countrysides' and four 'Seasides'. At one point I was forced to spend the time between commentary periods at a Lord's Test Match, editing the 'Countryside' tapes *over the 'phone* via my secretary in an editing channel in Broadcasting House, Manchester. And I thought, 'This is madness. How on earth can I get "the feel" of a contribution, or decide which parts to cut and which to retain, at a distance of 200 miles with Trisha holding the telephone receiver to the loudspeaker?' This was rank bad management, not only of manpower but of resources and it was appallingly cavalier treatment of a programme that was one of Sport/OB's most important contributions to Radio 4. It was a hideous wrench to surrender my share of 'The Countryside' to London but it had to be done for the sake of a programme of which I was inordinately fond. It was, always has been, always will be important to *care* for programmes. 'The Countryside' and 'Test Match Special' are the products I have cared for most in my BBC life.

My first visit to the West Indies proved an interesting mixture of experiences. It is difficult to cover a tour by a side that is not only losing games but not playing well. It is difficult for players if they feel their countrymen reporting the tour are against them just as there are problems for reporters trying to preserve objectivity when they have a natural human sympathy towards the England team. Dramas like the team's expulsion from Guyana for petty political reasons and the tragedy of Ken Barrington's death in Barbados did much to knit the party – players and media – together, only for the Captain's (Ian Botham) obduracy in the face of fair and legitimate critical comment to drive them apart again. Before the tour I felt it was a mistake for Ian to accept the captaincy, just as his mentor, Brian Close, did, and by the end of it I felt it even more strongly. It was rather like watching a brilliant attacking rugby player who has no defence. Botham's heroic qualities were based on Gung-ho charges at the barricades; he could not cope with defeat.

Nevertheless, it was good to work on commentary with fine players of previous generations like Gerry Gomez, Everton Weekes and Rohan Kanhai, to recall great Tests of the past with them when we were off duty. It was good to visit lovely islands like St. Vincent and Montserrat, to greet good friends like Trevor Bailey and Jim Laker, Ollie Milburn and Don Wilson, Dickie Bird and Jack Simmons, who were combining pleasure with pleasure by taking holidays to watch some of the Tests. We saw the build-up to the Carnival in Trinidad with steel bands and calypso singers rehearsing, by day and by night, their party pieces like those of some Caribbean Meistersinger. We saw blazing sunsets fold away into the deep purple velvet of night, oceans of dazzling blue, plantations and fields of sugar-cane, volcanoes and palm-fringed islands, cruise liners, stately sailing ships and snarling speedboats. It was impossible not to love so much of it all, even though a fair amount of hard work was involved. A ·

newspaper correspondent on tour can suggest to his sports desk that the next game is of only minor importance and that he should take a couple of days off while the paper is fed by news agency copy. Not so the BBC representative. There is a deep-seated belief in Broadcasting House that anyone going off on a cricket tour in the English winter is heading for endless hours of lying around on sun-kissed beaches although evidence to the contrary stares them in the face.

Twelve to sixteen-hour days are not uncommon and in the middle of all the problems in Guyana I did one 24-hour stint, serving news programmes as well as sport, TV as well as radio. It wasn't too pleasant at the time but on reflection I would not have missed any of it. Any new experience has got to be useful to some extent. And at the end of it my schoolteacher wife and I managed a bit of holiday in Barbados during her Easter break so that the new English season was virtually upon us by the time we returned.

With John Arlott living in retirement on the Channel Island of Alderney, the new voice on 'Test Match Special' was, for a brief period, Tony Lewis, before he moved on to link the TV presentation of cricket. The music of his Welsh voice gave a welcome extra dimension to the radio programme and he was, of course, a shrewd and experienced observer of the game. I felt that his talents would have been more useful to TMS if they had been channelled into between-the-overs comments (as with FST and Trevor Bailey) rather than describing, ball by ball, the progress of an over. He was an expert in his own field and his expertise was not being properly directed. In the meantime, Chris Martin-Jenkins, after six or seven years as the BBC's cricket correspondent, and now a couple of years as Editor of *The Cricketer*, began to sound a little bit pontifical in some of his pronouncements during his commentary periods. During the Lord's Test against Pakistan in 1982, Chris made a comment that all-too-clearly was a bit of nonsense as far as Trevor was concerned and he patiently tried to gloss over it. Chris persisted with his point; Trevor, with excruciating courtesy, took a different view. And with a new over about to begin Chris rather dismissively finished off the exchange with 'Well, I'm sorry but I don't agree with you, Trevor.' This was a startling exchange by TMS standards! Fortunately, it was time for Trevor to hand over the summarizer's seat to Fred and he steamed out of the box breathing just a trifle heavily. I joined him on the balcony behind the commentary box and Trevor asked, through gritted teeth, 'Did you hear that?'

'I did,' I replied.

'What did you think?'

'I think it serves you right.'

'WHAT?'

'You have been covering up for Chris for the past eight years. . . .'

This surprised Trevor. He said, 'Oh. You've noticed?'

But at the next interval Fred had a little more to say. 'Did you hear that
— actually *contradict* Trevor?' he demanded. 'Who does he think he is?'
There has always been a certain amount of electricity in the air with Fred
and Chris operating in tandem.

One of the most curious aspects of TMS to my mind was that we never
got together to discuss our operation, to pool ideas and thoughts on what
we were about. In all the cricket I had known, and in most of my
broadcasting, this had been an essential part of our professional lives. It
was invaluable to bounce ideas off each other and, more important still, to
confess our faults and look at our shortcomings. The four older members
of the team – Brian, Fred, Trevor and myself – did this from time to time
in groupings of two or three but the whole six of us never once got together
with the producer or Head of Sport/Outside Broadcasts to talk about the
programme as such. Just twice a year we all met in a non-working context
– once at BJ's garden party during the Lord's Test and once at the
commentary team dinner in Broadcasting House. The first was a purely
social occasion with many other guests so that was not the time or place;
but the other could have been most usefully developed to take in a
searching analysis of our work. Unfortunately, the dinner had become
something entirely different from its original concept when it involved
only commentators, summarizers, the scorer and statistical genius Bill
Frindall, plus the producer. We now had all kinds of other BBC figures,
in addition to dignitaries from Lord's and it had deteriorated into a totally
uncritical mutual admiration society. We had, in fact, become smug and
self-satisfied and TMS standards had begun noticeably to suffer. Within
the next year a severely critical correspondence had started to develop in
the columns of *Wisden Cricket Monthly* and we did not all take *that* as
seriously as we should have done. It was very much more comfortable to
gaze fondly at the flattering portraits in the Sunday supplements and the
feature pages than it was to consider the complaints in the correspondence columns. We were not as good as we used to be.

In November 1981 I flew to India with Keith Fletcher's team, managed
by Raman Subba Row, with considerable misgivings about the organizational back-up. There were to be six Tests in India and one, an inaugural
one featuring the newest member of the ICC, in Sri Lanka plus three
one-day Internationals in India and two in Sri Lanka. Several anxious
discussions with Slim Wilkinson had yielded only assurances that Tony

Lewis would join me for commentary on the First Test in Bombay and the solitary Test in Colombo, where we would be reinforced by Henry Blofeld. Tony would also be with me for the first one-day game, in Ahmedabad, and an Indian freelance based in London, Ashish Ray, would join me for commentary on four of the Indian Tests. I knew Ashish as a likeable chap but I had no idea of his capabilities as a commentator. No provision was made for inter-over summarizers and I would have to enrol players from the tour party IF the manager agreed and IF the players themselves were willing. It was a specialist role and we were to have non-specialist operators, IF they agreed! Oh yes – and we were to have a 'local' scorer, another unknown quantity. It seemed an extraordinarily hit-or-miss approach to a long and important tour. I suggested that for the two other one-day internationals, in Jullundur and Cuttack, plus the Final Test in Kanpur, we use as a commentator Michael Carey, at that time Cricket Correspondent of the *Daily Telegraph*.

Mike was a friend of mine to whom I had given a first taste of cricket broadcasting with Sport Spotlight in the old North Regional service. I was happy about his cricket knowledge and I knew he could talk so it seemed that with a bit of hard work we would get through. Yet I would have been a good deal happier to know that we had experienced back-up on a more regular basis. The organization as a whole left a lot to be desired. The First Test went well, with plenty of incident although England lost the match. In the meantime, for reasons that utterly escaped me, Slim had sent out Peter Baxter, the cricket producer, 'to take some of the pressure off me.' What was needed was a *broadcaster*. With more than seventeen years of production experience, I needed another producer like a hole in the head. But Peter, it now transpired, fancied trying his hand at voicing some of the reports and interviews that were required at the end of a day's play.

Now this is something which requires a bit of experience. After a day's commentary you sit back and wait for London's 'extra requirements', which can be anything between three and eight reports of different durations. With your notes of the day's play and a scorecard in front of you the requests come . . . 'One minute fifteen seconds for the lunchtime Sports Desk.' You start the stop-watch and *ad lib* seventy-five seconds of the day's highlights. 'Forty-five seconds for the ten o'clock Desk.' Bang – you rattle that one off. 'Two minutes for the main Sports Desk at 6.45.' Bang – what next? An interview is suggested with Ian Botham, or David Gower, or whoever is the star of the day. Off you go with the tape recorder and then spend a bit of time working out how to operate your gear through the Indian communications system. On this trip it worked well and the

Indian technicians were good. The trouble was that Peter could not *ad lib* his reports. He had to write them out, time them to the various durations required, then try to record them in one 'take'. It did not always work. Very soon I reverted to recording the reports myself while Peter went to do the interview. It did not take a psychologist to work out that he was not too pleased about it but since the alternative was missing the bus, which we shared with the Press party, between ground and hotel and getting back as best we could much later, it seemed to me the obvious course of action.

After the eventful First Test, the series was played on a series of pitches that rendered a clear result, win or lose, unlikely, and commentary became increasingly hard work, trying to impart a modicum of credible competitiveness into description of the play. Not all the players we recruited as inter-over summarizers were of equal fluency and very often, half-way through an over, one found oneself scratching around to think of a point to put to one's sparring partner when it ended. It was manifestly unfair to expect them all to slip easily into the idiom. And so we ground our way around the sub-continent. Peter and I had little in common to talk about in off-duty hours, not even the day's play, which we viewed on completely different wavelengths. Mike Carey, with whom I played endless games of Scrabble in the evenings, or Peter Laker (*Daily Mirror*) who was a fellow film-buff as well as an engagingly humorous companion, kept me company on most evenings while Peter, son of an Army senior officer and Wellington-educated, spent much of his time with John Thicknesse (Harrow and Oxford), of the *Evening Standard* – understandable enough.

And so we came to Jullundur, in the far north, for the second one-day International match in which I looked forward to being joined on commentary by Mike Carey. We shared a room in the Skylark Hotel – not one of the world's top ten establishments by any manner of means – and disenchantment with our accommodation was followed by disillusionment about collaboration on the morrow. A telegram awaited Mike from his sports editor specifically forbidding him from carrying out any broadcasting. Negotiations between the *Daily Telegraph* and the BBC's Head of Sport/Outside Broadcasts had apparently foundered. More to the point, no alternative help was suggested from Broadcasting House when I recorded a preview that evening. I would have to do the match solo!

Now to explain what happened less than a year later it is important to understand the implications of what now followed in Jullundur. Peter Baxter diffidently suggested that *he* should join me for short spells 'when I needed a break.' I spent most of the night considering the implications of this since sleep was not easy in the Skylark. Peter had very little experience of broadcasting and none of commentary and I was far from impressed by his knowledge of what was happening out in the middle. On the other hand, a single voice commentating for something like five or six hours was unacceptable in pure broadcasting terms. By morning I had decided (a) to enlist as summarizer a player with whom I had a good rapport and with whom I had could develop the day's transmissions on something like the lines of TMS at home – Graham Dilley; (b) not to call in Peter unless I was absolutely dropping with exhaustion. I did not think then, I do not think now, that TMS is a vehicle for enthusiastic amateurs.

It was a chilly morning, the start delayed because of mist which shrouded the ground. It warmed up for a couple of hours in the middle of the day and then the cold descended once more. Throughout it all, G. R. Dilley remained steadfastly at my side without a break, maintaining a cheerful and at times colourful dialogue. Without him the whole operation would have been impossible and he will always have a special place in my affections amongst modern cricketers. While it was cold, we shivered; when it was hot, we perspired; when the mouth dried up – as it naturally did during something like five hours of continuous talking, we dare not sip a bottle of mineral water for fear of a need to go in search of a toilet. When it was all over, Graham was still smiling broadly, brushing aside my fervent thanks with the response that 'he had really enjoyed it,' and seemed as fresh as a daisy. The decrepit old commentator was drooping visibly. It was then that the players decided they did not want to follow the schedule of driving the relatively short distance to Amritsar, there to sleep in a comfortable bed and spend the following day viewing the most sacred place of the Sikh religion, the Golden Temple, before flying to Delhi. The majority view, and naturally enough the media party had to keep the players in their sights, was that we should all now drive for eight hours over the pock-marked surface of the Great Eastern Trunk Road to reach four-star comfort as quickly as possible. Since the match had ended, Mr Baxter had not addressed a word to me; he spent the trip to Delhi sitting, like Achilles in his tent, some distance from me on the bus. I was too tired to concern myself and when we reached the capital I went to bed and slept for twelve hours.

Now if we could have sat down and talked about our differences it would have made sense to me but that, alas, is not Peter's way. We got on with the job with an outward appearance of civility. Nevertheless, it came as a surprise when he announced that he had engaged Steve Whiting, Cricket Correspondent of the *Sun*, to share commentary with me on the third one-day International in Cuttack and the sixth Test in Kanpur – without any consultation of any kind. This was really a bit cavalier. The appointment was not (shall we say?) a success and there were considerable rumblings back in Broadcasting House. As Steve had mentioned to me that his school came into the 'public' category I was moved to remark to Peter that this did not automatically impart an ability to be a radio commentator on cricket. When we reached the final stages of the tour in Sri Lanka I very quickly discovered that Peter had immediately acquainted Henry Blofeld (Eton and Cambridge) with the comment. 'Test Match Special' was beginning to take on the aura of a small-town gossip circle rather than one of BBC Radio's more popular programmes. The full extent of the pettiness of it all became apparent a few months later, back in England.

News reached me from London that Peter had sent a note to Slim Wilkinson (in his office five yards away – the BBC absolutely loves memos) saying that if I went to Australia the following winter, he didn't want to go. This caused some mild amusement on my part but no great excitement. There could be no question of Peter going in any case because the way we always covered tours to Australia was by the Cricket correspondent (acting/unpaid or not) joining the ABC commentary team on the Tests, just as Alan McGilvray joined TMS in this country, and reporting other games in the normal way. A producer was certainly not necessary. Oh, how I had underestimated that young man! He put together a scheme for the BBC to mount its own TMS in Australia based on the fact that Brian Johnston was going to visit one of his sons who lived in Sydney, that Chris Martin-Jenkins would be there for part of the tour as Editor of *The Cricketer* and that Henry Blofeld spent part of every winter in Australia. By getting himself involved in various ways and by recruiting on an *ad hoc* basis a number of former Test players who would also be in Australia at certain times, Peter had put together a neat little package which, somehow, he 'sold' to Slim. It was going to cost twice, or three times as much as covering the tour in the usual style but it would certainly provide jobs for the public schoolboys! And the first I knew that the scheme had been accepted was when Slim 'phoned to say, 'Sorry, but you won't be going to Australia in the winter.' I hurried off to London and asked for an explanation. Slim, lamely, said it was *cheaper* to use the TMS method than to send me! This would have insulted the intelligence of a mentally retarded zombie. It would cost just the same to send Peter, an unnecessary producer, as it would to send me as commentator/reporter; on top of that expense came the fees for all the other freelance broadcasters (including Brian, Chris and Henry) and at least a contribution towards their expenses in moving about an enormous country like Australia.

I insisted on Peter being called into the meeting, confronted him with the story of his note to Slim and eventually he admitted it. Slim, now high and dry, tried to bluster his way out of the dilemma by insisting it was cheaper to do it his way. When I challenged him to back it up with figures he had no answer. A second meeting was arranged and this time my Head of Radio in the North, Michael Green, backed my case and finally played a trump card.

It was manifestly unfair, he said, that I should do the year-round work of cricket correspondent but have to miss out on the tour to Australia; that I should have to do the 'rougher' tours and miss out on the best one of all. He, therefore, would find the money from his own budget for me to join the TMS operation Down Under. It would have the effect of strengthening the commentary team while not affecting Slim's own budget in any way. There was no answer at all to this so Slim asked for time to think it over. Eventually, when Michael and I were back in Manchester and far away from any eyeball-to-eyeball encounter, he telephoned to say, 'Sorry, but my decision still stands.' I appealed to the Director of Radio Broadcasting and received a dose of bromide by way of response. . . . 'He had every sympathy with me but had to accept the decision of his Head of Sport/Outside Broadcasts . . . only time would tell if it was the right decision.'

Now came a new twist. *The Sunday Times*, in their Inside Track column (it was therefore an anonymous piece) printed a wholly untrue story in exceedingly unpleasant terms saying that I had been banned from the tour because of a complaint by the Indian High Commissioner in London to the Director-General of the BBC about my reports from India the previous winter. I obtained from the DG's Office, The Secretariat, an assurance that no such letter was ever received. In any case, if there had been a complaint at that level it would most certainly have bounced down the chain of command until it reached me. No one had so much as whispered a mention of it. It was a complete phoney. But someone will always believe such tales. Dear old Brian Johnston, with no experience of journalism and the checking of facts, printed the story in his book *The Chatterboxes* without even consulting me! And I am still waiting for the correction and apology asked of the *Sunday Times* by my solicitor. Newspapers seemed to have changed a good deal since my day – and not for the better in terms of morality.

For six years, from 1974 to 1980, I had enjoyed being part of the TMS team as much as anything in my career. During that time, under Cliff Morgan and Bob Burrows, the head of department had kept a watchful eye on all output and all producers, whether in London or the regions. It was a benevolent regime; we were all regarded as responsible adults, experienced in our craft, and it would have been a churlish character indeed who failed to respond to that sort of lead. Matters involving revolutionary changes of policy – like mounting a full-scale TMS production in Australia *without* the only staff commentator on cricket – would have been discussed with all the people involved. In the short space of two years I had become sickened and disillusioned with the way the situation had changed so drastically. And this at a time when I was voluntarily doing, without any reward or even titular recognition, an important job as well as the one I was basically employed to do. Right. If this was the way they wanted to play it there was only one course of action open to me. I told Slim that with effect from the end of the 1982 cricket season I would simply be the senior OB producer in the North. I would do the job thoroughly and conscientiously but I would do no more broadcasting, either on cricket or anything else. And for the following eight months the aldermanic voice was silent.

Throughout the winter all requests from London for 'voice pieces' on a wide variety of subjects were firmly refused. At one point Slim tried to wave a big stick by telling me to 'broadcast when asked to do so or resign.' I replied that I was employed as a producer, not a broadcaster, that I most certainly would not resign and that if he tried to sack me I would slap the BBC with the most spectacular wrongful-dismissal case it had ever known. An uneasy silence followed, until spring, when the first whispers began to be heard about my re-joining 'Test Match Special' in the summer. First, my leader in the North tried, then Brian Johnston 'phoned, talking in terms which – I must say – touched me, of my value to the TMS team. But the blatant, childish injustice of my exclusion from Australia had inflicted deep wounds. I would miss TMS like mad; in many ways it smacked of cutting off my nose to spite my face. But it was essential to make clear my sense of outrage at the pettiness of it all.

Brian – bless him – tried again, this time drawing my attention to the fact that next winter's tour (1983-4) would be to New Zealand. He knew how I loved the country and was sure I would not miss the chance of another visit. What Brian did not know was that when retirement came, in October 1984, I was seriously considering going to live there, so the tour didn't really matter. But the campaign warmed up and pressure started to come from all directions. The only part of it to which I paid the slightest attention came from the listening public. All of us in TMS, I imagine (we rarely discuss such matters), have our own particular correspondents and we all (I hope) are grateful for them. It is always useful to know what the listeners think but more importantly, in my view, is that we have been able to develop friendships with people we have never seen and, indeed, can never expect to see. Some write more regularly than others and for many years I have carried on a correspondence with people in New Zealand, India, South Africa and every part of England, Scotland and Wales, not just about cricket but about a great variety of other matters. I know whole families of people I have never met and it gives me great pleasure. Now, as the 1983 season approached, many of my friends began to write as usual to say how much they were looking forward to TMS being on the air again in England. It was difficult to know how to tell them I would not be on parade.

Finally, the solution to it all came from New Zealand, from a man named Iain Gallaway who might be styled the Brian Johnston of cricket commentary in that country, – well-liked, totally respected, a delight to work with. He is a lawyer who has worked for many years as a freelance broadcaster on cricket and rugby and he now wrote that he was contemplating retirement himself and what, he asked, could give him more pleasure than sharing what would pobably be his last season of commentary with DM? No one – but no one – in Britain would have made me change my mind. Iain did. I arranged a meeting with Slim, was headed off by BJ while lunching at the Rugby Club, near Broadcasting House, urging me not to be too uncompromising (advice which I completely ignored), and had a completely cards-on-the-table confrontation with HSOB. I was sickened by the 'Hello-old-boy' greeting, as though we were bosom pals. Only after receiving the firmest possible assurances of no-more-messing-about did I return to the fold.

Relations with Peter Baxter after that were inevitably a little strained but we both put on a civilized front and got through the next two seasons on a basis of (at least at my end) 'it's the programme that matters.' While I was in New Zealand in early 1984 Slim Wilkinson retired and we now had a woman Head of Sport and Outside Broadcasting, Miss Patricia Anne Ewing. I had known Pat since she was recruited by Cliff to the department; I liked her personally and had a profound regard for her professionally. As soon as I returned from tour she wrote to ask if it would mean anything to me to be officially designated cricket correspondent and when I replied that it certainly would she promulgated the appointment in terms which made it, in effect, retrospective. It felt rather like being posthumously canonized!

When I reached retirement age on my sixtieth birthday, 3 October 1984, I signed a three-year contract to commentate on cricket and golf as a freelance. I worked at my desk in Manchester until precisely 5.30 p.m. on the 3rd, cleared the drawers of my desk, said goodbye to my colleagues and left for the last time – to think those deep philosophical thoughts that must fill the minds of everyone on such occasions. For the first time I began to wonder how many years I had left. I wondered about finances, about all the things my wife and I still wanted to do in life and whether we could afford them; what I would do with all the spare time that now stretched out ahead; how I would cope without some sort of routine which had always told me what was required in each working day.

At least two of these matters were resolved very quickly with a commission to write a biography of that complex character Geoffrey Boycott and another, from a different publisher, to write a book about my native county, to be called, *Fred Trueman's Yorkshire*. The idea for this originated with Fred, and it gave me immense pleasure to write about people and places I had loved all my life. *Boycott* was a different matter and I approached the task as a bit of good, old-fashioned reporting – get the facts and get them right – as I had been taught the trade forty-four years earlier. After that, other commissions began to come with gratifying regularity and I have produced two books a year since retirement. The wheel had turned full circle; I was back writing for a living and though it was on a grander scale than the first few paragraphs I had seen, with such delight, in the *Craven Herald and Pioneer*, it gave me no more – but no less – pleasure.

It was important now to accept that I was no longer a member of the staff of the BBC. It had been a surprise to find Chris Martin-Jenkins returning as Cricket Correspondent, not re-joining the staff but working on a contract which enabled him to retain his position as Editor of *The Cricketer*. If I reflected that some people are indeed blessed by the Gods – to be appointed as BBC cricket correspondent once would be privilege enough for most people; for it to happen twice . . . phew! – it was a thought I had to keep to myself. It was now no longer my place to offer advice to anyone unless it was sought. It was, in the cricket context, as if I had never spent twenty years on the staff, seventeen of them in a senior post. On the golf scene, happily, things were entirely different. The producer, Gordon Turnbull, was a most pleasant young man and it was a joy to work with him. John Fenton, who was effectively golf correspondent, had been my closest friend within the Corporation since I joined; Renton Laidlaw was a specialist who had forgotten more about the game than I would ever know; Chris Rea, with whom I usually shared on-the-course description of tournament play, was an ex-Scottish international rugby player and British Lion so we were never short of topics to discuss; and the other commentator was George Bayley, a good mate from North Regional broadcasting days who shared my passion for opera. I had been working with them all for many years in between my cricket commitments and production duties. There was no backbiting or skullduggery in this area of broadcasting, no knives, no double-dealing. We all liked and/or respected each other and there was never any question about our dining together every evening of every tournament. Each morning we planned the day's operations *together* – who would do what, *how* we would tackle it. It was a model OB operation.

With my elder son a member of the European tour, golf commentating had a special interest for me, naturally enough, but – that apart – it was a thrill to be with the great players of the world throughout the whole of the Open Championship and other tournaments . . . Nicklaus, Watson, Trevino, Ballesteros, Miller, Weiskopf, Irwin, and later Faldo, Lyle, Woosnam and Langer. It's not a bad thing, when one sits back to rake over sporting memories, to recall having watched the final round, shot by shot, of open champions like Watson at Muirfield and Turnberry, Nicklaus at St. Andrews, Norman at Turnberry, Ballesteros at Royal Lytham, Lyle at Sandwich, and to have a better-than-grandstand view in every case.

I finally gave up golf commentary after being saturated for two years in succession at Sandwich, then Turnberry. The weather in 1987 was unbelievably cruel and the unfortunate thing about Turnberry is that there is only one road out to the north where most of the accommodation is located. Soaked to the skin and needing to drive more than thirty miles to Ayr along roads choked with traffic before one could climb into a hot bath, finally brought the realization that in my sixty-third year it was not really the most sensible way of spending four days of 'summer'. There was quite a lot I wanted to do in life yet and contracting pneumonia was not high on my list of priorities. Retirement to New Zealand had proved impractical, since my wife was the only child of a widowed lady and we could not simply abandon her. Consequently, we settled for a winter visit each year, taking in Australia, where our younger son had settled, and a further exploration of the USA, a country we had first 'discovered' in 1978. We try to see at least two different states each year and, with fingers crossed, I hope it will be possible to take in all fifty of them before the final whistle sounds. So far we have followed the trail of the old pioneers from St. Louis to Oregon and California, probed the legends of the Old West in Deadwood, Laramie, Cheyenne and Tombstone, lingered in the Confederate 'south' of Virginia, Kentucky, the Carolinas, Tennessee and Georgia and disported ourselves in the tourist traps of Florida and Hawaii. It's a country of endless fascination and marvellous contrasts. With each new pilgrimage it is impossible to avoid reflection upon my earliest days in West Yorkshire and how impossible it would all have seemed then, even if one's fancy had been capable of such flights. Most of all I like to think of the friends this life has given me – not so much the famous and celebrated but all the people with whom contact has enriched my three-score years and what? It then becomes so much easier to forget the shabby and the shoddy. . . .

12 *Hawkeye – The Bravest Man I have Known*

The most courageous man I have ever known, Neil James Napier Hawke, born in Cheltenham, South Australia, a couple of months before the outbreak of the Second World War, was a great big bear of a man, ruggedly handsome, who got right to the top in two sports – cricket and Australian Rules football – and could have done it at golf as well had there not been a conflict of interests during his cricket-playing days.

He stepped into the record books at the Kennington Oval on 15 August 1964, firstly by preventing a Freddie Trueman hat-trick, which would have given the Yorkshireman, simultaneously, his 300th test wicket, and then, after luncheon, finally succumbing to Trueman who thus became the first man in history to reach that mark. Hawke modestly suggested that it was the only way *he* was ever going to be remembered in the record books. He was, in fact, a good cricketer who took 83 wickets at 19.80 on that 1964 tour. His first-class career with three Australian state sides brought him 458 wickets (average 26.39) and 3,383 runs (23.99) with a top score of 144 not out. He was, therefore, well equipped for a career as a league professional when he settled in the north of England for several years after his first-class career had ended, playing with Nelson and with East Lancashire, both clubs in the Lancashire League. But he was, my Australian friends assure me, an even better practitioner on the wide open spaces of 'Rules' stadia.

After the 1966-7 tour by Australia to South Africa, Hawke paid a brief visit to Barbados to play for a World XI and then came to England to take up a contract with Nelson. He settled very quickly indeed into the new atmosphere of league cricket with the help of an experienced captain, Frank Taylor, who knew every player in the league inside out. Hawke took 99 wickets in helping Nelson to the championship and was looking forward to making it 100 (a not inconsiderable achievement with the limited number of games) when the last opposition batsman was due to come to the wicket. His captain promptly declared and Hawke's love affair with northern cricket very nearly came to an abrupt end. He was required by Australia on their 1968 tour to England and lingered after the end of the trip to play on a West Country tour with a cosmopolitan collection of Test and county cricketers.

The following summer he was back in England and Nelson, renewing acquaintance with a gorgeous blonde, Elsa Miles, whom he married on 10 June 1969. Nelson were more than usually popular on their visits to other grounds after that, just as another side had been some years earlier when *their* pro had a seasonal relationship with a film starlet. League fees were good (Hawke was paid £1,100 a season) but not good enough to support a Hawke lifestyle that involved the consumption of pretty formidable quantities of beer and fairly regular visits to the betting shop. On one occasion he backed three horses in doubles and a treble and all of them won at odds of ten-to-one, ten-to-one and seven-to-one but this was an exception to the general rule, as it is with most punters.

To supplement his income in a more orthodox fashion, Neil took a part-time job with the *Evening Star* newspaper in neighbouring Burnley while Elsa took a boutique in Nelson's shopping centre, which was opened by his old adversary, F. S. Trueman. It was about this time that Fred's first marriage broke down and he moved, with his second wife, Veronica, into a bungalow in the Yorkshire Dales no more than twenty miles from Nelson. And shortly after that, Peter Parfitt retired from cricket with Middlesex to take a tiny village pub (with cottages and a barn adjoining it) about half-way between the Hawke and Trueman home-steads. Within five years Parf had incorporated barn and outhouses into a huge and magnificent country hotel with dining room and even a dance floor. It was at the official opening of this that I first saw the delectable Elsa and was not disposed to wash my face for a week after her bestowal of a chaste salutation. It was a merry gathering with the Truemans and the Hawkes joined by Farokh Engineer, the former Lancashire and India player (resident in Manchester) and a host of other cricket notables. Thereafter, Neil, Peter, Fred (sometimes with Brian Close substituting) and myself played a lot of golf together, spoke at winter dinners together and enjoyed a quadriform friendship in which laughter played a major part and which was, I think, important to all of us.

During this time, Lancashire were on the verge of offering a contract to Neil and a dramatic, last-minute change of heart saw them opt, instead, for Clive Lloyd, and what a significant move that turned out to be!

When Nelson slipped down the league table in Hawke's third season with them he was asked to take a cut in his fee of £350. Neil, pointing out that because he had settled in the town the club saved a substantial figure by not having to cover air fares from a distant land, said he was willing to take a fee of £850 but not to drop as low as £750. An approach came immediately from the East Lancs club, based in Blackburn, and he spent four seasons there during which two championships and a Worsley Cup-final win were achieved. But results apart, Hawke was described by Jim Kenyon, one of the best-known personalities in Lancashire League cricket, as 'the most unselfish professional he ever played with,' and very, very few mercenaries have earned an accolade like that.

He was a category one golfer and a dynamic force when he became captain of Nelson Golf Club, starting a celebrity am-am tournament which was as popular amongst the visitors as it was with club members. At the same time he took a particularly keen interest in and gave a lot of help to a young man from Burnley called Hogan Stott who went on to become a professional. That was Neil Hawke – a magnificent sportsman himself, he was always willing to help others to enjoy *their* sport. He was, in consequence, immensely popular in the part of England where he had made his home. He found, as all visitors have done, that Northerners are firm in their belief that nothing is ever as good as in days-gone-by, and at Nelson in particular Neil discovered that every pro at that club automatically lived in the shadow of Learie (Lord) Constantine who, since his first appearance there forty years earlier, had been a god in the eyes of the local populace.

Nelson at the end of the 1920s was in the grip of as much poverty and deprivation as other industrial towns and, once a week, sport was one important safety valve or escape hatch from it. Constantine's popularity as a cricketer was so immense that I remember once being transported over the border, via three different bus routes, just to gaze upon the great man – six-hitting batsman, fast bowler and a fieldsman of such electrifying speed of reaction that he raised that unsung aspect of cricket to an art form in itself. Later professionals at Nelson have always been judged by his standards. And at East Lancs, Neil found that he had to stand comparison with Ray Lindwall. Life as a league pro is far from being all beer and skittles. But in the end it was the English weather that brought to an end the Hawke love affair with life amongst the Poms.

He longed for the sunshine of his native South Australia, or for South Africa, where he had many friends in a country that he liked, but Elsa was not keen to venture abroad and to adopt a completely new lifestyle. The marriage might not have survived if Neil had not become involved, in the 1970s, in a new business venture which flourished from the start – pool tables. It was a 'phone call from the Australian Trade Commission that drew his attention to something that was already highly successful in Australia and Neil bought two of the tables as an experiment. They were coin-operated and he placed the first one in a pub called the Shooters' Arms run by the former Burnley footballer Tommy Cummings. The second, placed in the Corporation Hotel, Burnley, attracted the interest of that's pub's owners, the brewing giant, Bass Charrington, who promised to 'instal' the tables in other pubs if Hawke could get hold of them. There were just twelve others available in this country at the time and by cashing in a couple of insurance policies, and getting the backing of a friendly bank manager, Neil grabbed them. Within months the enterprise had taken off; part-time journalism with the *Evening Star* had been abandoned, professional cricket had slipped to the back of his mind and a new commercial life had opened up. He *could* have played league cricket as an amateur after reaching the age of thirty-six (1975) but after experiencing a bit of wrangling with the Lancashire League over which club he could join (Nelson or East Lancs) Neil decided to concentrate on golf as his principal leisure pastime and left cricket behind, though he retained his personal friendships within both clubs. With a handicap of two he was in increasing demand for pro-am tournaments and the celebrity am-ams, which were becoming highly popular as fund-raising efforts. He also qualified for the British Amateur Championship and enjoyed a visit to play in it at Little Aston.

Side by side with all this, his business developed but now began to experience competition from other firms anxious to cash in on the pool-table boom. Finally he sold out to a larger firm based in Blackpool and was given a seat on the board. Then, the sudden deaths of three business associates of a similar age to his own caused him to step back and think. His philosophical reflections were interrupted by an emergency dash into hospital himself for the removal of an intestinal blockage but the irrepressible Hawke humour enabled him to bounce back rapidly. In the middle of a 'friendly' fourball (with intensely competitive undertones), Brian Close and I unexpectedly found ourselves two up in a match against Neil and Peter Parfitt. As we stood on the next tee, Hawke suddenly whipped up his shirt to reveal an enormous operation scar running from breastbone down to the navel and growled, 'That's *my* handicap, mate. And we're still going to beat you.' They did.

Despite this, and many other, happy social occasions, and despite a considerable success in business, Neil could not come to terms with the English climate. When A.F.M. Leisure (of which he was a director) started to explore the possibility of introducing pool tables to South Africa he begged Elsa to join him in a new life there. She declined. It was not difficult to appreciate her point of view. She had built up her own business – the boutique – and her Northern canniness compelled her to weigh the security and the personal friendships she enjoyed at home against the risks of a brand-new venture in a country she did not know at all. And those of us who liked them both viewed with concern their failure to resolve the problem. In the end, Neil went to South Africa alone, still hoping that Elsa would, in due course, join him. Before leaving Nelson he went for a purely social evening to Nelson Golf Club where the Captain, John Holding, called an unusually large gathering to order and announced the honour of Life Membership to his predecessor, Neil Hawke. He wept.

He decided to go to South Africa via a nostalgic visit to Australia, and on a spur-of-the-moment visit to Cheltenham racecourse he met, and fell immediately in love with, the lady who was to become his new wife, Beverley. The South African enterprise immediately lost its appeal and Neil applied for the post of secretary-manager of Port Adelaide Cricket Club. He was never to know whether the application would have been successful. . . .

On 5 July 1980, Neil and Beverley had been to a cocktail party in Adelaide at which he had nibbled some peanuts. On the afternoon of the 6th he was attacked by severe stomach pains, whipped into hospital and renewed acquaintance with Dr Donald Beard whom he had known years before as a club cricketer. It was now a different relationship. 'I approached surgery,' Neil said later with a wan smile, 'confident in the knowledge that I would soon have relief from intense pain. What transpired thereafter now seems like a never-ending nightmare.'

In point of fact one particle of one of those peanuts had caused a blockage, and in the following months of agony and hallucination Neil was proclaimed clinically dead twelve times. He developed blood poisoning and gangrene, and experienced liver and kidney failure. His heart had to be reactivated on a dozen occasions and in one day he needed blood transfusions totalling sixty litres. For months, local newspapers, radio and TV stations – with obituaries of one of South Australia's favourite sportsmen prepared – issued hourly bulletins on his condition. He spent those months with his abdomen opened up, a confused mass of tubes which were used to feed and evacuate a tortured body. When a tracheotomy was added to his surgical requirements and halting speech was impossible, Beverley (who rarely left his side for a moment) pasted Scrabble letters onto a piece of cardboard to achieve a measure of communication. Neil spelled out his words by pointing to one letter after another. Eventually, the surgeons, only after much experimenting, managed to graft pieces of skin from his legs to cover the gaping hole which was the lower part of that once-magnificent frame, but throughout all this time, because the liver failure precluded the injection of pain-killing drugs, Neil Hawke hovered between life and death in a crazed, unreal world of agony. Huge ulcers developed on his back because of the need to lie for weeks and months in one position. And still he fought back, inspired by Beverley's devotion – he will have no other explanation of it – which so vitally supplemented the ministrations of the hospital staff. He had been silent, incapable of speech, for months; jaundice had turned his skin first yellow, then almost orange.

Amidst all this, the legal formalities of his divorce from Elsa had been completed and he was able to think about marrying the lady without whom he knows he would never have survived the nightmare. This took place at the home Beverley had prepared, but even then the skin grafted onto his stomach failed and new grafts from his other leg had to be applied. He was married sitting in a wheelchair wearing a new dressing-gown and pyjamas.

Through the long months of convalescence he somehow found the will and the strength to write to his friends, not only those in Australia who had supported him and prayed for him, but to some of us 10,000 miles away who had despaired for him, to friends in Nelson, Burnley and Blackburn, and to Fred Trueman, Peter Parfitt and myself. The three of us anxiously but eagerly swopped notes when a letter arrived and we found one common factor: not once, even by a single syllable, did Neil complain about any aspect of his suffering; not once did he mention the pain or the moments when he had hoped for a release from it all; not once did he fail, in any letter, to laugh at his immobility and incapacity. It was the most incredible testimony to a triumph of the human spirit I have ever known. But there was more – much more – to come.

Modern surgery clocked up something like six or seven 'firsts' during Neil's months in hospital and he became a text-book case. Exactly how much of his internal system was removed, I do not know, but it all left him with the entire nether end of his torso held together by grafted skin and secured by a huge body belt. Inside it was what resembled a huge bag of water. *And in this state Neil attempted to return to golf.* A letter arrived describing his first venture on to the practice ground at West Lakes with Beverley (to whom he had introduced the game shortly before his collapse) 'hitting six-irons sweetly into the distance beside me while I struggled to make contact with that little white object grinning evilly at me from the tee.' 'Eventually,' the letter continued, 'after what seemed a lifetime and must have been at least half-an-hour, I managed to get a touch and scuffed the ball about three feet ahead. Two great big tears rolled down my cheeks.'

And as I read that, two even bigger ones rolled down mine.

Still the Fates had not finished with Neil Hawke. In July 1990 a letter arrived from him with the news that he had suffered a stroke, which had impaired his sight and mobility and had caused a certain amount of brain damage. Once again Neil's three hand-written pages uttered no word of complaint, only deep, deep concern that Beverley would again have to take over responsibility for their joint lives. Neil had been running a business as a middle man between the manufacturers of leatherwork and earthenware and major retail outlets, as well as doing a certain amount of writing for a newspaper, *The News*, in Adelaide.

It had been going well on my last visit to Adelaide; he and Bev had a nice home and, having become born-again Christians, they spent much time travelling around Australia lecturing, using slides of various stages of what Neil called 'my flirtation with death' to illustrate their narrative. Now he had been struck down again. How much could one human being be asked to bear? And still his first thought was for his wife.

Neil now wrote, 'I feel for Bev who has been a wonderful and uncomplaining support. Her never-wavering faith convinces her another miracle is possible but I have had ten bonus years and I have no right to be greedy. I regret that I portray gloom as I would not like my friends to think I am ungrateful for a full and memorable life. I recall blitzing nine birdies on my first visit to Ghyll (Barnoldswick) Golf Club and taking golf balls off Parfitt – no mean feat, you must agree? Dear friends, thank you for being special and treasured people and for the happy times we spent in each other's company – the odd joust or two on the golf course, the occasional jar and swapping a yarn or three. Should anyone contact me, make no reference to doom as Bev believes the impossible takes a little longer. She vets all my mail and the standard joke is pensioner pie for the Hawke visitors and bring your own tea-bag. Look after yourself and cheers to our mutual friends.'

And then the bit that administered the emotional *coup de grâce*: 'This epistle has taken three hours which gives an indication of what a laborious exercise it has been.' I wept for a dear, brave, unselfish friend.

What could one do now to help? Learning from other sources that a dinner for Neil's benefit was to be staged in Adelaide in August, I went to the Edgbaston Test Match in July 1990 and set up a tape in the BBC radio control-point on which a succession of great ex-players and broadcasters recorded messages of tribute, of shared pleasures, of good wishes. That could be played to the assembled throng in August. What about something to auction, or raffle, to raise a dollar or two? Fred weighed in with a print of an oil painting by the Yorkshire-based artist, John Blakey, and, this being the final Test appearance of Sir Richard Hadlee, I thought. 'How about the ball used by the new cricketing knight on his farewell appearance?'

Well it seemed a good idea at the time. . . .

The rest of the story, as I wrote it in my letter to Neil, went like this:

'I asked Alan Oakman, the Warwickshire assistant secretary, if I could have the ball with which Richard had taken the last England wicket when they were bowled out for 435, and he readily agreed. The umpires, Barrie Meyer and John Holder, retrieved the ball for me and Richard autographed it. The umpires then added a certificate of authenticity, which read, "With this ball Sir Richard Hadlee took his 426th and last wicket in Test cricket. Edgbaston, 6 July 1990." Now let me explain that New Zealand had lost two wickets overnight and it seemed quite unlikely that they would be able to avoid the follow-on. Also, every day of that Test was dogged by rain and bad light so it was a pretty safe assumption that Richard would not bowl again. It just goes to show that one should never take anything at all for granted in cricket and as that was my 100th as a commentator I should most certainly have known better.

'New Zealand showed better resistance in mid-innings, England's bowling was less incisive and in due course the follow-on was avoided. Not only that, but R. J. Hadlee suddenly produced another five-wickets performance in England's second innings for a record 36th time and the ball with which he did that was certainly going to have to go to him, if only to enrich the archives of the New Zealand Board of Control. So I had typed out another "certificate": "With this ball, Sir Richard Hadlee took the 425th and 426th wickets of his Test career in his 85th and final Test, Edgbaston, 5-10 July 1990." '

This was duly signed by the umpires once more, so with egg on my face (and in the hope that a confession of Pommie incompetence would give the ball some slight novelty-appeal) I parcelled it up and sent it off to Adelaide. I didn't know if anyone would buy it at auction, but I did know that Neil would enjoy the tale.

From Adelaide in July came the news that Neil had been given four to six months to live by the specialists who had worked so hard to help his recovery. The news was, of course, kept from him but it was clear that he had few illusions when he wrote to me on 20 July:

'Satan is becoming irritated that I won't join his team. He has promised I can bowl downwind but I don't believe him.'

Remarkable words from a man said to have suffered brain damage from his stroke – an intriguing mix of Neil's irrepressible humour and his Christian faith.

Less than a month later, on the first day of the Second Test against India, I received a phone call at Old Trafford from Gavin Easom, an Australian journalist who was organizing the dinner: would I fly out as a surprise guest for Neil at the dinner on 31 August? Of course I would. A number of commitments had to be shuffled around but that meant nothing compared with the opportunity to see my friend again, albeit in tragic circumstances. In the Cornhill marquee at close of play I mentioned the call to John Hampshire, one of the umpires, and he asked: 'What can I do to help?' The following evening, before I had had time to make a suggestion, John returned to the subject in the most positive way possible. He said, 'I've got one of the match balls for you, autographed by the captains, and on the last day I'll get one of the stumps and get the captains' signatures on that, too. Will they be any good to you?'

And so, as I flew out of Manchester Airport, courtesy of Quantas, on Monday evening, 27 August, my luggage included one stump and one cricket ball. It was, in its way, a particularly interesting stump because it was one of a set which bore a bit of advertising and was the first, other than cricket equipment (e.g. Duncan Fearnley's distinctive trade mark), to be seen in a Test in this country. The red triangle symbol of Bass beers caused a few flutterings in the BBC TV dovecote when a close-up zoomed in on the stumps, and brought immediate representations to the TCCB. But it remained on view throughout the Test. I knew that would amuse Hawkie, too.

It did indeed, especially when I was called from hiding behind a potted palm in the Adelaide Hilton International Hotel on the night of 31 August 1990 – still brandishing the stump from Old Trafford – to greet the astonished Hawkeye. 'Why are you carrying that?' asked Tony Charlton, one of the two comperes. I replied, 'I always go armed when visiting the Colonies,' which caused Neil to choke, 'Typical. Absolutely typical.' The Prime Minister, Bob Hawke, seemed less amused than his namesake but the sell-out 'house' showed no disposition to lynch me and the evening proved a glittering success.

It had been brilliantly organized, single-handed, by Gavin Easom, of *The News*, for which Neil had written. In addition to the Prime Minister, the guests included the Governor of South Australia, Sir Donald Dunstan, and the Premier of the State, Mr Bannon. Co-compere with Tony Charlton was radio personality Ken Cunningham and the speeches reflected equally Neil's involvement in cricket and Australian Rules football. I was shocked by the appearance of my friend but mercifully Gavin, with splendid foresight, had previously shown me recent pictures of Neil so to some extent I was able to disguise my reaction from the cameras of Channel Nine television. Autographing menus was so clearly a tremendous effort for Neil but he stayed, signing scores of them and shaking as many hands, until 2 a.m. and I feared it all might have been too much for him. He was in a complete daze by the time Beverley shepherded him home. Yet less than twelve hours later he was 'completing my education' by introducing me to the mysteries of Aussie Rules at a game between Norwood and North Adelaide, then going on to a 6 p.m. wedding reception. This from a man whose once-magnificent physique had undergone more severe torments and punishment than the human frame was ever intended to withstand. On the day I left Adelaide to spend a few days with my son in Sydney, Neil was taken back into hospital. And just three days after that came the news from England that Sir Leonard Hutton had died. There was more to growing old gracefully than savouring such delights as had eluded one previously in life. There was the constant and ever-present sadness of losing one's friends and heroes.

But if Hawkeye had accepted the inevitable in his mind, his body still battled on. On 17 October, from his hospital bed, he still found the strength to write a letter of thanks for my presence at his dinner. My God! If only I could make him understand what a privilege it was to have been asked, and to have been able to go. Now his handwriting showed the composition of a letter to be even more of an effort . . . 'my balance and recall is hopeless.' But still no complaint, still his thoughts and concern were for Beverley . . . 'She won't face the inevitable. She still believes I can recover. I have told them (the doctors) to go to any lengths necessary to try and grab a few more days. . . .'

And his last sentence was for some of his friends: 'Hope to get the tape of the night (a video-recording of his testimonial dinner) to you to relive. Regards to Veronica and Fred.'

In March 1991 he wrote again, his handwriting firmer and steadier, his tone buoyant and confident: 'A new course of drugs seems to be working. I went back to writing for *The News* last week.'

IT IS UNBELIEVABLE.

13 *Heroes and Friends*

It is difficult to evaluate just how much Len Hutton meant in my life. At a time when every Yorkshire schoolboy I knew read every word written about the county's cricket team and cherished childish dreams of following in the footsteps of one or other of them, Hutton was the greatest idol of all. I was nine years old when I was taken to my first Test Match and saw Bradman score 304 at Headingley in 1934. Four years earlier Leonard Hutton had watched, transfixed, the same batsman on that same ground score 334. And in 1938 it was my immense good fortune to be taken to London for only the second time in my life on the day when Hutton surpassed Bradman's record score. If The Don was the greatest batsman the world has ever seen (and that is indeed my view for what that is worth) then Hutton was his chief disciple. It seemed the ultimate heresy to read, in later years, that Leonard, during the earlier part of his career, had been regarded as a dour batsman, intent before all else upon consolidating an innings. In my mind one did not think of him in any critical terms. He was Yorkshire's opening batsman and to youngsters of my generation that put him very close to God. When he took 364 runs off an Australian Test team it did not matter to us that the tourists' bowling strength had been seriously weakened by injury; it was just a natural progression in the career of a young man, only six or seven years our senior – but light-years ahead in every other sense – who was, to us, destined to scale every peak. And if the war had not taken five years out of his life, who knows what he might have done?

Leonard followed the Herbert Sutcliffe tradition of being a magnificent batsman when conditions were technically difficult, on a worn or rain-affected pitch. It was his legacy from the earliest years, perfecting his defensive technique on the more unpredictable pitches of junior league cricket before graduating to the Bradford League. But, in the classic

157

opening mould, he could take an attack to pieces by controlled aggression, once established, and thus make matters easier for the men who followed. The two strokes for which I best remember him were the cover-drive, a masterpiece of timing achieved because of his immaculate balance at the crease, and the late cut, that epitome of grace and delicacy which is now unfashionable in the era of Samoan warclubs as bats. Hutton's weighed 2lbs 20zs – and he could make the ball *fly* to the boundary.

Sutcliffe was twenty-one years older than his partner of the second half of the 1930s but he admired and respected the younger man's ability. It has been one of the great privileges of my life to spend long hours talking cricket to both of them and neither of them ever referred to the other with anything but professional respect. It has been one of the highlights for me that two men I hero-worshipped as a school boy later became my friends, because two or three hours spent discussing the technical mysteries of the game were worth an entire season of watching and learning alone, no matter how intense one's concentration. The game has certainly changed but some of the basics will always remain unaltered – if a batsman is playing properly. Nothing will ever convince me that Bradman, Hobbs, Sutcliffe and Hutton would not have been great in any era against any bowling.

Sir Leonard was an enthusiastic golfer in his spare time and became an accomplished player, only to have to give it up, to his intense regret, in his last few years because of back trouble. We last played together at Ganton, the splendid east Yorkshire course ten miles inland from Scarborough, in 1976. It was the brilliantly hot summer of West Indies dominance in Tests and after a one-day International in Scarborough he invited me to join him at Ganton the following day. My left foot was giving me one or two problems at the time and my wife was aghast when I said I would rise early to drive from our hotel to Ganton. 'You are not going to play golf with *that* foot?' she inquired. 'Whenever the great man asks me I will walk over broken glass for a game,' I replied.

There were signs on the first tee of the parched course prohibiting smoking but after three holes Leonard said, 'I don't know about you but I'm going to have a cigarette.' (It was a habit I had picked up from an ex-fiancée after surviving the first twenty-four years of my life without tobacco). So, like a couple of guilty schoolboys sneaking off behind the bicycle shed, we looked around for officials and green-keeping staff before slinking furtively behind the gorse. By the time we reached the eighteenth tee I had won by two-and-one and I could not have been more delighted, even though my left foot was now squelching around rather painfully in its shoe. A two-ball had mysteriously appeared in front of us and while we were waiting for them to clear the fairway we sat on a bench beside the tee.

Len handed over a Dunlop 65 which had been the stake on the match and asked, conversationally, 'Have you ever heard of a belladonna plaster?'

'No,' I replied. 'It sounds like a herbal remedy of some kind.'

'That's right,' he responded. 'My mother swore by them. Now I have a lot of back trouble, as you know, so yesterday I asked Dorothy to see if she could find one in Scarborough while I was at the cricket. She scoured just about every chemist's in the town before she found one. I'm wearing it now so I just want you to know that your win has only been achieved against an old man with a bad back playing under a severe handicap. Right?'

'Of course,' I demurred. Then I took off my left shoe, pealed off the once-white sock, which was now bright, blood-stained red, and went through the motions of wringing it out. Replacing the sock without a word or change of expression, I stood up, said, 'It's my honour, I think,' and resumed play.

Sir Leonard did not utter a word until we reached the eighteenth green. Then, as Lady Hutton emerged to join us for lunch he rushed over to her explaining, 'I've just seen the finest trick of all time, Dorothy. Don carries round a blood-stained sock with him!' Yorkshire pride would not admit that the one handicap was greater than the other. We understood each other.

Golf, which I did not take up until I was nearly forty – and never mastered – has played a big part in the enjoyment of the most recent one-third of my life. It was the traditional form of relaxation for county cricketers on Sundays before the 40-overs matches were inflicted on them. Some hospitable club was always willing to extend the courtesy of the course to visiting counties and they were days of fierce competition mixed with a lot of laughter. Then came the days of the Celebrity Am-ams to boost players' benefits and this really *was* combining pleasure with pleasure – playing some of the best courses in the country, making new friends and giving a bit of help to old ones. Before the start of each season the Lancashire team used to relax after training with an occasional game of golf in which I joined them, and this led, in due course, to a day at my own Manchester club, Denton, with the cricketers of Lancashire and Yorkshire and the footballers of United and City all playing together.

At that time the D'Oyly Carte Opera Company used to play a seven-week season at the Opera House and they were given the run of Sale Golf Club during their stay in Manchester, culminating in a match against the host club. With a number of friends in the company, I was invited to join in this match – as a D'Oyly Carte team member. Fortunately, no one ever asked me to sing. But when the Sale Club finally ended this courtesy I immediately persuaded the Denton G.C. Committee to extend a similar facility to the singers. The result was a most cordial association which continued until the company, sadly, folded. We provided a trophy to be contested annually and were rewarded with a Sunday night of splendid music towards the end of the D'Oyly Carte season. Never was the Denton clubhouse so filled with members.

All this led in turn to a close association between some of my cricketing mates and the D'Oyly Carte Company and many a singing night in a pub resulted, featuring Yorkshire cricketers and the G & S professionals if they both happened to be playing in the same place on the same dates. Not all pubs, of course, were willing to have the sound of late-night revelry echoing from their premises but one willing soul was an aunt of Philip Sharpe who was the licensee of the Queen's Head in Horsforth, when the D'Oyly Carte boys and girls were playing at Leeds Grand Theatre. The following year – auntie having moved to a remote country hostelry – Philip was unwilling to surrender such an opportunity to indulge in his love of singing and twenty or thirty of the company crowded into his bachelor flat in Weetwood. The accoustics were not those of the Grand Theatre, or even the Queen's Head, but I think it could have been accurately reported that an enjoyable time was had by all.

Twenty years or more on, P. J. Sharpe, in between spells as an England Selector and specialist observer to the later Dexter regime, is still an enthusiastic member of the York Light Opera Company and on one evening of their annual production a gathering of those Yorkshire old boys and afficionadoes who happen to be in the country fills most of one row of the stalls of the superb Theatre Royal in York, followed by a musical party at the Sharpes' – John Hampshire, John Waring, Barrie Leadbeater, Jim Love, Richard Hutton, along with their wives, plus members of Philip's other sporting fraternity, hockey. One regular on these occasions is Anne Nicholson, widow of the much-loved Tony, who usually brings her son and daughter, too. This, probably more than anything else, provides one with a reminder of the quite remarkable cameraderie of the Yorkshire team of the 1960s. I was abroad at the time of Tony's funeral which, I was told, was something like the massive tribute paid to Roy Kilner, a man held in similar affection by the Yorkshire cricket public. 'Nick', my golf partner for many years, earned the accolade from F. S. Trueman, no less, of being 'the best bowler never to play for England.'

Fred, like Philip Sharpe, is another player whose friendship has endured for more than thirty years and as I have written more with, and about, FST than anyone else I shall not labour the point here except to say that no fast bowler, before or since, has kindled anything like the same excitement for me. When Yorkshire's players of more recent vintage *asked* the Committee to abandon tradition and sign an overseas player for the county, I really thought he would burst a blood vessel. The team of the sixties would have died rather than address such a request to headquarters. More than that, they would have fought to the death to resist such a move. But everything changes and not all change is synonymous with improvement.

In the last ten years or so has come an increasing awareness of a generation gap opening up between myself and modern players. It was, of course, inevitable, and it was accentuated by the closeness of my relationship with players of the previous era. That does not mean that it became necessary to surrender close links with the game altogether; merely that they had to be adjusted to a different plane. The Yorkshire players of today would be no more anxious to have a drink with me at close of play than I would be to hear an expansion of their view that the time had come to import overseas players for the county. This was, quite simply, the ultimate heresy and it is not mere jingoism to say so. What were the players trying to achieve, apart from drawing closer attention to their own shortcomings which were already painfully clear? They didn't seem to know with any degree of unanimity. Some quite simply yearned for greater success which might bring greater financial rewards. Others (batsmen, needless to say) wanted some form of retaliation to the bouncers directed at them by other counties' imported fast bowlers – a fine reason indeed for casting aside a century of proud tradition! – but it was put, nevertheless, as a serious proposition. No one seemed to have decided who the noble fellow was who would stand down to make way for the new recruit.

Leaving for a moment matters of sentiment and pride, let us consider the practical problems presented by the players' petition of 1989 and a section of Committee thinking in 1990. Such a radical break with tradition, if it came about, would give rise to pangs of conscience amongst the Membership the moment it was done. The Members would immediately be assailed by doubts, by retrospective questioning of the wisdom of their radical action. It would, therefore, be necessary for the new man to dispel the doubts and fears by showing straightaway that he could play a major role in reversing the decline of the club as far as results were concerned. Was there such a player, anywhere in the world, who was eligible and available? Of course there wasn't. And even if one were available, would not the pressure on him be greater than any man should be expected to withstand? Of course it would.

There was some pointless, vote-catching rhetoric from one section of the Committee about a 'quick solution having to be found or else. . . .' But there was no quick solution available. More than twenty years had gone by since a county championship had been won; it might take another twenty years to put things right but Yorkshire's only salvation lay in their own hands.

We had got to start asking ourselves why standards in the leagues had dropped with the result that there was now no longer a queue of promising youngsters knocking on the door at Headingley and challenging for a place in the Colts and later the first team. We had to discover why talented players from Yorkshire still turned up in other counties, not to the same extent as in the past but still in significant numbers. We *knew* why the conveyor belt of grammar school products had broken but we still had to question whether things were right in harnessing the ability of boys in other schools. In the winter of 1989/90, for instance, I was approached by the father of a thirteen-year-old bowler who told me that Northants were interested in his boy. He, a good Yorkshireman, wanted some assurance that his native county was also interested. I checked the Northants connection and found there was indeed a considerable interest in the lad. I then checked with Headingley – *and found no one there had ever heard of him*! Yet this boy had recently been chosen as the outstanding prospect from all the schoolboys of his age seen at the Lord's nets during that winter! Why, then, was he not 'on the books' at Headingley?

The answer was tragically simple. He attended a school where the headmaster did not believe in competitive sport (Heaven help us!) and so his name had not been forwarded through schools channels to county headquarters. That was quickly put right and the boy began to receive special coaching at once. He made the county team in his age group but now we saw another disturbing aspect of the handling of schoolboy cricketers in Yorkshire. In the nets he was bowling to a batsman of known outstanding ability – Liam Botham, son of Ian. The younger Botham (to whom I at one time read bed-time stories while he sat on my knee, I reflected) was getting on to the front foot and driving 'my' protégé around merrily. Like any self-respecting Yorkshireman, the bowler dropped one short to discourage the practice. And he was taken off, rebuked and told to sit out the rest of the session!

Now Ian Botham had long since announced to the world that there was no way *his* son was ever going to play for the county of his birth and that he would, when the time came, go to Worcestershire. He would, before that, go to a public school outside Yorkshire. No one would suggest for a moment that these plans should preclude a full opportunity for Liam to be coached as regularly and as expertly as possible during his earlier education, wherever he was ultimately destined to play. There might possibly be those who would approve of the solicitude shown to him in protecting him from bouncers (even if they were bowled by one of his own age group), though I am damn sure his father would not have been one of them. But what of the Yorkshire-born boy who wanted to play for Yorkshire? What of the thirteen-year-old genuine fast-bowling prospect (a rare breed indeed) who was prevented from using a basic, recognized method of discouraging a batsman from driving ball after ball with gay abandon? What encouragement had been given to him to develop his natural talents? If this was an indication of Yorkshire Schools' Cricket Association's method of operation – though it would be wrong to suggest it was more than an individual action by one teacher-coach – it suggested a possible cause for concern.

From top to bottom, the county's talent-spotting and recruitment systems need overhauling. It needs to be done painstakingly and expertly. It will take time and it will take patience, both on the part of the management and the Membership. But it is the only way because there is no short cut if Yorkshire are to retain any semblance of the respect with which they were once regarded all over the world. All that is left now is the exclusivity of the county's playing personnel but the roots are there, embedded deep in the broad acres. They have been neglected for too long; they must be tended and nurtured.

There are serious problems, too, at committee level. We find our cricket run by a large, unwieldy body of three separate and distinct factions: (1) those of the old guard who would like to revert to the cosy, gentlemen's club which existed when the team was great and no close supervision of the team's cricket was necessary; (2) the new radical faction who are concerned more with ousting the old guard than anything else but cannot suggest replacing it with anything better; (3) the merest handful – I can count two, just possibly three – who work hard, conscientiously and industriously for the greater future glory of Yorkshire cricket. As a whole, it is not an encouraging base on which to rest hopes of a brighter future.

Repeating that there is no easy or quick solution, what I would like to see is a headquarters structure of Chief Executive responsible for all matters of administration and finance; a cricket manager concerned entirely with selection, coaching staff and playing-personnel matters; a marketing manager charged with finding sponsorship and with fund-raising; and a committee, of no more than ten, to act in the role of a board of directors with the same sort of brief as if the county was a limited company. That, in my view, is the first step to be taken to restore some sanity to an organization that has become a laughing stock throughout the game for an ability to work efficiently only to one end: self-destruction.

There can be no argument about my personal sentimental attachment to matters of tradition. To anyone brought up in the 1920s and 1930s an attitude of reverence towards Yorkshire cricket was inescapable. The White Rose was synonymous with supremacy and we were all a part of it. To have been closely involved with the teams of the 1950s and, more particularly, the 1960s was to have those schoolboy impressions confirm-ed and strengthened. That is why I sympathize with those who have grown up during the past twenty-two years. They have missed something that was very, very special in the game of cricket – indeed, something unique. They have, in our own language, known 'nowt no better.' Friends in Surrey look back on their great years of 1952-8 with quiet and pleasant satisfaction, as do those of Worcestershire and Essex in more recent years. But they do it without the blazing passion of a native-born Yorkshireman. It is difficult for others to understand our attitude; do we even think it worthwhile to consider theirs? Probably not, for we are different. There can be no doubt about that. That it is usually considered by outsiders to be an unpleasant difference does not trouble us unduly. Except that when our highly individual character makes us objects of ridicule, then we should most certainly take stock. And take action.

14 'Neighbours' and Pantomime

Blood-ties and other connections have meant that Fred Trueman and I have enjoyed a closer relationship away from the TMS commentary box probably than any other pairing. We have often stayed together when working on a Test Match in London; we have been involved in a lot of literary collaboration; our wives are good friends; and we understand each other rather well. None of that is difficult to appreciate.

What is not so easy for me to explain to myself is the pleasant companionship I have enjoyed with Brian Johnston for so many years. Our backgrounds could not have been more different, with Brian's family connections with banking and steel, his education at Eton and Oxford, and his (distinguished) wartime service in the Guards Armoured Division. One obvious explanation is, of course, that BJ is one of the nicest people I have ever known – kind, generous, caring, wholly unselfish and unfailingly charitable. I have never heard him utter an unpleasant word about anyone in well over twenty-five years of our acquaintance. I have seen him actually *hurt* by the vituperative outbursts of others, usually me! That accounts, perhaps, for my liking for the man but does not completely provide a reason for my deep respect. In trying to rationalize this I have taken the devil's advocate role and told myself, 'It's not too difficult to take a more wholesome view of life when you have never really had to struggle to get where you want to get.' But that doesn't add up because with others that sort of advantage has provoked resentment on my part; with Brian it never has.

Next I tried to equate it with my schoolboy, *Hotspur*-magazine-induced, regard for the public school system and saw Brian, perhaps, as an idealized figure, the 'Deadwide' Dick Doyle of Red Circle School. It simply did not make complete sense when I ranged it alongside my intense dislike of other products of the same system. For many years I had been forced to accept a grudging envy of one quality in this fraternity – the *self-confidence* of the public schoolboy – until enlightenment came from the most unexpected quarter. Over dinner one night in Auckland I mentioned the matter to 'Billy' Ibadulla who was acting as a summarizer during the current Test series and he looked at me in astonishment.

'Don, how can you have got it so wrong?' he exclaimed. 'They are not self-confident at all. It's a smoke-screen they put up to hide the terrific sense of insecurity they feel. Haven't you noticed? They stick together. They are never comfortable except in the company of their own type. But confident – no.'

Now that *was* interesting, coming from a Pakistan-born cricketer who had played for Warwickshire, lived in Birmingham and then spent years in Australia and New Zealand! But he had seen a lot of the public school fraternity in English county cricket and he was an extremely shrewd observer. One could see that his ideas made a good deal of sense. But I would have bet my last half-crown that they did not apply to BJ. The two of us were linked by a common love of laughter. He has called me 'the worst giggler' in the box whereas any fit of giggling in which I indulge is invariably induced by Brian himself. If I were to list the principal reasons for my affection for 'Test Match Special' they would be (1) the privilege of watching and talking about a game I love; (2) involvement in a popular and successful piece of Radio; and (3) the degree of relaxed fun I experience with BJ. Throughout the season we carried out a marathon series of pencil-and-paper word games during which, for no reason which would be obvious to anyone else, we frequently reduced each other to paroxysms of half-suppressed laughter. We usually led the chorus which greeted any manifestation of commentary-box wit. We contrived to find something funny in the most obscure passages of day-to-day routine. Out of season, we kept in touch with each other by letter, postcard or telephone. Obviously we found something in common; what need was there for an explanation of it? In 1989 we found more common ground of a less likely nature. . . .

Four or five years ago I lingered a little longer than usual over my lunchtime soup and sandwich and found the one o'clock News on television was followed by an Australian soap opera called 'Neighbours', which I had neither seen nor heard of up to that point. I watched with idle interest the preparations of a group of Melbourne teenagers for their school dance and the metamorphosis of a dowdy young lady who seemed to be known as 'Jane the Brain' – bespectacled and straight-haired – at the hands of a few of her chums. She fancied, it seemed, a pleasant but earnest young man called Mike who, entirely understandably, was not in the least interested in Plain Jane. However, in the course of a couple of scenes, with spectacles discarded, hair coiffed and make-up applied, the Ugly Duckling was transformed into a very fine swan indeed. Jane was a beauty, or, in more characteristic Aussie terminology, a Beaut. And suddenly I was hooked on 'Neighbours', along with, it transpired, most of the school-age population of Britain.

Jane was the grand-daughter of, and lived with, a fearsome dragon of a lady named Mrs Mangel and during the course of the first Test Match the following summer, her name cropped up in one of Brian Johnston's conversations in the TMS box. 'Are you a "Neighbours" fan, BJ?' I inquired. His eyes lit up. 'Certainly, Alderman,' he replied. 'Watch it every day. Are *you* one of us?' And yet another conversational gambit was introduced to the commentary box. It evoked incredulity in 'The Boil' and 'Jenkers', a blank stare from 'Blowers' (despite the fact that he spends every winter in Australia) and a disbelieving grunt from Sir Frederick: 'I don't know what they're on about.' The character of Mrs Mangel clearly fascinated Brian while I (twelve years younger) of course maintained an unrealizeable (perhaps unhealthy) interest in the now-beauteous Jane. 'Neighbours' quickly became part of our TMS lives.

We watched the first five minutes of 'Neighbours' on the television monitor in the commentary box and the poor soul waiting to start the afternoon's operations at 1.35 p.m. had to contend with this chatter as he tried to listen on his 'cans' for the announcer in Radio 3's London studio cueing over to him, as well as the excited shouts of the two oldest British viewers of 'Neighbours' alongside him. If Brian was the man waiting to take up commentary it was my job to keep him informed and it became a regular thing for TMS listeners, pining for the latest score from Lord's, Trent Bridge, or wherever, to have to listen first to an up-date on what was happening in Ramsey Street, Melbourne! Somehow we managed to get away with it with a minimum of complaint from cricketing listeners and then, in 1989, came Alan Border's Australian tourists and with them the ABC commentator on his first visit, Neville Oliver. He later confessed to having had some doubts about how he would get on with a bunch of toffee-nosed Poms with plums in their mouths. He was not prepared for the 'Neighbours' Appreciation Society.

Now 'Neighbours' is broadcast in Australia on one of the independent commercial networks and ABC's television department did not look with favour at all on the regular and enthusiastic plugs for a rival programme which was going out over the Australian airwaves via their simultaneous transmissions of 'Test Match Special'. Increasingly, Neville Oliver (or 'Doctor No' as he was christened by Brian as soon as his initials appeared on the commentator's rota) complained to BJ – echoing the lamentations of his colleagues in Australia: 'For God's sake, Jonners, give it a rest. They're going mad back home. And in any case, how the hell can you and The Alderman watch rubbish like that?'

We carried on, unrepentantly and unsympathetically. Just before the Fourth Test it came to my notice that two major characters of 'Neighbours' – a middle-aged couple called Madge (played by Anne Charleston) and Harold (Ian Smith) – were to take part in pantomime around Christmas at the Davenport Theatre, Stockport. They were also about to get married, purely in the context of the serial. I waited for the right moment. . . .

Rain, inevitably, interrupted play at Old Trafford, and with Brian, Fred and myself involved in a 'chat' session, I gently slipped into the conversation a question to BJ. 'Do you know where Madge and Harold are going to spend their honeymoon, Brian?' I asked, innocently. Fred immediately quit the box with a snort of disgust; Brian was suddenly excited. 'Alderman, what do you know, old man? Tell us.' Note that 'us'. Whether our cricket listeners were interested or not in an Australian soap opera they were going to get the information. But that is the wrong way of looking at the TMS operation. The whole essence of this type of broadcasting is to carry on a conversation that *involves* the listening public as part of it.

So I felt pretty sure we were on to a good thing now as I replied, 'Stockport'. It was not difficult to imagine a great deal of attention now being focussed, out there beyond the microphones, on this wild irrelevance under discussion during a break in the Fourth Test Match. Who on earth would think of going to Stockport for a honeymoon? So *Dick Whittington* at the Davenport Theatre got a substantial plug as well as 'Neighbours'.

A little later in the day, when we were chatting outside the box, Brian said, 'Alderman, we must go to the show. Can you fix it up?' And so arrangements for Christmas festivities involving two members of the TMS team were put in train. Jack Edge, managing director of a group of cinemas and theatres, which includes the Davenport, was more than helpful and passed on to Madge and Harold in Australia our invitation to them to join us for dinner after the show. A date of 11 January was fixed and BJ and I were delighted when the message came back from Melbourne that Anne and Ian would be delighted to join us for a meal. So far, so good.

During the Sixth Test, at The Oval, Brian greeted me, bubbling with laughter. 'We have a request from another member of the "Neighbours" fan club who would like to join us and meet Madge and Harold,' he chortled. 'John Paul Getty III.' This rocked me a little. I had heard of Mr Getty, of course; I had seen him described in newspapers as the seventh richest man in Britain, or something of the sort. But I had also read that he was a man who shunned publicity, and with the amount now being dispensed about the 'Neighbours' stars appearing in a Stockport pantomime it was difficult to see how he was going to be able to pay a quiet, private visit to see *Dick Whittington*. I was also intrigued about how he came to be involved with (a) 'Neighbours' and (b) Brian Johnston, vast though BJ's circle of friends is. He explained. Mr Getty had given substantial financial backing to the building of the new Mound Stand at Lord's. Brian had been invited to lunch in one of the hospitality boxes at the top of the stand during that summer of 1989 and, together with an impressive gathering of cricketing dignitaries, had been startled when John Paul Getty III arrived late for lunch because, he said, he had been watching 'Neighbours'.

Immediately, he and BJ went into a corner to compare notes. One really can't see too many from the higher echelons of MCC being able to contribute knowledgeable views on the lives of Madge and Harold, Charlene and Scott, Mike and Jane, Paul and Gail, and Helen and Jim, so the two of them had virtually a clear field. And they continued after that meeting to swop their thoughts, sometimes on an exchange of visits, sometimes by telephone. When Brian was able to give JPG news of the pantomime appearance, the tycoon was immediately enthusiastic. He would drive with Brian up to Stockport, see the show, join the dinner party and ask a lot of questions of our two guests.

Jack Edge took the news well. I am sure he felt strongly that someone was trying to pull his leg when two elderly cricket commentators placed a request for pantomime seats and a meeting with two of his stars. When they said they were being joined by one of the world's richest men he must have been tempted to say, 'Try the other one. It's got bells on.' But he soldiered on with courtesy and dignity and made the arrangements. Things, however, now began to get complicated. . . .

I went off to do a bit of work in South Africa during the month before Christmas, leaving Brian to handle any adjustments which might be necessary, including the booking of hotel accommodation for the three of us and our ladies. Brian wrote to Jack Edge, confirming one or two arrangements and inquiring whether Jack was, in fact, a Lancashire comedian of that name who had entertained him thirty or forty years ago. He wasn't, but that didn't matter quite so much as the fact that Brian's handwriting is not the best the world has ever seen and his signature is virtually indecipherable. In fact I have often thought of taking one of Brian's letters to a chemist's shop to see just what would be dispensed, for two or three lines of his writing make the average doctor's prescription seem utterly legible. Somehow, Jack Edge took the letter to be from John

Paul Getty, and replied to *him*, although he posted the letter to the address at the head of Brian's letter! It duly arrived, addressed to Mr J. P. Getty at BJ's home in St. John's Wood where my colleague pondered over the mystery for a day or two, then took the letter round to the Getty residence and passed it on.

I am unable to disclose what the country's seventh richest man thought about a letter from Stockport explaining that the writer was *not* a former Lancashire comedian, because I have never met Mr Getty, for reasons which will, I hope, become clear (or at any rate less *unclear*) a little later in this tangled tale. On my return home for Christmas, Brian telephoned to report that hotel rooms were booked at the Alma Lodge, a few hundred yards from the theatre, but that he had not had any reply to his letter to Jack Edge! Would I check that all was well with our planned visit to the show and dinner with Madge and Harold? I did and it was.

Two days before the big day, Brian 'phoned again to say that JPG was less enthusiastic about being chauffered northwards and was exploring the possibility of coming up by helicopter! Somehow this news leaked out to the Press and there was renewed interest in that quarter. Not too many people, I suppose, travel 200 miles by chopper to view a performance of *Dick Whittington* in Stockport. At 10 a.m. on the morning of 11 January BJ 'phoned again. JPG had decided against the flight on the grounds that the helicopter was just a little bit expensive at £2,700. I was inclined to agree, but then I don't have millions of oil revenue pouring into my bank account. The bad news was that Mr Getty had decided not to see the pantomime after all and would I therefore cancel two of our six seats? I must say that Jack Edge took this in a most gentlemanly way and was not one whit less cordial in his welcome for having two of his best seats left on his hands at the last minute.

We had forgotten about the Press and in particular the won't-take-no-for-an-answer branch of the Fourth Estate – the photographers. We had agreed in advance to have pictures taken with the two stars in their dressing-room but only the local weekly paper representative was now interested in this mundane shot. What the nationals wanted was the normally reclusive Mr Getty stepping out for a night at the theatre – in Stockport. And, of course, they were now not going to get it. We were unable to convince the photographers that JPG was not going to be present and throughout most of the performance they prowled around the theatre in search of the quarry who was 200 miles away. What they missed – which I felt would have made an excellent pic – was a septuagenarian BBC commentator joining lustily in the choruses and shouting (along with hundreds of small children) 'Oh no you won't,' etc, in best pantomime tradition. And dinner with Madge and Harold was extremely pleasant.

Brian loves the theatre and has a special affection for panto. In fact he was once due to play Alderman Fitzwarren in a professional production a few years ago and I was prepared to cancel the winter trip abroad so as to see it. Alas, for reasons I have never fully understood, the project was cancelled. The history of the stage is the poorer for it. A lovely man, BJ. More than anyone or anything else in broadcasting, I shall miss him.

15 *Senior Producer to Senior Citizen*

Retirement, as I have suggested, leads to philosophical revisions. In my case I was fortunate that 'what to do with spare time' did not apply; there wasn't any, though the opportunity was there to find it if time were needed to do something special. That is the chief bonus of retired status. There are others (apart from travel concessions!). In fact, following the life-begins-at-forty school of thought, it seems to me that new pleasures become available in each decade. The seventh is no exception, though necessarily you do begin to look at long-term projects in a new light: shall I be around to see it happen? The weeks and months and years do seem to pass very much more quickly and you certainly find yourself going to bed at night wondering, 'Did I really make the most of today?' But by and large you find yourself becoming more tolerant of things that enraged you twenty years earlier, and most of all you start to count up your blessings as you look back on that you have done with your life (or what life has done to you).

It is alleged that the older one gets, the more one reverts to childlike ways. Well, I don't think it has happened to me yet but most certainly I find myself thinking more and more about my childhood, my schooldays, my adolescence. In particular I think of those earliest days at Bracken Bank where the world as I saw it, and in which I could expect to spend most of my life, was strictly limited. Then, there was absolutely no possibility – even by the most extravagant exercise of imagination or the most fanciful flights of optimism – of my seeing the Taj Mahal by daylight and by moonlight as well, the Pyramids and the Sphinx, a sunrise tinting the Himalayas with rose-pink or a sunset setting the Caribbean skyline ablaze. There could be no thought of flying round the world a dozen times, visiting South Sea islands like Tahiti, Fiji and Hawaii; no dreams of sailing a 40-footer amongst the West Indian islands or looking up 12,000 feet at Mount Cook from one of its glaciers; no hope of watching Test Matches and Rugby internationals from the best viewpoint in the ground. Yet it has all happened; all these wonders, and many more, have come to pass. Best of all, by the time one has reached the mid-sixties one can appreciate these miracles with humility and gratitude and not simply with smug complacency.

If you are very foolish, you allow your thoughts to stray into areas of hostile envy of younger men now streaking with unprecedented speed to 'the top' for reasons unconnected with ability or industry. This is no time to dwell on such things. You have to tell yourself that it has happened in every era and probably always will. Now is the time to return to the precepts of childhood and don't speak unless you are spoken to. In senior citizenship it is merely a matter of changing the words: don't offer advice unless it is solicited.

This was the philosophy I took into retirement, which was to involve a certain amount of broadcasting and a lot of writing. The latter was good – very good. Publishers commissioned books and I wrote them. There was a requirement to provide manuscripts on time and to make them accurate and interesting. That was not expected to cause problems to anyone who had taken the trouble to learn his trade properly and I was content to be judged on my results. There have been twelve books in six years to add to the half-dozen 'ghosted' for cricketing friends in earlier days, plus newspaper and magazine articles. One hopes there will be more.

Broadcasting, too, was good at first. The initial three-year contract was followed by a lady's-and-gentleman's agreement between Pat Ewing and myself that I would do a certain amount of Test commentary and county cricket reporting each summer. No further assurances or detailed guarantees were thought necessary on either side. Two friends understood and respected each other. In 1988 I wrote to Pat to say I thought the time might be coming for me to step down and give a younger man the chance to gain commentary experience. She replied that she hoped I would stay so that TMS could be transported intact from Radio 3, when the broadcasting frequency was lost to the BBC, to the new Radio 5 channel she was to head. A new Head of Sport/Outside Broadcasts, Larry Hodgson, took her place.

Meanwhile I had been giving help and advice to certain local radio stations, when asked for it, contributing some thoughts to regional television, and doing what I could to encourage a young man, Dave Edmundson, of Radio Lancashire as a cricket commentator/reporter. He was by no means ready to be proposed at this stage for 'Test Match Special'. The only candidates on the horizon, in my view, were Pat

Murphy, a staff producer in Birmingham who actually did, and was happier doing, more broadcasting than production, and Andy Smith, formerly on the BBC staff in the Sports Room, now freelance. Both had gone to a great deal of trouble to learn their cricket at grass-roots level (i.e. by watching a lot of county cricket and spending a lot of time talking to and listening to the men who played the game for a living). Additionally, both had sound, basic journalistic experience; both had done a lot of writing. Of the two I felt Pat's claims were more advanced than Andy's but no one else even remotely on the horizon appeared to have the necessary qualifications to warrant immediate grooming.

When I had been involved in informal conversations about 'the future' I had already suggested that 'Murph' ought regularly to be doing the Radio 2 job on Tests (contributing short reports throughout four days of the week, getting in a little commentary work on Sport on Two on Saturdays) so that he could spend a fair amount of time in the TMS box between his own transmissions and get the 'feel' of our particular operation. Pat had the confidence and friendship of many experienced first-class players, notably Bob Willis and Jack Bannister. He 'ghosted' a syndicated column for David Gower. He had written more than twenty books either in collaboration with, or about, county and Test cricketers. He continually sought to improve his knowledge of the game and to gain, when it was possible, more experience of commentary. I commended him on a number of occasions to those in London who now dictated the course of events and met with a far-from-enthusiastic response. Pat was 'an abrasive personality'; he 'upset people'; he 'made waves'. All this was probably true but as I saw it that was not the point at issue. Did he know the game and could he talk fluently and intelligently about it? The answer to that was unarguably 'Yes'. Whatever others thought about him as a person was, therefore, largely irrelevant. I had encountered enough of a negative attitude in my own time to want to see it being directed at a colleague. All right. If I were to be cast away on a desert island with 'Murph' I would no doubt want to kill him after a week but if I were asked whether I would be happy with his description of what was happening out in the middle during a Test Match when I was listening on my radio, then the answer would be 'Yes'. And that, after all, is fundamentally what the average listener wants. The refinements, the *bon mots*, and the humour all come later when one has got the confidence that comes with experience; the basics are essential.

In 1989 and 1990 some extra air-time was squeezed out of Controller, Radio 3, to put on 'Test Match Special'-like days of broadcasting during the quarter-finals and semi-finals of Benson and Hedges Cup and

Natwest Trophy games. Now we started to introduce new commentators and summarizers, men being given their first taste of what it is like to keep talking as intelligently and entertainingly as possible when not much was happening. It wasn't as difficult as in a Test Match, of course, because limited-overs games provide infinitely more incident but it was extremely useful practice for the new boys and the idea was good. 'Semi-experienced' performers like Peter Edmondson and Anthony Gibson could obviously benefit because they did a lot of work for local radio stations and so could Pat Murphy and Andy Smith. But Peter Baxter now started introducing himself to commentary work and as I saw it this was not on.

The cricket producer's job was by now very much a full-time occupation with the multiplicity of Tests around the world and regular tour coverage to organize. And in my view Peter had neither the cricket knowledge, nor the words, to think in terms of promoting himself to TMS. He was a frequent user, for instance, of a phrase that took us back to old-fashioned commentary: 'He played *pretty* well.' Had he ever put himself in the position of a listener and asked himself what the expression meant to him? At best it was meaningless in terms of enhancing a listener's picture of an innings; at worst it was insultingly patronizing to the professional cricketer concerned. I had once asked Henry Blofeld, after a particularly over-the-top performance, 'Have you ever wondered what listeners in Oswaldtwistle and Cleckheaton think about your style of commentary?' And Henry had replied, 'My dear old thing,' (of course), 'No. Should I?' (Just as I often asked myself if listeners in Bognor Regis and Cheltenham Spa could accept my North Country idiom.) I told him, 'You should care about what *all* listeners are thinking.'

And that, I honestly believe, is where TMS has tended to lose its way in recent years. We have become far too self-satisfied and self-indulgent. We have not paid enough attention to an increasing note of criticism in the columns of newspaper critics and in our personal postbags. We have dismissed unfavourable comment far too easily and basked in the light of the more appreciative correspondence. It is still, incidentally, weighted in favour of TMS but is not unequivocally so. In Charles Max-Muller's day (much as I detested what he represented and resented his personal attitude to my aspirations) he would have put a stop in an instant to monologues about buses and helicopters, butterflies and pigeons, 'thoughtful-looking' or otherwise. So, most assuredly, would Cliff Morgan. But for far too long we had been left virtually unsupervised. No one in authority in Broadcasting House was listening to the programme output with a remotely critical ear. Our Heads of Outside Broadcasts had been content for too long to believe that they had a winner in the cult following of TMS and that no correction of style and discipline was required.

It disturbed me deeply and I began to retire more and more into my broadcasting shell. Updates of the score began to figure more frequently than usual in my commentary periods because no one else seemed interested in correcting the shortcomings of others in this department. And letters began to arrive from regular correspondents asking, 'Why have you stopped enjoying yourself?' The answer was that I had become desperately afraid that TMS was deteriorating into, as one columnist wrote, 'a caricature of itself'. Nevertheless, I received a message that the Managing Director, Radio, had given me a commendation for my work on the 1990 Old Trafford Test against India and that the minutes of the Programme Review Board duly reflected this. 'Thank God,' I thought, '*somebody* in Broadcasting House is listening.' Then, I mused, more realistically, 'It wasn't a match I felt I had done well at all. There was nothing actually to commend my commentating. I had simply been doing my job in a workmanlike way – absolutely "straight" and factually. If that is now singled out for commendation perhaps it might suggest to someone in Outside Broadcasts that other aspects of TMS are not in perfect health.' It didn't.

When the quarter-finals of the NatWest Trophy came round, the Alderman was used only because one of the new boys had to cry off. He was not required for the semi-finals and final, and was called up for the Benson and Hedges Final only because Chris Martin-Jenkins took a holiday. But surely the whole idea of 'blooding' aspiring commentators was to have them working alongside experienced broadcasters? Two final straws broke this particular camel's back. For twenty-six years, when radio reported the Yorkshire-Lancashire match, mine had been the voice describing this biannual tribal confrontation. It brought a lot of good-natured chaffing from both sides – the Yorkists because I lived in Lancashire, the Lancastrians because I was Yorkshire-born. But at least I had an understanding of what the game was about and it still has a special significance to all North Country folk. Now, without the elementary courtesy of a word from the producer, or the Editor of Sport on 2 (which, rightly or wrongly, I believed would have been the decent thing to do after twenty-six years), dear Henry was sent up from London to cover the match. Because he was going to be commentating for Sky TV the following day, in Chesterfield!

I didn't even know about this 'team change' until I went to Headingley, seated myself in the crowd under the impression that BBC radio were not featuring the match and was immediately accosted by a spectator, watching the game and listening to his transistor: 'Wot's thar doin' dahn 'ere and wot's that bloody fooil doin' up yonder.' He nodded in the direction of the commentary box. No doubt I was a far from disinterested party but it did seem that to have Henry my-dear-old-thinging around Headingley at a Roses Match was as absurdly anachronistic as appointing George Best to introduce 'Songs of Praise'. That was straw No. 1.

No. 2 came during the Old Trafford Test. A week earlier, on the NatWest quarter-finals we had introduced two voices new to cricket commentary – Nick Stewart and Julian Tutt. Nick I knew as the man who used to bring up the daily odds from the bookmakers City Index to the commentary box; Julian was a sports assistant in the Radio Sports Unit; neither had previously been involved in live commentary. While three or four of us were having a rare dinner together during the Second Test we were joined by Jim Swanton who put to Brian Johnston the hypothetical point: 'Supposing you were to break a leg before the next Test – is there anyone ready to step in?' And before Brian had time to reply, Chris Martin-Jenkins answered with four names: 'Baxter, Murphy, Stewart, Tutt.' The list was interesting, the order of the names fascinating. So this was the way the wind was blowing . . . Baxter first, Murphy second, and two others whose experience was so far limited to one day. But . . . Nick Stewart was a Harrovian and Julian Tutt was educated at Sandhurst. Their debuts the previous week had not sounded to me as likely to merit an immediate rise to stardom. Were the Smiths, the Edmondsons and the Gibsons, who at least had spent rather a long time gaining experience and polishing their technique, now to be completely passed over? The producer and the cricket correspondent were very close to each other so it was not difficult to see the way things were moving. I resolved in that moment not to have anything to do with it if the situation developed on the lines that seemed likely. Was anyone else noticing what was happening? Well, at least one listener was! At the beginning of September, my first rugby match of the new season, I met Bill Beaumont, former England captain and now a radio and TV personality. But Bill is also a TMS listener and his opening remark now took on a great significance. Without any preamble at all he said, 'I see the public school lot are taking over again. Why?' Why indeed?

In the past 1990 season TMS had at times reached such a shambles of personal indiscipline that the programme has sounded somewhere between Gussie Fink-Nottle's speech day address and the Monty Python Twit-of-the-Year contest. Bill had noticed, not so much as a broadcaster himself but as a listener to the programme. I wondered how many other listeners had gained a similar impression because TMS regulars are amongst the brightest and most involved listeners. I had written to Head of Outside Broadcasts expressing personal disquiet about commentary appointments some weeks earlier and received a reply that he 'didn't know what I was talking about.' I now wrote in more detail to Mike Lewis, who, as Editor of Sport, was closely involved with all the departmental output. His reply was – quite unintentionally, I am sure – one which nevertheless insulted my intelligence. Most importantly it indicated that commentary assignments were being made, at best with the personal convenience of certain individuals in mind, at worst with the use of 'the public school lot' being given precedence. The wheel had turned full circle. I had battled against the system once; I was not prepared, approaching the age of sixty-five, to take it on again. Life was too short; I had more useful things to do with what was left of mine. If no one any longer cared about the quality of programmes, irrespective of personal favouritism, then it was the BBC's problem and it should no longer concern me. I had spent years, seventeen of them, meeting people who thought '"Test Match Special" must be a lovely way to make a living,' people who longed to get involved and to enjoy the reflected glory of what had been created by others; people who thought they could simply ease gently into a place in it all without any of the effort and expertise which had gone into creating the modern TMS. John Arlott's words of warning, offered long ago at The Oval, now came back to me. At last I fully understood their significance.

Faced with Hobson's choice of begging to be allowed to commentate or allowing myself to be ignominiously squeezed out, it was time for me to call it a day. There would be those who would miss The Alderman – my postbag told me that – but of greater importance than personal considerations was that the voice-mix of 'Test Match Special' would lose the variety that every programme of that kind needs. A bland chorus of public school tones might sound splendid to those immediately involved but it was not going to be entirely popular with listeners in general. Whatever the public thought of me personally – and, believe me, in my part of the world they left no one in any doubt of his shortcomings! – it was important to cricket-lovers in northern England to feel that somehow their interests were represented in the commentary team.

They had been a long time without it before The Alderman joined. They looked like being a long time without it in the future. I hadn't managed to beat the system but I had given it a good try.

One final comment on TMS, in answer to a thousand queries: the title 'The Alderman' was bestowed on me by Brian Johnston, *but he doesn't know why*. Probably it seemed a good idea at the time.

*

Seventeen years in the TMS commentary box involved working with a wide variety of colleagues at home and abroad of different nationalities, background and styles.

First of all, at home, there were the two definitive TMS men, Trevor Bailey and Freddie Trueman, providing a complete contrast in themselves and yet dovetailing perfectly into the general pattern. One of the greatest delights about working with Fred is his utterly marvellous inconsistency. He believes with passionate sincerity that what he is saying at any given moment is the absolute truth, yet it can be (and often is) the direct opposite of what he was saying, with equal earnestness, only a couple of minutes earlier. The trick is to recognize this, and to harness it – rather like tacking into a Force 5 or 6 wind.

On one occasion we were working together at Old Trafford while the West Indies (class of '88) were hurling in their short-pitched deliveries with the usual monotonous regularity. Suddenly Fred launched into a bitter denunciation of the tactics and offered the view that never in his bowling career had he bowled with the intention of hitting a batsman. I pinched myself to make sure I was actually awake and that this was not a wildly improbable dream. At the end of the next over I questioned him: 'Wait a minute, Fred. Are you saying that at no time did you seek domination over a batsman by bowling *at* him?'

'That's right,' replied our hero. 'I wouldn't set out to hit a man deliberately.'

My brain reeled and the years rolled back. I remembered those blood-curdling threats to 'pin that bastard to t'----ing sightscreen.' I recalled those mornings when he sauntered into opposition dressing-rooms, marking an imaginary cross between the eyes of the quaking opposition. I thought of generations of players ducking and weaving; of others clutching a bruised ribcage or being helped off for X-ray. When FST found a pitch to his liking it had happened with some frequency. But Fred obviously believed what he was now saying. This was not the time for argument. It was one of those moments when you have to know your man, to understand that distance has lent enchantment to some of Fred's memories. It was the time for subtlety – or the nearest approximation I could manage.

I took a deep breath. 'In that case, Fred,' I responded, 'an entire generation of batsmen passed through the 1950s and 1960s with a complete misunderstanding of what your bowling was about.'

'That's right,' agreed Fred.

I turned my attention back to the cricket before us – not, however, without a passing thought to a Roy Ulyett cartoon which is proudly displayed on one wall of Fred's home. It shows a West Indian mother warning her fretful child: 'If you don't go to sleep I'll send for Freddie Trueman to chase you.' It is one of Fred's most treasured momentos. Mrs Trueman, meanwhile, was telephoning Mrs Mosey: 'Are you listening to this?' She was.

FST's greatest value to the commentary team (apart from his dramatic contrast in style with Trevor) is his profound knowledge of what is happening out in the middle at any given moment. Forget, if you will, his oft-professed bewilderment: 'I just don't know what's going off out theer.' He knows all right. What he really means is: 'I don't know *why* it is happening.' His impatience with and critical attitude towards modern cricket is based on having played at a time when the game was indeed different (as modern practitioners are quick to tell us) in that it was played more correctly. He had to bowl at players who played through the line rather than across it. And if any of his opponents did play across the line it was because they were possessed of a genius not known today (e.g. Compton). They had gifts which modern cricketers have largely forgotten or never enjoyed in the first place. But Fred knows bowling inside out and this gives him a greater perception of what good batting is about. And within the commentary team he is at his best in those rain-stops-play sessions when he is reminiscing with someone he likes and respects. Throw him the right sort of bait-ball and he will play a conversational innings to be relished.

Trevor was already established on 'Test Match Special' when Fred arrived. He had worked with the Old Guard and slipped just as easily into the idiom of the new. His natural intelligence was allied to the experience of having done it all at top level – a man who had opened Test batting and bowling, who had been third or even fourth seamer and shored up the middle order batting, a county captain of many seasons with all the tactical and strategic know-how that brings. His personal sense of humour was particularly geared to upsetting the opposition at the most highly charged moment. Who else could have appealed against the light in brilliant sunshine with one over to go before luncheon against the Australians in full attacking cry? Who else could have taken just under six hours to reach 50 in a (then) rare televised innings in Brisbane? And yet he was so often the ideal man for the job in Tests, whatever was required of him with bat or ball.

He brought all these qualities to Test commentary. In all the hours I worked with him I cannot recall ever feeling the slightest disquiet or concern. One knew instinctively that if one got into any sort of trouble he would come to the rescue; alternatively, if the commentary was flowing he would complement it at the end of the over with a suitably apt, but brief, comment. With some summarizers you find yourself, in mid-over, wondering if you can think up a question to put to stimulate discussion. Not so with T. E. Bailey. Never. Whether he is adding something pertinent and enlightening to the commentary or contributing one of those terse, Mr Jingle-like (John Arlott's felicitous description) additions, he is always, absolutely, on the ball. Though he was an amateur for all but the last five of his twenty-one years in first-class cricket (when everyone became simply 'cricketers'), in the commentary box he has always been the complete professional. It is tragic that he has been so sparingly used in recent years and has turned, increasingly, to phone-in operations. He is undoubtedly the best summarizer I have worked with, anywhere in the world, and that includes Rohan Kanhai, Gerry Gomez, Everton Weekes, Bruce Taylor, John Parker, Jeremy Coney and Hanif Mohammed, as well as a host of English Test players.

We shall return to summarizers in a moment but let us digress briefly to look at overseas broadcasters. Probably the two best-known in this country are Alan McGilvray, of Australia, and Tony Cozier, the Barbadian. McGilvray was a first-class player with New South Wales and was a highly respected commentator in his own country and in New Zealand as well. This is worth noting for any Australian in any field who wins respect on the other side of the Tasman Sea has got to be very, very good at his job! McGilvray followed the Antipodean style of talking seriously, and in low-key style, about the game. That he knew cricket inside out goes without saying. He played with and against Bradman and could speak knowledgeably about all the great Australians of his day. Mostly it was delivered in a flat, but never boring, monotone with the more extreme emotions – anger, admiration – reflected in subtle nuances of the voice that he rarely raised above pianissimo.

His commentary colleagues could and did admire McGilvray but he was not an easy man to love. He was far from gregarious, rationed his socializing on tour to a bare minimum and laughter was not a major influence in his life. I suspected that he never *really* approved of the British style of commentary or sympathized with our attitude to the game. His long-running feud with John Arlott was carefully covered up in TMS operations and while he himself played his part with a gentlemanly avoidance of any overt clash it occasionally made life a trifle difficult for his colleagues. But there could be no doubt about his qualities as a cricket broadcaster and when he was in the right mood he could provide some magic moments. One rain-stops-play interval in which he and Freddie Trueman talked right through the session on great men they had played with will remain with me as long as I live as a prime example of cricket 'chat'. He spoke of retirement on at least three tours before he actually called it a day and we wondered just how the ABC would replace such a legendary figure when he retired.

In the event the Australian Broadcasting Corporation sent Neville Oliver in 1989 and they could scarcely have made a better choice. The Tasmanian was relatively inexperienced in international commentary and he confessed to worrying about how he would fit into the BBC operation with a bunch of 'toffee-nosed Poms with plums in their mouths.' He astutely decided to play it by ear and after initially being amazed at the relaxed style of TMS he found he fitted in perfectly. This was in direct contrast to McGilvray, a resolute individualist who had his own style and the Poms could like it or lump it. Norman had not been a great player at top level so he had no standards to defend. He warmed to Brian Johnston's welcome and played along with Brian's schoolboy humour and practical jokes. He was helped, of course, by following an extremely well-organized and successful Australian side; it is never easy to be on tour with a side that loses matches consistently. So as Neville was able to report one victory after another to the folks back home his natural good humour was enhanced by the atmosphere in the commentary box where he marvelled at the Poms' ability to absorb so much punishment. The result of all this was that we got more approving letters about the visiting commentator from the listening public than ever before.

In the West Indies, commentators grow almost as fast as players. In any commentary box you can expect to find anything up to a dozen people who are ready, willing and able to take a turn at the microphone. The visiting Englishman never knows who will be describing play before or after him. The West Indians' natural love of the game is possibly equalled only by his willingness to talk about it on the air. Consequently, I have broadcast in the company of men I had never seen before and undoubtedly will never see again. But apart from the odd glimpse of 'Reds' Perreira during World Cup series, the only one known to listeners in this country, since Roy Lawrence retired, is Tony Cozier. Calm, good-humoured, knowledgeable, he has been the ideal man to keep a sense of proportion amidst the wholesale rejoicing of British-based West Indians during the past fifteen years or so. Tony gets through an immense amount of work on tour, serving TV and Radio at home and in the country he is visiting, as well as writing thousands of words in serving his newspaper interests, too. Yet he never flaps, rarely shows signs of irritation and thoroughly enjoys his cricket.

Until his retirement in 1989, New Zealand's regular tour commentator was Alan Richards, a low-key, absolutely sound, broadcaster in the

McGilvray mould. A former player with the Auckland first-class side, Alan brought technical expertise to his commentary while retaining a splendid impartiality. (There is a great danger on tour of adopting a them-and-us complex.) He followed New Zealand through some of their lean years to see the days of glory when they scored wins over all other ICC teams.

It is BBC practice not to include an Indian or Pakistan commentator in the commentary team in this country because they are required from time to time to describe the game in the vernacular, say twenty minutes in the hour, and therefore the TMS operation would become impossible. In fact the aforementioned Alan Richards, on his first tour of Pakistan, took his place in their national radio commentary team and was startled to find one-third of the broadcasting was carried out in Urdu. He spent a rather uncomfortable time wondering what the listeners back home were making of it all! In England, we get round the problem of putting the opposition point of view by using an extra summarizer – an Anglicized Indian or Pakistani like Farokh Engineer or Mushtaq Mohammed. Both these have lived here for twenty or thirty years and in all truth are more familiar with the England players than their opponents. However, they are welcome in the Indian/Pakistan camp and can provide the right touch of information about the visiting players. Both are also good companions and fit well into the TMS operation.

In recent years we have seen the introduction of a number of new summarizers in England. In the late 1980s, Robin Jackman, formerly of Surrey and England, came home from South Africa (where he coaches in Cape Town) for a summer holiday and joined us in two or three Tests. His offerings have been sound commonsense born of a lot of county cricket experience. As a reward for his assistance on England tours abroad, Mike Selvey (Cambridge University, Surrey, Middlesex, Glamorgan and England) has been invited to join us for a number of matches. He, too, brings a wealth of first-class experience to bear in his comments and he operates for commercial television as well as writing for the *Guardian*.

The extension of ball-by-ball commentary to the quarter-, semi-final and final stages of the NatWest and Benson and Hedges competitions in the last two or three years has made it possible to try out more former and current players with a view to the future. They have provided some interesting contrasts. On the one hand we have, for instance, Mark Nicholas, the Hampshire Captain, a man of sharp intelligence and wit who recognizes that he is working with commentators who are top-class professionals in their own right and he seeks to complement their work. On the other, happily, I can recall only one instance of a player who has quite simply taken the view that experienced commentators count for very little and that his views are of paramount importance – rightly or wrongly. That is David Gower whose intolerant attitude to the media generally is pretty well established.

For reasons that have always escaped me we clutter up the commentary box at Benson and Hedges and NatWest Finals with extra summarizers, which causes all kinds of problems for the commentator. It means we have two summarizers working with one commentator and it is only courteous to include a word from both between the overs and so one problem immediately is time. Also, one is inevitably inexperienced in this particular role so if the more experienced man offers an obviously pertinent comment, one has to think up something to help out the other. They sit on opposite sides of the commentary box and in turning to them there are technical difficulties like going 'off mike'. There are, in fact, lots of problems to contend with and we could easily avoid them by sticking to the traditional formula.

Now David Gower does not particularly like me, a view he is perfectly entitled to take but not to the extent of bringing it into the box and seeking to score points there. That is not only discourteous, it is unprofessional. Thus, during the 1990 B & H Final, when I said, 'Two catches so far at square leg for Phil Neale – one a brilliant diving effort, the other a more straightforward one,' David immediately commented, 'Oh I wouldn't say the second catch was straightforward.'

No one had said it was. We were now dealing, not with a matter of cricketing fact or opinion, but with simple semantics, in which most commentators are a little more skilled than Mr Gower. Later in the day he made a similar intervention and again it was an attempted points-scoring exercise. It would have been too easy to point this out on the air but that would have been discourteous to the guest-summarizer. It would also have been unprofessional. I like to think that TMS listeners, who are a highly intelligent band, spotted the difference.

No one else, in my experience, has adopted this attitude. We have worked harmoniously with players like Vic Marks, Jon Agnew, Derek Underwood, Bob Taylor and Mike Hendrick (a particular favourite of mine). We all have our favourite collaborator but I have never heard any of my colleagues utter a word of criticism of any. In the Old Trafford Test of 1990 we were joined by David Lloyd who was not only a sheer delight as a new colleague but an instant success with the listeners.

David not only has a superb knowledge of the game (as a Lancashire and England player, a coach, and a first-class umpire), he is a most entertaining after-dinner speaker and a brilliant natural droll. Rain had stopped play in the Second Test against India, and David, Fred Trueman and myself were holding the fort. Fred had received a letter from a listener who had bred a hybrid flower which he wanted to present to FST who, like any good Yorkshireman, was not averse to accepting something for nothing and was talking about *his* garden (which is, indeed, a delight). David intervened with a remark that he, too, had been involved in laying out his new garden, which included a fish-pond. Fred issued a friendly warning: 'Watch out for herons. I had some fish in a pond and the herons have pinched them all except one. I think that's too big for 'em.'

With the exquisite timing of a great professional comedian David hesitated fractionally then, with just the right touch of pathos, he responded, 'We don't get a right lot of herons in the middle of Accrington, Fred.'

I have never heard a better remark, a more sublimely timed one-liner, uttered in seventeen seasons with 'Test Match Special' – and there have been a lot. The listeners seemed to agree, too. Three months after the season had ended, the letters were still coming in.

16 *Retirement*

There is an ancient tradition of retirement to Morecambe by people from my part of West Yorkshire – from Bradford, Keighley, Halifax and the smaller towns and villages in between. From Leeds and beyond, Yorkshiremen tend to drift eastwards. The watershed, therefore, must be somewhere around Pudsey. Morecambe has long been known as Bradford-by-the-Sea for its number of West Riding-born settlers and it had long occupied a special place in the affections of both my wife and myself as the nearest place in which one could spend a seaside holiday. When the M61 was opened from the outskirts of Manchester to the M6 near Preston, it became feasible to commute to my office from Morecambe. So began an early rehearsal for retirement in the time-honoured spot.

It was once a favourite watering-hole for the thousands who emerged each summer from the cotton mills of Lancashire and the woollen factories of Yorkshire to spend, respectively, 'Wakes' and 'Feast' weeks at the coast. It was then a flourishing centre for the bucket-and-spade holiday when children asked for little more than sunshine in which to spend their time at the water's edge, and for the parents there were theatre shows, pierrots and concert parties.

In those far-off days of the 1920s and 1930s even a modest 'family room', in a cheap boarding house was beyond our purse so we stayed at the
home in Lancaster of an aunt (my father's sister – a fact I kept very quiet during the cricket season) and her husband, my Uncle Charlie. He was a man who fascinated me because, as far as possible, I was kept away from him. The dark family secret was that Uncle Charlie DRANK! He was a master clogmaker, the last, I believe, to work in Lancaster, and on Friday nights, after being packed off to bed early with my cousins, I lay awake to listen for that great rumbling bass voice to be raised in song – only to be

immediately 'shushed' by my aunt. *Pas devant les enfants*! Coming from two long lines of teetotallers and having had the evils of drink spelled out with crystal clarity to me in my Primitive Methodist Sunday School, Charlie Cragg, seemed to symbolize the massed forces of depravity. Whether because of this, or despite it, I know not, but I loved him. I used to make unauthorized visits to his workshop to watch him carving out wooden soles with marvellous dexterity. Then he and his two 'men' (employees) fixed the shaped leather uppers to the wooden soles with tiny brass nails, and a pair of clogs materialized in seemingly no time at all to be placed, graded by sizes, alongside others in the shop window. To me it was a place from the pages of the Brothers Grimm.

My lasting memory of Lancaster in those days is of the smell, distinctive but not unpleasant, from Williamson's linoleum factory beside the River Lune. Half a century later I still deliberately sniff the air, expecting to scent that manufacturing process. Over the whole scene brooded the castle of the Dukes of Lancaster and their forebears. Its Norman keep and superb curtain walls give it the appearance of one of the best-kept fortresses in Britain and I indulged my interest in history by spending every moment I could in the castle. The great hall (still used as an Assize Court) engaged my attention for hours with its walls hung with the heraldry of kings and dukes and high sheriffs of the county. For years now it has been used partly as a prison and so the areas available to tourists have been limited but happily a more general access seems probable in the next few years.

Lancaster positively reeks of history so I was perfectly happy to roam its streets when we were not actually *at* the seaside. On other days we travelled the three or four miles into Morecambe by bus or train to lie around on the beach or wander into the amusement arcades where one spieler attracted his crowds by standing with a snake curled round his shoulders. I remember a ship being systematically broken up on the long stone jetty which jutted out into the bay opposite the Promenade station and the lines of charabancs along The Front, their drivers competing with each other to attract holidaymakers with their invitations to visit 'Seven Lakes', 'the Yorkshire Dales', 'Arnside and Silverdale', or simply to try 'a mystery tour'. There was a rose garden at Heysham Head where we sat amongst the fragrance of the flowers and watched a concert party sing, dance and perform sketches; there were two piers with old-time dancing and tea-rooms, anglers and penny-in-the-slot machines. We had the 'revues' of Ernest Binns' Arcadian Follies and there was the Alhambra Theatre where the actor-manager Archie Collis staged comedies and farces, which were the very stuff of seaside holidays for the tired mill hands of the industrial North.

One man who played there regularly was Joe Gladwyn, sometime proprieter of the 'chippie' in 'Coronation Street', but later immortalized as Wally Batty, henpecked husband of the formidable Nora in 'Last of the Summer Wine'. A lovely chap, Joe used to come into the BBC Club every Friday lunchtime, to drink two halves of shandy – no more, no less – and our conversation never failed to touch on his character parts at Morecambe Alhambra in the summer shows.

Joe's accent was purest and richest Lancashire but I suppose to the BBC Drama Department we all sound the same whether we come from the 'Summer Wine' country of Holmfirth (West Yorkshire) or Greater Manchester! However, when David Jacobs once introduced a record made by Joe of a bit of unmemorable verse called 'What have they done to my Christmas?' and called it 'the authentic voice of the West Riding of Yorkshire,' I really couldn't let it pass. I sent David a light-hearted reproof and he replied with a postcard saying it was his producer who had given him the information. And, with obvious delight, David added that his producer came from Bradford! Clearly he had been away from home for too long.

And there was, of course, the sea, mysteriously coming and going twice a day. No one thought about pollution, and no foreigners told us our beaches were not clean. This was our own Magic Kingdom, the creation of God with adjustments by Man, and we did not inquire how it had come about. We simply loved it.

Much of that childhood fantasy remains with me. Even in the height of the modern holiday season when traffic crawls at a snail's pace from one end of the promenade to the other I still take that route from my home in the quaintly named suburb of Bare to the West End (opposite) because the view is unparalleled anywhere around the English coastline. Take any one of the streets that run at right-angles to the promenade so that the bay suddenly springs up in front of you and the sight will take your breath away. Across seven miles of sea (or, at low tide, of sandbanks) are the Lakeland hills with peaks like Scafell Pike, Coniston Old Man and the Langdales individually identifiable. On some days they are distant, remote; on others it seems as though you could throw a stone and reach them. The sunsets turn the bay into a suffusion of pink and black and silver. The air is like a sleeping-draught and my guests from afar find themselves nodding off in a chair long before the time to retire.

I love Morecambe today in an entirely different way from fifty years ago, which is perhaps as well because it is an entirely different place. The views, the sunsets and the air are unchanged but there is no longer a theatre; we do not even boast a cinema of any kind. We have bingo halls and slot-machine arcades in abundance but one pier has long since been swept away in a gale and the other is out of commission. The saddest sight is of a young couple with small children on a rainy day (yes, it does sometimes rain in Utopia) wondering how on earth to entertain their complaining offspring. One man used to be employed to 'sell' the resort to the nation's holidaymakers; now we have a huge staff, divided into an intriguing number of departments, carrying out sundry esoteric assignments at high cost – and they pull in nothing like the number of visitors Morecambe used to have! The magic has gone and all the 'hype' and PR in the world cannot replace it because the attitudes of children and their parents to summer holidays have changed.

Blackpool, a few miles south as the gulls fly, saw the need to move with the times and acted accordingly. Morecambe stood still and then gently started to move backwards. The Tourism Department, with astonishing regularity, produces plans for the resort in the twenty-first century while failing to notice that it has barely scrambled into the twentieth. Blackpool took its own steps to modernize its image; Morecambe has always cried out for someone else to do it. A high proportion of letters to the local paper, *The Visitor*, make the same inquiry: 'When is the Council (or someone else) going to do something about. . . .'

The most sensible suggestion I have seen in all those letters to the Editor is to cash in on the few (but immensely valuable) assets that remain and which cost nothing, or very little: the natural environment and a quite splendid Parks Department. It would not take much effort or finance to change Morecambe's image to that of 'the town of flowers'. The hoteliers on the seafront, in particular, but in the other streets as well would not take much persuading to double or treble their displays of hanging baskets and improve their gardens. The Parks Department would not go on strike if asked to double or treble the number of promenade displays they are asked to undertake at the moment. This could be synchronized with the staging of a major flower show, seasonally in spring, mid-summer and autumn, each of which could rival the annual event in Southport. There is a greater variety of birdlife in and around the bay than in almost any other section of the British coastline and a wonderful RSPB reserve at Leighton Moss. Instead of mourning the loss of the Wakes Weeks multitudes which are gone, never to return, the town could become a Mecca for nature-lovers, bird-watchers and those who value some of the better things in life.

In all this I am once again playing devil's advocate because, to be quite honest and in common with many other retired people, I don't want the place cluttering up with holiday-makers. Most of all I don't want the town filled with candy-floss-eating, paper-hat-wearing, motor-cycle-roaring masses who turn it into hell on earth. Quite selfishly, until the Community Charge sent the cost of living soaring (and that is largely the fault of a profligate Socialist regime at *county* headquarters) I was content to look with amused tolerance at the mismanagement and misdirection at local level. And at local foibles. Every year I drive a motorcar in the USA, in Australia and in New Zealand. I have, in the past, driven in at least a dozen other countries. There is nowhere in the whole world as dangerous as Morecambe on a Saturday morning when the shoppers are out in full force. The large percentage of elderly people who live here has given rise to standards of motoring that are nothing less than terrifying. Those without cars, on the other hand, regard the motorists as having no right at all to be on the roads and they cross when and where they feel like doing so, without warning, without signal, without thought. Drivers signal left and turn right with unflagging regularity; they pull out from parking spots without a glance to see if anything is approaching; they never – but *never* – give a thought for anyone or anything else on the road. And the general bedlam has been compounded by those whose duty it is to site pedestrian crossings, bus stops, traffic lights and the like. Most of these appear to have been positioned by idiots or non-drivers or both. A friend of mine, a former commander in the Met, used to talk about the dangers of fighting the criminal populace in London. 'Danger?' I used to say to him. 'You don't know what it is until you have driven around Morecambe on a Saturday morning.' Rush hour in Paris has nothing on it; negotiating Marble Arch at 8.30 a.m. is child's play by comparison; even driving out of San Francisco in one of six nose-to-tail lanes of moving vehicles can be contemplated with relative equanimity.

But it is endearingly slap-happy, just the same. I can be deep in the Lake District in forty minutes, in the Yorkshire Dales National Park in a similar time, at the Scottish border in an hour. At home we have the natural wonders of the bay and its wildlife. A flock of sheep come to my back fence to eat out of my hand and be patted on the head. A heron occasionally fishes optimistically in a tiny stream fifty yards away; the magpies forage industriously in the sheep's fleeces and the lapwings nest on the golf course. It's as near to the perfect retirement spot as I can imagine and there is so much that is close to my heart. Morecambe bumbles along at just the right pace and in the right sort of (just) controllable chaos. One morning my wife, reading from the columns of the local paper, spotted that a group of local blind people had been 'entertained by *a conjuror*!' With a bewildered little laugh, she said, 'This place has got to be the nearest one can get to "Clochemerle". Why don't you write a novel about it?'

Now there's an idea. . . .

Epilogue

In November 1990 came the announcement that Christopher Martin-Jenkins was to join the *Daily Telegraph* as Cricket Correspondent the following April (i.e. after the England tour to Australia). He was thus voluntarily relinquishing for the second time the job widely regarded in cricket circles as the best in the world. Most people in the game would give their eye-teeth to be appointed the BBC's cricket correspondent. Here we saw a man who had got the position twice – and given it up twice! The political in-fighting within the BBC now started all over again and I was glad to be clear of it. Brian Johnston and I talked on the 'phone about Chris's successor and reached complete disagreement, though in a perfectly civilized and pleasant manner. He wanted to see Peter Baxter (a public schoolboy) in the job despite – as I saw it – a serious lack of knowledge of the game itself, surely the prime requisite? I wanted it to go to Pat Murphy, a grammar schoolboy who had gained his cricketing knowledge the hard way.

Then, in the following month, politics of a different kind shook the country and Mrs Thatcher was deposed from the Premiership. Though saddened by events which led to this, I was obviously going to be happy about the choice of her successor as Prime Minister, John Major. The Member of Parliament for South Ribble, Robert Atkins, was a good friend of mine. I had introduced him to 'Test Match Special' and he regularly visited us in the course of a cricket season. On a visit to the Commons, a few years ago, to dine with him, I had been introduced to the Financial Secretary to the Treasury – then John Major – and had instinctively liked the man who was a great cricket supporter. As Robert became, successively, PPS at the Ministry of Trade and Industry, then to the Minister of Transport and finally appointed Minister of Sport, John Major's career rocketed to Chancellor of the Exchequer, then Foreign

Secretary and ultimately to Prime Minister. It was good to know that both men were great friends of 'Test Match Special' even though the decision had been made by me to leave the programme behind. The most heartening thing was to know that a grammar schoolboy could become the leader of the country.

But could he have become the BBC's cricket correspondent? Ah, now that's another matter altogether.

Index